D1453134

THE INTERPRETATION OF
THE BUDDHA LAND

BDK English Tripiṭaka 46-II

THE INTERPRETATION OF THE BUDDHA LAND

by

Bandhuprabha

Translated from the Chinese of Hsüan-tsang
(Taishō Volume 26, Number 1530)

by

John P. Keenan

Numata Center
for Buddhist Translation and Research
2002

First Printing, 2002
ISBN: 0-9625618-2-7
Library of Congress Catalog Card Number: 2001098895

Published by
Numata Center for Buddhist Translation and Research
2620 Warring Street
Berkeley, California 94704

Printed in the United States of America

052803/4342 z5

A Message on the Publication of the English Tripiṭaka

The Buddhist canon is said to contain eighty-four thousand different teachings. I believe that this is because the Buddha's basic approach was to prescribe a different treatment for every spiritual ailment, much as a doctor prescribes a different medicine for every medical ailment. Thus his teachings were always appropriate for the particular suffering individual and for the time at which the teaching was given, and over the ages not one of his prescriptions has failed to relieve the suffering to which it was addressed.

Ever since the Buddha's Great Demise over twenty-five hundred years ago, his message of wisdom and compassion has spread throughout the world. Yet no one has ever attempted to translate the entire Buddhist canon into English throughout the history of Japan. It is my greatest wish to see this done and to make the translations available to the many English-speaking people who have never had the opportunity to learn about the Buddha's teachings.

Of course, it would be impossible to translate all of the Buddha's eighty-four thousand teachings in a few years. I have, therefore, had one hundred thirty-nine of the scriptural texts in the prodigious Taishō edition of the Chinese Buddhist canon selected for inclusion in the First Series of this translation project.

It is in the nature of this undertaking that the results are bound to be criticized. Nonetheless, I am convinced that unless someone takes it upon himself or herself to initiate this project, it will never be done. At the same time, I hope that an improved, revised edition will appear in the future.

It is most gratifying that, thanks to the efforts of more than a hundred Buddhist scholars from the East and the West, this monumental project has finally gotten off the ground. May the rays of the Wisdom of the Compassionate One reach each and every person in the world.

NUMATA Yehan
Founder of the English
Tripiṭaka Project

August 7, 1991

Editorial Foreword

In January 1982, Dr. NUMATA Yehan, the founder of the Bukkyō Dendō Kyōkai (Society for the Promotion of Buddhism), decided to begin the monumental task of translating the complete Taishō edition of the Chinese Tripiṭaka (Buddhist canon) into the English language. Under his leadership, a special preparatory committee was organized in April 1982. By July of the same year, the Translation Committee of the English Tripiṭaka was officially convened.

The initial Committee consisted of the following members: (late) HANAYAMA Shōyū (Chairperson), BANDŌ Shōjun, ISHIGAMI Zennō, KAMATA Shigeo, KANAOKA Shūyū, MAYEDA Sengaku, NARA Yasuaki, SAYEKI Shinkō, (late) SHIOIRI Ryōtatsu, TAMARU Noriyoshi, (late) TAMURA Kwansei, URYŪZU Ryūshin, and YUYAMA Akira. Assistant members of the Committee were as follows: KANAZAWA Atsushi, WATANABE Shōgo, Rolf Giebel of New Zealand, and Rudy Smet of Belgium.

After holding planning meetings on a monthly basis, the Committee selected one hundred thirty-nine texts for the First Series of translations, an estimated one hundred printed volumes in all. The texts selected are not necessarily limited to those originally written in India but also include works written or composed in China and Japan. While the publication of the First Series proceeds, the texts for the Second Series will be selected from among the remaining works; this process will continue until all the texts, in Japanese as well as in Chinese, have been published.

Frankly speaking, it will take perhaps one hundred years or more to accomplish the English translation of the complete Chinese and Japanese texts, for they consist of thousands of works. Nevertheless, as Dr. NUMATA wished, it is the sincere hope of the Committee that this project will continue unto completion, even after all its present members have passed away.

It must be mentioned here that the final object of this project is not academic fulfillment but the transmission of the teaching of the

vii

Buddha to the whole world in order to create harmony and peace among humankind. To that end, the translators have been asked to minimize the use of explanatory notes of the kind that are indispensable in academic texts, so that the attention of general readers will not be unduly distracted from the primary text. Also, a glossary of selected terms is appended to aid in understanding the text.

To my great regret, however, Dr. NUMATA passed away on May 5, 1994, at the age of ninety-seven, entrusting his son, Mr. NUMATA Toshihide, with the continuation and completion of the Translation Project. The Committee also lost its able and devoted Chairperson, Professor HANAYAMA Shōyū, on June 16, 1995, at the age of sixty-three. After these severe blows, the Committee elected me, Vice President of Musashino Women's College, to be the Chair in October 1995. The Committee has renewed its determination to carry out the noble intention of Dr. NUMATA, under the leadership of Mr. NUMATA Toshihide.

The present members of the Committee are MAYEDA Sengaku (Chairperson), BANDŌ Shōjun, ISHIGAMI Zennō, ICHISHIMA Shōshin, KAMATA Shigeo, KANAOKA Shūyū, NARA Yasuaki, TAMARU Noriyoshi, URYŪZU Ryūshin, YUYAMA Akira, Kenneth K. Tanaka, WATANABE Shōgo; and assistant member YONEZAWA Yoshiyasu.

The Numata Center for Buddhist Translation and Research was established in November 1984, in Berkeley, California, U.S.A., to assist in the publication of the BDK English Tripiṭaka First Series. In December 1991, the Publication Committee was organized at the Numata Center, with Professor Philip Yampolsky as the Chairperson. To our sorrow, Professor Yampolsky passed away in July 1996. In February 1997, Dr. Kenneth K. Inada became Chair and served in that capacity until August 1999. The current Chair, Dr. Francis H. Cook, has been continuing the work since October 1999. All of the remaining texts will be published under the supervision of this Committee, in close cooperation with the Editorial Committee in Tokyo.

MAYEDA Sengaku
Chairperson
Editorial Committee of
the BDK English Tripiṭaka

Publisher's Foreword

The Publication Committee shares with the Editorial Committee the responsibility of realizing the vision of Dr. Yehan Numata, founder of Bukkyō Dendō Kyōkai, the Society for the Promotion of Buddhism. This vision is no less than to make the Buddha's teaching better known throughout the world, through the translation and publication in English of the entire collection of Buddhist texts compiled in the *Taishō Shinshū Daizōkyō,* published in Tokyo in the early part of the twentieth century. This huge task is expected to be carried out by several generations of translators and may take as long as a hundred years to complete. Ultimately, the entire canon will be available to anyone who can read English and who wishes to learn more about the teaching of the Buddha.

The present generation of staff members of the Publication Committee includes Diane Ames, Marianne Dresser, Eisho Nasu, Koh Nishiike, and Reverend Kiyoshi Yamashita, president of the Numata Center for Buddhist Translation and Research, Berkeley, California. The Publication Committee is headquartered at the Numata Center and, working in close cooperation with the Editorial Committee, is responsible for the usual tasks associated with preparing translations for publication.

In October 1999, I became the third chairperson of the Publication Committee, on the retirement of its very capable former chair, Dr. Kenneth K. Inada. The Committee is devoted to the advancement of the Buddha's teaching through the publication of excellent translations of the thousands of texts that make up the Buddhist canon.

Francis H. Cook
Chairperson
Publication Committee

Contents

Contents

Translator's Introduction

The *Interpretation of the Buddha Land* (*Buddhabhūmyupadeśa;* Taishō Vol. 26, No. 1530, pp. 291–328) is a commentary on the *Scripture on the Buddha Land* (*Buddhabhūmi-sūtra;* Taishō Vol. 16, No. 680, pp. 720–4). This scripture consists of an introductory description of the setting in which it was preached by the Buddha; the main body of the text, which treats the five factors that constitute a Buddha land, i.e., the Pure Dharma Realm and the four wisdoms: mirror wisdom, equality wisdom, discernment wisdom, and duty-fulfillment wisdom; and a concluding section of two illustrative similes and four summary verses.

The place of the *Scripture on the Buddha Land* within Mahayana history remains a subject of controversy. One of the concluding similes and all the summary verses are directly parallel to verses 56–9 and 82–5 of the "Bodhi Chapter" of the *Ornament of the Scriptures of the Great Vehicle* (*Mahāyānasūtrālaṃkāra,* Taishō No. 1604) and, according to the commentaries of Asvabhāva and Sthiramati,[1] were taken from the *Scripture on the Buddha Land.* This would mean that this *Scripture on the Buddha Land* was anterior to the *Mahāyānasūtrālaṃkāra* and was among the earliest Yogācāra texts.[2] However, the *Scripture on the Buddha Land* is never mentioned by any Yogācārin earlier than Asvabhāva. Its style is furthermore quite systematic and reflects more of a *śāstra* genre. These reasons lead others[3] to think that it is a late (fourth century) composition.

It should, however, be noted that the *Scripture on the Buddha Land* does not reflect a defined Yogācāra lineage. There is no mention of the basic themes of the *ālaya* (container) consciousness, the development of consciousness (*vijñāna-pariṇāma*), or the three patterns of consciousness (*trisvabhāva*). The text may well have been quite early and yet not have been considered an authority by early Yogācāra thinkers, and thus it would not have been quoted by them. It would then represent a tangential lineage, perhaps closer to the Maitreyan corpus, with its emphasis on wisdom and original purity, than to the classical Yogācāra of Asaṅga and Vasubandhu, with their emphasis on the samsaric nature of empirical consciousness.

In any event it was later considered to be a Yogācāra text and taken as a prime source on the nature of wisdom. Śīlabhadra (529–645) composed a commentary on it entitled the *Exposition of the Buddha Land* (*Buddhabhūmivyākhyāna;* Peking ed. No. 5498), preserved in its Tibetan translation. This commentary constituted the basic layer of the present Chinese text, which is attributed to Bandhuprabha and others and which, having added new material from the Dharmapāla–Fa-hsiang tradition of Yogācāra, is twice as large as Śīlabhadra's Tibetan text. Almost all the additional material has been drawn apparently from the *Ch'eng wei-shih lun* (translated by Francis H. Cook and published under the title "Demonstration of Consciousness Only" in *Three Texts on Consciousness Only*, Numata Center, 1999). The *Ch'eng wei-shih lun* is the principal doctrinal authority of Fa-hsiang, the East Asian version of Yogācāra founded by Hsüan-tsang and his disciple K'uei-ch'i. This would imply either that the *Interpretation of the Buddha Land* was composed in India by Bandhuprabha and others by drawing additional material from a no longer extant Sanskrit version of the *Ch'eng wei-shih lun,* or, if one judges the *Ch'eng wei-shih lun* to have issued in China from Hsüan-tsang himself, that the additional passages of the *Interpretation* also issued from his hand.

The present text contains both the rather straightforward commentary of Śīlabhadra as well as additional material from the Dharmapāla–Fa-hsiang tradition, with its strong emphasis on the enduring structure of other-dependent (*paratantra*) consciousness even within the realm of the perfected (*pariniṣpanna*) wisdom.[4]

The overall theme of these texts is that the Pure Land is not a physical location, but a symbol of the mind of wisdom—constituted by the five factors of the Pure Dharma Realm and the four wisdoms. These four wisdoms, grounded on the Pure Dharma

Realm, present the varied structure of wisdom as conceived by Yogācāra thinkers. Mirror wisdom and equality wisdom are nondiscriminative, while discernment wisdom and duty-fulfillment wisdom distinguish the nature of bodhisattva tasks and carry them out in the world. Thus the overarching context for these texts is the tension created between the critical awareness and "deliteralization" tendency of Yogācāra, and the Pure Land cultus, with its veneration of many Pure Land Buddhas and its hopes of being born in the Pure Land.

Note on Terms

Throughout the text, the term Scripture, capitalized, refers to the *Scripture on the Buddha Land,* the subject of this commentarial text; the term Commentary, capitalized, refers to this text itself, the *Interpretation of the Buddha Land.* The lower-case terms "scripture(s)" and "treatise(s)" refer generally to other Buddhist texts. The term Dharma, capitalized, refers to the overall Buddhist teaching or "law," while the lower-case term "doctrine(s)" is used to denote specific teachings or doctrines within the Buddha-Dharma as a whole.

Technical terms throughout have been rendered in English; in many cases, the corresponding Sanskrit term has been provided in parentheses on first appearance of a term in the text.

THE INTERPRETATION OF
THE BUDDHA LAND

Composed by Banduprabha and others
Translated by Tripiṭaka Master Hsüan-tsang
of the T'ang Dynasty

Introduction

I bow down in reverence before the supreme, prospering field,
Before the [Buddha in the] three bodies, the [Dharma of] the
    two truths, and the Sangha of the One Vehicle.
Now, according to my ability, I will present this treatise,
So that the Dharma may continually abide and deliver the
    multitude of beings.
Having examined the teachings of all the masters, I have
    already been purified,
But, being concerned lest those of meager intelligence fail to
    understand,
In order to lead them to engender the eminence of
    purification,
I will summarize and interpret the Land of the Sage.

The Commentary explains: This *Scripture on the Buddha Land* is
the embodiment of universal wisdom and of universal wisdom in
its entirety,[5] which are liberated from the [two] obstacles of passion and to knowledge. [Such wisdom] is able to open on awakening both for oneself and for all sentient beings in regard to all things
and all their characteristics, just as one might awaken from a dream
or just as a lotus flower might open up its blossoms. This [embod-
iment of wisdom] is what is meant by the Buddha land.

This means that the support, practice, and content [of the
Buddha land] are precisely the enjoyment of phenomena as of one
unified taste, as the Pure Dharma Realm, mirror wisdom, equality wisdom, discernment wisdom, and duty-fulfillment wisdom.

The term Buddha land refers to this support, practice, and content of Buddhahood. The term Scripture means that this meaning

runs through and upholds it, for the Buddha's sacred teachings run through and uphold both the meaning they explain and the beings they convert. Understand that the Buddha land expounded in this Scripture is of extreme benefit to sentient beings. The title *Scripture on the Buddha Land* is chosen in virtue of its contents, just as the *Scripture on Dependent Co-arising* (*Pratyītyasamutpāda-sūtra*) and the *Scripture on the Accumulation of Gems* (*Ratnakūṭa-sūtra*) [reflect the content treated in those texts].

The overall meaning summarized in this Scripture is that the Buddha land, which is established on the perfections of the Bhagavat's Pure Land, the perfections of its good qualities, and the perfections of its assembly, is a phenomenal wisdom all of one unified taste which is enjoyed both separately and in unison in the five factors which constitute that Buddha land. [That Buddha land] is supported on the Dharma realm, endowed with all good qualities, and differentiated into the three bodies (*trikāya*).

Thus we will explain in due order the location of the Tathāgata abode, the good qualities [of that abode], the nature of its assembly, and the differentiations in the meaning of that land. The location of his abode refers to the Buddha land, that is, his broad, extensive palace, adorned with eighteen kinds of perfection. Its good qualities refer to the Buddha Bhagavat's twenty-one kinds of eminent qualities. Its assembly refers to that incalculable assembly of great disciples and great beings (*mahasattvas*) who perfect all kinds of wondrous qualities. The different meanings of that land refer to the five factors of this wisdom land, which both individually and in unison enjoy phenomena as of one unified taste. All this will be explained in detail later.

There are three parts to this Scripture. The first explains the cause for the arising of this teaching. The second deals with the explanations of the teaching. The third treats the devout practice 291c which was carried out as a result of this teaching. [The first part] explains in general terms the occasion on which this Scripture was first heard and in specific terms describes the lord of the teaching and the actual location in which it arose. Since those to be converted

2

by the teaching are themselves the cause in virtue of which this teaching arose, the part [that describes them] is entitled "The Arising of the Teaching."

The second part is entitled "The Content of the Teaching," since it explains the differences in the doctrines enunciated in this true and sacred teaching.

The third part is entitled "The Practice Based on the Dharma," since it explains how the assembly that had heard the Buddha's teaching at that time was elated and put it into practice.

Part One

Chapter I

The Arising of the Teaching

The Scripture says: "Thus have I heard: At one time the Bhagavat...."

The Commentary explains: The phrase "Thus have I heard" in general refers to the enunciation of what has already been heard. The transmitter of the Buddha's doctrine says, "This is precisely what I have heard."

In general there are four kinds of meaningful discourse. The first is analogical. The second is exhortatory. The third is responsive. The fourth is authenticating. Analogical discourse is exemplified by the sentence, "Monks are like treasures." Exhortatory discourse is exemplified by the sentence, "This is the manner in which you should recite and understand the scriptures and treatises." Responsive discourse is exemplified by the sentence, "What I am preaching is precisely what I have heard." Authenticating discourse is exemplified by the sentence, "For you, I must think this, do this, and say this." Such discourse is thus authenticated [as the words of the Buddha].

[There are three opinions on how many kinds of meaningful discourse are involved in the presentation of this scripture.] The first opinion holds that only authenticating discourse is possible here. When assembled, all the bodhisattvas ask, "Please speak just as you have heard." The bodhisattva who transmitted this doctrine then spoke, assuring them and saying, "I must indeed speak just as I have heard, for it is in this manner that faith may be examined and confirmed." This means that in all instances his discourse was in conformity with and in no way different from that doctrine he had previously heard [from the Buddha].

The second opinion holds that responsive discourse is also involved. When questions arise, [the transmitter of the doctrine] must have responded with exactly what he had heard. Therefore he said, "Thus have I heard."

The third opinion holds that all four kinds of discourse are involved. [The Scripture discourse] is analogical in that the phrase "Thus have I heard" implies identity to what is now being enunciated [by the transmitter]; it is exhortatory in that, when it was spoken, the assembly must have been enjoined to listen to the content of what was heard by the transmitter.[6]

The word "I" refers to the conventionally erroneous view of the aggregates. The word "hear" refers to the auditory perception of the consciousness that evolves from the ear organ. It is by disregarding these distinctions that people generally say, "I hear."

[There are two opinions on the nature of the cause of this Buddha discourse.] The first opinion holds that it was in virtue of the enabling cause of the Tathāgata's compassionate vow that images of words and meanings were produced in the consciousness of the hearer. Although these words and images did depend directly on the power of [the hearer's] own good roots, yet, since he received strong conditioning [from the Tathāgata vow], it is called Buddha discourse. Thus when the Scripture says, "I hear," it means that the mind [of the hearer] was itself transformed through the power of his ear organ.

The second opinion holds that by the power of the enabling cause of good roots and the power of the primal vow, images of words and meanings were produced in the consciousness of the Tathāgata. These images arose from the good roots whereby the Buddha benefits others, and are thus called Buddha discourse. Although the mind of the hearer did not apprehend them, yet, because similar images became present, he said, "I have heard."

Understand that the phrase "Thus have I heard" implies the avoidance of any increase or decrease [in the content of what was

292a

heard]. It means that [the transmitter] declared [this Scripture] in accord with the doctrine heard from the Buddha and not according to any explanation concocted by another. Such a hearer had the profound ability to avoid the errors of either adding to or subtracting from that which he had heard. He was not like the fool who lacks such ability and is thus incapable of avoiding these errors. The transmitter of the Buddha's doctrine, when he gathered up that doctrine, based himself on the Tathāgata's doctrine and began by saying these words in order to lead sentient beings to revere, respect, believe, and accept [that doctrine]. He said that his words and meanings are established with neither increase nor decrease, just as he had heard them from the Buddha. And we, having correctly heard, must truthfully reflect on and assiduously cultivate them.

The phrase "at one time" refers to the time of hearing and refers to a continuous series of moments without interruption. The period of speaking and hearing is generally said to be one time. If this were not so, then syllables, words, and phrases would be different when they are spoken and when they are heard. How then could words be the same [for both speaker and hearer]?

Alternately, he who enunciated [this doctrine] has attained mystic formulae (*dhāraṇīs*) and, in one word, in one instant, he was able to convey all doctrines. Or, when he who heard had attained the pure ear, in one instant, when he heard but one word, everything became unobstructed to him. Because of such experiences, [that hearing] is said to have occurred at one time.

Or again perhaps because the time is not differentiated from the period when that assembly perceived it, the text says "at one time." This means that the phrase, "at one time," refers to the coming together of the common characteristics of speaking and hearing. Time is something that is conventionally established among conditioned things. Or it is a state of mind in which images, are all conventionally established in dependence upon material forms. Thus it is included among those karmic formations unassociated with the mind].

[It is objected,] why then do we not explain [time] by dividing it [into the sequential moments] as [done] below [in the text itself]? if we speak only of one time, then the divisions of day and night could not be established or identified in speaking! [Our] opinion is that [the time when this Scripture was spoken] is not determined. Thus we cannot ascertain whether it was spoken just in one moment or in a continuity of moments. Therefore in general terms its images are said [to have occurred] at one time.

The term Bhagavat comes from six interrelated meanings. The first is mastery, the second brilliance, the third majesty, the fourth renown, the fifth blessedness, and the sixth nobility. As a verse says:

> Mastery, brilliance, and majesty,
> Renown, blessedness, and nobility.
> These six meanings are all attributed
> To the term Bhagavat.

292b   Since all Tathāgatas are endowed with these qualities and do not lack any of them, they are called Bhagavats. This is to be interpreted as meaning that since all Tathāgatas are never bound by any passion, they are masterful. Since they are consumed by the fire of flaming wisdom, they are brilliant. Since they are adorned with the thirty-two major marks, they are majestic. Since they are recognized as being replete with all eminent qualities, they are renowned. Since they are approached, revered, and praised everywhere in the world, they are blessed. Since their merits are always active and bring benefit and peaceful joy to sentient beings through skillful means (upāya) without ceasing, they are noble.

Furthermore, since they are able to destroy the four inimical forces,[7] they are called Bhagavats. These four inimical forces are the passions, the aggregates, death, and the demon.

Thus Buddha is designated by these ten qualities [of the six meanings of the term Bhagavat and the four abilities to destroy inimical forces]. The reason why the transmitter of the Tathāgata's teaching placed this name, Bhagavat, at the beginning of all the scriptures is that it is honored over all the world. Even heterodox

8

teachers all refer to their founders as Bhagavat. This one name encompasses a multitude of good qualities, and, being unlike other names, it is always placed at the beginning of scriptures. Later we will discuss all these good qualities of the Buddha.

Chapter II

The Good Qualities of the Pure Land

The Scripture says: "...[the Bhagavat] dwelled in a great palace, which was ornamented with the seven luminous gems and which emitted a great light that completely illuminated immeasurable world-realms. Its immeasurable configuration was well apportioned in its distribution of dwellings. Its unlimited horizon was unfathomable. Its domain surpassed anything in the triple world. It arose from good roots beyond those that transcend this world. It was characterized by perfectly purified and masterful conscious construction. It was the support of Tathāgatas. It was the cloud gathering of the assembly of all great bodhisattvas. It constantly had as servants an immeasurable number of gods, dragons, humans, and all manner of supernatural beings. It was sustained by enjoyment and delight in the taste of the great Dharma. It brings about meaning and benefit for all sentient beings. It destroys the oppressive, defiled proclivities of passion. It expels all inimical forces. It is arrayed by the Tathāgata to surpass all [other] arrayments. Its paths are great memory, great understanding, and great practice. Its vehicles are great quiescence and wondrous insight. Its entrance gates are the deliverances of emptiness, imagelessness, and wishlessness. It rests on a kingly collection of great, jeweled lotus flowers, ornamented with innumerable collections of good qualities."[8]

The Commentary explains: This passage explains the perfections of the Tathāgata's abode, for it describes the Pure Land of the Buddhas. Since the Pure Land is characterized by eighteen kinds of perfection, it is termed completely perfected. These eighteen fullnesses are: color, configuration, extent, domain, cause, result, lords, confreres, servants, sustenance, action, beneficence, fearlessness, abode, paths, vehicles, entrance gates, and foundation. These eighteen phrases manifest the eighteen perfections. 292c

11

This means that that august palace of such perfections is called the Buddha's Pure Land. This Scripture reports the manner in which the Buddha abides in that great palace.

But, [it may be asked,] is this the enjoyment land or the transformation land of the Buddha? [There are three opinions on this question.] The first opinion holds that that land was a magically transformed land and that the Buddha who preached this Scripture was the transformation body (nirmāṇakāya), because a great number of word-hearers (śrāvakas) dwelled in that land, were present before the Tathāgata, and listened to him preach this Scripture. They were elated, received it in faith, and put it into practice. Because of this manifestation of the Buddha's mind, his pure, world-transcendent conscious construction became phenomenally perceptible in the enunciation of this eminent Dharma. He magically created this land in the presence of all kinds of sentient beings and caused them to become elated and to embark upon practice. Instantaneously he magically created a pure Buddha land by the supernatural power of his wondrous transformation body, and they were led quickly to attain insight. If this were not so, the numerous word-hearers would not have gained insight.

The second opinion holds that that land was the enjoyment land and the Buddha who preached this Scripture was the enjoyment body (saṃbhogakāya), because this land was unlimited in measure, and its paths, vehicles, and entrance gates were all actually merits. Moreover, it is taught [in the last chapter of the *Summary of the Great Vehicle (Mahāyānasaṃgraha)*] that that land was enjoyed everywhere as purified, pleasurable, irreproachable, and masterful. Furthermore, the *Scripture on the Explication of Underlying Meaning (Saṃdhinirmocana-sūtra)* says: "They attained birth above the triple world." Moreover, the Buddha who preached this Scripture was endowed with the twenty-one kinds of true qualities, as will be explained later. When he preached other scriptures, such Buddha qualities were not enumerated. If he magically created this Pure Land by means of his wondrous [transformation] body in order to benefit the multitudes and lead them to gain insight, this would have been clearly stated, as it is in other scriptures. But it is not so stated here. Thus this land is an enjoyment land of the enjoyment body. The multitude of word-hearers and so forth were magical creations of the Buddha, or, perhaps, they were the bodhisattvas who appeared in these bodies, because they are the assembly to whom this doctrine is addressed in that adorned Buddha land.

But [it is objected to this second opinion,] if this be true, then this land would have been both seen and heard only by bodhisattvas above the earth. Why then was this Scripture codified and preached to the bodhisattva who transmitted this doctrine in this land of the transformation Buddha?

[It is answered that indeed it was codified and preached] in order to show that universal wisdom and its abode do transcend all worldly states, for thus it shows [that the Buddha] desires to cause those who are to be converted to engender gladness. This was done in order to lead them to elicit the vow to be born into that Pure Land of Buddha, to see Buddha, to hear that doctrine, and to cultivate its causal force. It was done in order to engender eminent joy for sentient beings of broad, victorious understanding and for all bodhisattvas. It was done because he desires to strengthen such a victorious understanding of superior aspirations. These are the reasons this Scripture was codified and preached. Moreover, that doctrine was preeminent for those who heard its proclamation. In such a case, the transformation body, which in its phenomenal defilement is not preeminent, could not have proclaimed such words. Thus this Buddha is the enjoyment body dwelling in an enjoyment land, and he preached this Scripture for all bodhisattvas from the first stage up to the last and caused them to codify and preach it.

293a

But, [the objection continues,] if this be the case, then why did he not state that this doctrine was specifically addressed to them? Even if he did not identify its location, who could claim that he did not know it? He clearly could have identified it! Since all beings are so perplexed, he should have stated it explicitly.

The correct opinion is that when Śākyamuni preached this Scripture, a great multitude on this earth saw his transformation body dwelling on this lower earth to preach this teaching, while a great multitude above this earth saw his enjoyment body preaching this Scripture in the Buddha's Pure Land. Although what they heard was identical, what they saw was different. Although all were elated, received it in faith, and put it into practice, yet some understood in a shallow manner and others understood deeply. The transmitter of this doctrine witnessed to the Buddha's good qualities in the presence [of the word-hearers] in order to lead sentient beings to hear about his eminent, wonderful vow, to cultivate its causal force, and to be born into the Pure Land. Thus the assembly of those who saw the Victor said that the Bhagavat dwells in utmost victory and they discoursed on the Tathāgata's merits.[9]

The First Perfection: Color

The phrase ["the Bhagavat dwelled in a great palace, which was] ornamented with the seven luminous gems" [according to the original Sanskrit grammatical form] means either that that palace employed seven jeweled adornments, which were luminous, or that, because that great palace was adorned with the seven gems, it was luminous. These seven gems are gold, silver, aquamarine, sapphire, emerald, red pearl (they are generally called red pearls because they come from worms and insects, or, perhaps, because their center is red), and quartz. These are what is referred to as the seven gems. In truth the Pure Land is beautifully arranged and adorned with limitless, wonderful gems, beyond the awareness of people on this earth.

The phrase "it emitted a great light that completely illuminated immeasurable world-realms" means that that great palace emitted a great light and illuminated all the numberless realms, or, perhaps, because that great palace in its essence encompassed these limitless realms, it emitted a great light and illuminated everything.

These first two phrases treat the perfection of color in Buddha's Pure Land.

The Second Perfection: Configuration

What is its configuration? The phrase "its immeasurable configuration was well apportioned in its distribution of dwellings" means that the wondrous configuration of that great palace was well apportioned in limitless dwellings, or that the limitless configuration of that palace was well apportioned in those dwellings, for the word limitless [in the original Sanskrit] can [grammatically] modify either the word "configuration" or the word "dwellings." The phrase "that configuration was well apportioned" means that that apportionment was laid out by placing priority on understanding.

But, [it can be asked,] how can it be that the pure mind of the Buddha became phenomenally characterized? [We answer that] this was not done by some worldly craftsman working from the outside. The meaning of the sentence that its configuration was well apportioned by placing priority on understanding is that the Buddha Bhagavat, previously when he was a bodhisattva, developed the wisdom of skillful means and by his earnest practice vowed to adorn this Buddha land. From the power of that vow of his previous practices, when he had attained the result [of awakening], the Buddha's pure conscious construction became manifested in this manner, even though he dwelled in the wisdom of no fabrication. It was this that caused the conscious construction of the bodhisattvas to be similarly transformed. Thus there is no contradiction. All the other passages [that refer to the phenomenal aspects of the pure mind] should be understood according to this principle.[10]

293b

The Third Perfection: Extent

The phrase "its unlimited horizon was unfathomable" [in the original Sanskrit grammar] means either that because the extent which that palace encompasses is unlimited, it is unfathomable, or that because the extent of that palace is itself unlimited, and what it encompasses is unfathomable. Just as the directions of the compass are unlimited, so its extent is unfathomable.

[There are three opinions on the nature of the Pure Land of

the enjoyment body.] The first opinion holds that the land of the Tathāgata's enjoyment body, when proclaimed and manifested to those to be converted, cannot be determined as to its extent. Even though it may appear to be very extensive, yet it does have limits. But in order to perfect the wisdom of those bodhisattvas who are present in this land, it is said to be unlimited and its extent is unfathomable.

The second opinion holds that the land of the Buddha's enjoyment body is the universal Dharma realm (*dharmadhātu*), cultivated for three incalculable eons and influenced by unlimited good roots. World-transcendent bodhisattvas and even all the Tathāgatas are unable to fathom its unlimited extent. Therefore they consider it to be unlimited from time without beginning.

The third correct opinion holds that there are two kinds of lands of the enjoyment body. The first is that of the enjoyment body for oneself, which refers to the unlimited Dharma realm, cultivated by all Tathāgatas for three incalculable eons and influenced by unlimited good roots. It is this [enjoyment body] in which they themselves enjoy the great Dharma. From the first moment when they attain awakening until their last limit is exhausted, they continue without change. Even the bodhisattvas with all their merits cannot see this land. But they can hear about it. It is this Pure Land that is considered to be without limits. Even though all the Buddhas see it, yet even they are unable to fathom the limits of its extent. The second is the enjoyment body for others, whereby all Tathāgatas lead the multitudes of world-transcendent bodhisattvas to enjoy the great Dharma. This body for others advances and cultivates victorious conduct and is manifested as appropriate. Whether superior or inferior, large or small, it is subject to change and undetermined, just like the transformation body. It is thus that the Pure Land is considered to have limits. The world-transcendent bodhisattvas and all Tathāgatas completely fathom its extent, but in the world it is said to be unfathomable. Thus the phrase "its full extent is unfathomable" should be understood by means of this distinction.

The Fourth Perfection: Domain

We have now explained the perfection of extent, but how is it dissimilar to other places in the triple world? The phrase "its domain surpasses anything in the triple world" means that the location of that great palace transcends anything that might be found in the triple world. It is dissimilar to this world, where covetousness and craving for the objects of the two obstacles [of passion and to knowledge] hold sway and ever increase. These [cravings] and those [obstacles] mature and become the dominant results [of life in this world]. But one cannot grasp that Pure Land by the covetousness of this world, because it is liberated from the two obstacles and does not produce such dominant results [like those in this world]. It is like unto cessation, which transcends the realm of all the results of maturation in the triple world.

[It might be objected that] if this be so, then the Pure Land is not included in the triple world. Then it must be uncontaminated. And if it is included in the category of uncontaminated but conditioned things, then it must be identical with the truth of the path and goodness itself. How then can that Pure Land employ material form, voice, smell, and so forth as its own characteristics? It has been taught elsewhere that of the eighteen realms [which support perception and are thus necessary for such material forms, voices, smells, and so on], fifteen are contaminated, while eight may be morally neutral. [Thus if the Pure Land is uncontaminated, it cannot be characterized by such contaminated, or at best, neutral, material forms, and so on.]¹¹ 293c

[There are three opinions on this question.] The first opinion holds that the eighteen realms [necessary for perception], whether contaminated or uncontaminated, are all entirely good. When it is said that of the eighteen realms, fifteen are contaminated or eight morally neutral, this refers to the gross characteristics of the objects [perceived in] the lower vehicles.

The second opinion holds that the Pure Land is a magical creation of the concentrated mind. Although it appears to be characterized by the five senses and their respective objects, it is not included within them at all. It is not attainable by the five senses in their worldly operations. Just as blue is the content of the concentration of totality [and is not a material object elicited from worldly perception but is elicited from the concentrated mind, so the Pure Land is not apprehended by means of worldly perception]. Its material forms arise from mastery and are comprised in the Dharma realm. Therefore, although the Pure Land does employ material form and so forth as its own characteristics, yet it is uncontaminated and good. There is no contradiction here!

But, [it may be further objected,] if this be so, then the five sense consciousnesses of the bodhisattvas would not have that blissful land as the object [of their perception. And we know that they do perceive that land. Thus there is still a contradiction].

[We answer that] although they do rely on their own powers [of perception], and their own consciousnesses do mature, yet because of the [differences] in the grossness and subtlety of the images [in their minds, those minds] do not resemble the [concentrated mind of the Buddha, which engenders the Pure Land, and so do not parallel the case of the Buddha mind supporting the forms of the Pure Land].

[In that case, it is further objected,] it would be possible for the five sense consciousnesses of a Buddha, not being directed to the five sense objects, to have no content at all. [How could this be possible?]

[We answer that] the phenomenal activities of a Buddha in taking [sense objects] as their objects do resemble [worldly perception], but he is said to have these five sense consciousnesses only by conventional designation, while in reality he does not have them at all, since he constantly dwells in concentration. Other texts teach that by their nature the five sense consciousnesses are the essence of distraction, because they lack concentration. [Thus if a Buddha is in concentration, he does not really have the non-concentrated sense consciousnesses!]

[It is further objected that] if this be so, then [the consciousness of a Buddha] would not arise from the sense organs at all!

[We answer that] the five sense organs [of a Buddha] and their objects are conventionally designated as the five sense organs because they are described as being the same as those objects of sensation, but his objects of material form, and so on, are transformations of his concentrated mind. In truth, they are material forms produced from the mastery of the Dharma realm.

[But it is further objected that] if this be so, then the four wisdoms would not be simultaneous, because, [since a Buddha would have only the container and thinking consciousnesses,] the four wisdoms would then not be simultaneous, because many consciousnesses of the same kind [that is, wisdom,] do not arise simultaneously [in the same personal continuity].

[We grant that they are not simultaneous, for] there is no error in admitting that. [Thus a Buddha, without having the five consciousnesses of sensation, can at one time possess one wisdom and at another time another wisdom.][12]

The third correct opinion holds that the land of the Tathāgata is most profound and wondrous. It is neither existent nor nonexistent, neither contaminated nor uncontaminated, neither good, evil, nor neutral. It is not included within the teachings on the aggregates and the realms, but is enunciated differently as appropriate. When other texts teach that among the eighteen realms [of perception], fifteen are contaminated or eight neutral, this refers to the gross discrimination of sense objects by those in the two vehicles (i.e., of individually enliightened ones and word-hearers) and or by common worldlings and does not touch upon the profound sphere of all Buddhas and great bodhisattvas, for it is elsewhere taught that the Tathāgatas are not really included within the aggregates, supports, and realms [of perception], but manifest only what is good.

[The question then arises of whether,] if that be the case, the Pure Land is identical with or different from the triple world. [Again there are three opinions.] The first opinion holds that it is different, for some texts teach that it is located above the pure heaven of the gods, while others teach that it is to be found somewhere off in the west.[13]

The second opinion holds that it is identical because the Pure Land extends in its limits to the universal Dharma realm.

The third correct opinion holds that the land of enjoyment [for oneself] does extend to the universal Dharma realm and has no place in which it is not present. But it cannot be described either as apart from the triple world or as identical with the triple world. When it is that which is appropriately manifested to bodhisattvas, then the question of whether it is a purification of the world of material form, is located in the heavens, or is off in the west cannot be determined.

294a

The Fifth Perfection: Cause

[It is objected that,] since the Pure Land has such a perfection of domain, then it transcends the realm of the results of maturation in this triple world, and, like cessation, cannot have any cause. For, if it had a cause, then it would necessarily be included within this triple world. But, since it is taught that the Pure Land transcends this triple world, it must also transcend all the causes of this triple world. Its characteristic must then be said [to be the absence of cause]! How then are we to understand the phrase that "it arises from good roots beyond those that transcend the world"?

[We answer that] this means that that great palace has as its cause the good roots of both transcendent, nondiscriminative, and subsequently attained wisdoms. It is thus that it arises, for it does not lack a cause, but that cause is not the great god Īsvara, nor anything [similar] within the world of material form.

[It is objected that, in that case,] how can the Pure Land transcend this triple world and yet employ the transcendent, nondiscriminative, and subsequently attained wisdoms? Are not all pure states in this world, [such as subsequently attained wisdom,] caused by the process of maturation?

We do not teach that the Pure Land is caused by the process of maturation as are those other [worldly states]. It arises from a cause other than that, a cause similar to the highest worldly state of wisdom-patience which understands suffering. It employs both the basic, nondiscriminative wisdom and the subsequently attained, uncontaminated seeds of good states, and, by cultivating them for three incalculable eons, causes them to increase. This is the cause for the magical creation that is the Pure Land.

Nondiscriminative wisdom is termed world-transcendent. But its cause is the subsequently attained wisdom which goes beyond that and is termed the preeminent employment of those transcendent, uncontaminated good roots. In other words, the holy path of the word-hearers and the individually enlightened ones (*pratyekabuddhas*) is termed world-transcendent, while the good roots of Tathāgatas surpass even these and are termed preeminent. Therefore the Pure Land of the Buddha takes as its cause these uncontaminated good roots in the consciousness of the Tathāgata, and thus arises.

[There are two opinions on the nature of the causality of the Pure Land.] The first opinion holds that the Pure Land arises only from enabling causality, because it is external [to the minds of sentient beings].[14]

The second opinion holds that the Pure Land arises by direct causality, because [those uncontaminated good roots in the mind of the Tathāgata] are able immediately to produce it. If this were not so, then it would have no direct cause at all, because the images of external things [in the consciousness of sentient beings] cannot be its direct cause. All such external things have as their cause the permeation of internal states.

[It is objected against this second opinion that] if external things [have the internal permeation of seeds (*bījas*) in the container consciousness (*ālayavijñāna*) as their cause, then, since [external things] have a common existence, how can individual sentient beings have their own individual seeds? Since the direct cause would be common to all of them, then it would have to produce one common result [and there would be no individual seeds and no differences between sentient beings].[15]

[We answer that] it is indeed difficult for small minds to penetrate such a great teaching! [The above statement assumes that real atoms actually exist and that they account for the similarity of objects in consciousness.] But how could it be that external things are actually compounds unified from these many causes which are the atoms? [In our explanation] there is no contradiction between the individual evolutions of the maturing consciousnesses of [individual] sentient beings and the similarity of their support, [that is, the similarity of their container consciousnesses]. It is just like the light from many lamps, or things seen in a dream, for such images are similar because the same kinds of causes produce the same kinds of results. That which is not differentiated in its support [in the similarity of the container consciousnesses of individual sentient beings] actually becomes individualized and differentiated only by conventional designation. The Buddha's Pure Land is like this, for the magical creations of the individual conscious constructions [of Buddhas] encompass the universal Dharma realm. These [Pure Lands] are said to be common [to many Buddhas], because of the similarity of their grounding [within that Dharma realm]. Such is the perfection of cause in the Pure Land.

The Sixth Perfection: Result

What are the characteristics of its result? The phrase "it was characterized by perfectly pure and masterful conscious construction" means that that great palace was characterized by the Buddha's uncontaminated mind of utmost mastery. This is so because only conscious construction exists, and, apart from such conscious construction, there are no separately existing gems, or anything else [in the Pure Land]. This means that the pure mind of the Buddha in its transformations appears as these multitudinous gems, and so forth. As has already been explained, these objects are similar to those of a person who has entered the concentration of totality, focused on blue, and so on. These objects, which are manifested by conscious construction, are the pure conscious constructions associated with the Tathāgata's mirror wisdom, because they are directly caused by the uncontaminated seeds of the Pure Land, which he has previously cultivated for his own benefit. At all times

294b

and in all places, these objects do not wait upon any activity of thinking but manifest themselves spontaneously. This enjoyment land, adorned with its gems, has as its support the enjoyment body for oneself. But, as directly caused by the pure, uncontaminated seeds that benefit others, as manifesting Pure Lands, whether large or small, whether superior or inferior, as appropriate for the bodhisattvas, this Pure Land is also supported on the enjoyment body for others. This means that, as appropriate for bodhisattvas in the first stage, [a Buddha] manifests small and inferior [Pure Lands], and, as they develop through the other stages,these [Pure Lands] become large and superior, for this is how they function from the beginning [of the stages] until the final [attainment of awakening]. Such is the perfection of result in the Pure Land.

The Seventh Perfection: Lords

What of its lords? Every palace must depend on a lord. The phrase "it is the support for Tathāgatas" means that in that palace, all Buddha Bhagavats are lords, since only they are so preeminent. Only those associated with Bhagavats support and maintain it, for no others are capable of so doing.

Although the enjoyment body for oneself and its land encompass the Dharma realm, yet there is no contradiction here with the successive magical creations of its individual lords. And, although the enjoyment body for others and its lands are the magical creations of all Buddhas, there is no contradiction here with its being supported by lords either as a unified body [and land of many Buddhas] or as an individual body [and land of one particular Buddha].

The Eighth Perfection: Confreres

There must be confreres, for every lord gathers confreres around himself. The phrase "it is the cloud gathering of the assembly of all great bodhisattvas" means that that great palace constantly had a cloud assembly of innumerable great bodhisattvas. All those who stand before [the Buddha] are his assembly and they constitute a community of innumerable great bodhisattvas. Because they have become his confreres, there is no evil capable of injuring them. All the word-hearers are not like this at all!

This means that all the bodhisattvas from the first stage, although unable to assemble in the pure enjoyment land for oneself of any Buddha, yet are able to gather in a pure enjoyment land of the enjoyment body for others. Since in their own minds Buddhas are compassionate, they reveal lands, either gross or subtle, to these bodhisattvas as appropriate. The bodhisattvas, because of their own good roots and the power of their own vows, elicit images in their own minds similar to the Pure Lands produced by the Buddhas. Although their minds are each separately transformed, yet in their configuration they all resemble that one place. This is what is meant by their gathering together in that one [pure] land.

[There are three opinions as to whether] that Pure Land of those bodhisattvas above the world is contaminated or uncontaminated. The first opinion holds that it is uncontaminated, because in their own minds these bodhisattvas are equipped with the seeds and the vow power of an uncontaminated Pure Land, all of which are attained subsequent [to nondiscriminative wisdom]. By means of a magical creation within their own minds, they give rise to a 294c Pure Land and therein enjoy the great Dharma. The entire assembly of these bodhisattvas, from the first stage on up [to the last], realizes the truth of suchness, attains the true uncontaminated support and the true outflow from that reality, dwells in that Pure Land, and always sees all the Buddhas. Therefore that magically transformed land consists exclusively in the reality of the uncontaminated path.

The second opinion holds that it is contaminated, because in their own minds these bodhisattvas, at the stage of intensified effort, are equipped with the seeds and the vow power of a contaminated Pure Land. By the magical creation of their own minds, they give rise to this Pure Land and therein enjoy the great

Dharma. This is so because, even though these bodhisattvas realize suchness and attain a true uncontaminated state, still, in the first seven stages, passion does yet arise. Even until the tenth stage, there are still present the seeds of passion which have to be eliminated by the practice of meditation. The obstacle to knowledge is still present, because the container consciousness is able to support it and receive its permeations. Consequently this land consists of a morally neutral, contaminated nature. Now, that which consists of the conditioned truth of the uncontaminated path is most definitely good. But if in the ten stages the essence of the container consciousness was good and uncontaminated, then [the pure consciousness] of the Buddha land would not be capable of receiving any permeation at all, because it would not be capable of supporting contaminated seeds, [but the Pure Lands of the enjoyment body for others does just that]. The essence of the container consciousness is morally neutral and contaminated. How then could the Pure Land, which is a conversion of this consciousness, consist in a goodness that is uncontaminated? Furthermore, each sentient being has but one actual body, and, as long as he has it, it is contaminated. How then could a Pure Land of such a [contaminated] body be uncontaminated?

The third and correct opinion holds that the magical creations of the minds of the bodhisattvas are of two varieties. In the case of a Pure Land which is a conversion of the container consciousness, then, although its characteristics are pure and wondrous, yet it does consist in the contaminated truth of suffering, because it is an image of a contaminated consciousness, and because it is supported by a contaminated body. Likewise, those [Pure Lands] which are manifested by intensified effort are also contaminated. But in the case where those images of the Pure Lands are magical creations of the uncontaminated subsequently attained mind, [which is realized after the attainment of nondiscriminative wisdom,] then they consist in the truth of the uncontaminated path, because they consist in an uncontaminated image and arise from uncontaminated seeds. This is the perfection of confreres in the Pure Land.

The Ninth Perfection: Servants

Since there must be servants, the Scripture next teaches that "it had as servants an immeasurable number of gods, dragons, humans, and all manner of supernatural beings." This means that that great palace has as its servants only such gods and so on, for it does not have any other kinds of beings. The phrase "all manner [of supernatural beings]" includes *yakṣa*s, *gandharva*s, *asura*s, *garuḍa*s, *kiṃnara*s, and *mahoraga*s. The *mahoraga*s are great pythons.

But, [it is objected,] how can the Pure Land transcend this triple world, and yet have gods and so on as its servants? All such beings belong within this triple world!

295a [We answer that] the Pure Land simply takes on the appearance of these [gods and so forth] in order to be adorned, and thus there is no contradiction here. Or perhaps these various magical creations appeared in order to bring sentient beings to maturity, just as in converting King Kapphina innumerable universal monarchs (*cakravartin*s) appeared all about.[16] Or perhaps these innumerable magical creations were bodhisattvas in the bodies of the gods and the dragons and so forth, dwelling in the Pure Land in order to pay homage to the Buddha. Or perhaps the Buddha's own transformation bodies took on the forms of these gods, dragons, and so forth. But inasmuch as they are the servants of the Tathāgata, there is no error here. Such is the perfection of servants in the Pure Land.

The Tenth Perfection: Sustenance

What is the sustenance of those who dwell there? The phrase "it was sustained by enjoyment and delight in the taste of the great Dharma" means that, nourished by joy in the Dharma of the Great Vehicle, they were able to dwell there. This is the meaning of their sustenance.

But, [it is objected,] it has already been explained that "the Pure Land surpasses anything in the triple world." How then can there be any eating there? Furthermore, uncontaminated states of consciousness cannot be said to be eaten! Eating can nourish sentient beings in this triple world, but since these Pure Land beings have severed their existence [in the triple world] they should not be said to eat at all!

[We answer that] it is because [that taste of Dharma] is the cause which gives them nourishment that the word sustenance is used here. Now, even you will admit that when one is born into the world of form (*rūpadhātu*) and there enters a uncontaminated concentration, he is said to be nourished therein. He is not said to be nourished because in the past he has eaten, because the past does not exist. So it is with the above passage, for they are said to be nourished [in the Pure Land] inasmuch that [that taste of Dharma] is the cause which sustains them.

Although contaminated states are indeed obstacles to uncontaminated ones, yet, since they do sustain contaminated attachments [in the earlier stages of the path, those contaminated states] are said to nourish. In like fashion, uncontaminated states, although they sever contaminated states, yet do sustain those uncontaminated states. Thus they also can be said to nourish.

In this Pure Land all Buddhas and bodhisattvas subsequently attain the uncontaminated state and it can be said of them that they are able to enjoy the taste of the great Dharma and thus to elicit great enjoyment and delight. Furthermore, the wisdom of true reality enjoys the taste of suchness, and thus elicits great enjoyment and delight. It is able to sustain the body and prevent it from coming to harm. It can nourish good states and is thus said to nourish. Such is the perfection of sustenance in the Pure Land.

The Eleventh Perfection: Action

What kind of action does [the Pure Land manifest]? The phrase "it brings about meaning and benefit for all sentient beings" means that its [action] itself can bring about all meaning and benefit for all sentient beings, or that it can lead those sentient beings themselves to bring about all meaning and benefit. Because it manifests benefit, it is called meaning. Because it makes that benefit present, it is called profit. In the world it is called meaning, but transcendent to the world it is called profit. Because it avoids evil, it is called meaning. Because it supports good, it is called profit. Because it is blessed merit, it is called meaning. Because it is wisdom, it is called profit.

Although they are in the concentration of the abatement of all differentiation, yet, due to the power of the vow previously cultivated with intense effort, [Buddhas] are able spontaneously to bring about all meaning and benefit for sentient beings. Such is the perfection of action in the Pure Land.

The Twelfth Perfection: Beneficence

What is its beneficence? The phrase "it destroys the oppressive, defiled proclivities of passion" means that there one is far removed from the defiled proclivities of all passion and its oppression. All the passions are called defiled proclivities and they are the causes of oppression. Since these defiled proclivities of passion are not present there, the oppression they bring about is also absent there.

Furthermore, these passions refer to the one hundred and twenty-eight basic passions. The proclivities are lack of shame, and so forth. Defilements mean flattery, deceit, pride, and so forth. Oppression refers to the karmic actions that result from these. If the obstacle to knowledge and its inclination be termed a passion, then its arising is also termed a defiled proclivity. [But since] basic doubt is called a proclivity and its inclination a defilement, the obstacle to knowledge and its inclination are [better] said to be an oppression.

What is the beneficence of the Pure Land? It is precisely the elimination of these oppressive, defiled proclivities that is termed its beneficence. Just as a ruler of some worldly region, who might not actually cherish [his people], might be described as conferring beneficence on them because he does them no harm, just so the realization and attainment of liberation from those oppressive, defiled proclivities of passion is a conferral of beneficence, because

295b

it is an eminent, blessed wisdom. And so the Pure Land, being liberated from inner oppression, is perfected in beneficence.

The Thirteenth Perfection: Fearlessness

There must also be no cause for fear there and thus the Scripture next explains its perfection of fearlessness. The phrase "it expels all inimical forces" means that there [in the Pure Land] one is far removed from the [four] inimical forces of passion, the [impermanence of] the aggregates, death, and the demon, or that one can cause others to be far removed from these four inimical forces. These four are the causes of dread, since they can engender all kinds of dread. Since they are absent there, there is no dread.

The inimical force of passion refers to the one hundred and twenty-eight passions and their accompanying inclinations. The inimical force of the aggregates refers to the five aggregate heaps (*skandhas*) [that make up the illusory identity]. The inimical force of death refers to the fact that all internal contaminated states are impermanent. The inimical force of the demon refers to that ruler of the Paranirmitavaśavartin Heaven in the world of desire (*kāmadhātu*). Since these four can diminish and injure all good things, they are termed inimical forces. From these four inimical forces all dread arises. Because a Tathāgata is eternally apart from these four inimical forces, he is fearless. Bodhisattvas from the first stage are also freed from them, and thus lack any of the five fears [of poverty, bad reputation, death, falling into evil, or going before crowds]. Such is the perfection of fearlessness in the Pure Land.

The Fourteenth Perfection: Abode

That abode must also be eminent. Thus the Scripture next explains the perfection of its abode. The phrase "it is arrayed by the Tathāgata to surpass all [other] arrayments" means that the Tathāgata's abode surpasses all the arrayed abodes of the bodhisattvas or of anyone else. For it is only this abode that has been arranged and adorned by the Tathāgata himself. Therefore it surpasses all other arrayed abodes and is called the perfection of abode. Such is the perfection of abode in the Pure Land.

The Fifteenth Perfection: Paths

What are the paths along which one travels there? The phrase "its paths are great memory, great understanding, and great practice" means that there great memory, great understanding, and great practice are the paths to follow. Because they are that along which one travels, they are termed paths. This pathway has different names. Great memory is the wisdom perfected from hearing, for it articulates the unfailing meaning of what has already been heard. Great understanding is the wisdom perfected from reflection, for it rationally discerns and attains certitude. Great practice is the wisdom perfected from the practice [of meditation], for, in virtue of the force of such practice, it arrives at truth. Such memory, understanding, and practice are great because they arise by taking as their content the teaching of the Great Vehicle and are its results.

295c

Since it is by following these wondrous wisdoms that the Pure Land is traversed, they are called its paths. This means that they are called its paths because it is through these three wisdoms, as the cause for becoming a bodhisattva, that one realizes entrance into the Pure Land. As the great memory of all Tathāgatas, they are identical with nondiscriminative wisdom, since, in virtue of such memory, one peacefully abides in the truth of suchness. Great understanding is identical with subsequently attained wisdom, since it distinguishes all the conventional characteristics of the truth of all things. It is these two which bring about the enabling action of the Pure Land and therefore they are also called its activity. Since, due to these two wisdoms, one attains birth in the Pure Land, they are called its paths.

In other words, the practice of great memory is the practice of self-benefit, since it is uttered within, while the practice of great understanding is the practice of benefiting others, since it discerns externals. This is the sequence whereby a Tathāgata, by means of his wondrous understanding, gives rise to the two kinds of Pure Lands. Thus they are called its paths. Such is the perfection of paths there.

The Sixteenth Perfection: Vehicles

There must also be vehicles whereby one can ride along those paths. Thus the Scripture next explains that "its vehicles are great quiescence and wondrous insight." Quiescence means concentration, while insight means wisdom. The meaning of "great" is as explained above [in the last section]. Because these two are conveyances, they are called vehicles. Mounting upon this quiescence and insight, one follows along the appointed course and progresses along the path. Along that path, quiescence and insight are identified as vehicles. Such is the perfection of vehicles in the Pure Land.

The Seventeenth Perfection: Entrance Gates

There must also be entrance gates through which one enters by riding on those vehicles. Thus the Scripture explains that its "entrance gates are the deliverances of emptiness, imagelessness, and wishlessness." This means that these three deliverances are the entrance gates to that great palace. Deliverance refers to transcendent cessation. Great emptiness and the other two are termed deliverance gates. The Pure Land is entered through these gates. Emptiness means the absence of self, for selfhood is a state produced by clinging to what is entirely imagined. Taking this [no-self] as the content of concentration is what is meant by the deliverance gate of emptiness.

Image refers to the ten images of material form, sound, smell, taste, contact, male, female, birth, old age, and death. Since cessation lacks any image, it is called imageless. A concentration with such a content is what is meant by the deliverance gate of the imageless.

Wish means to seek after. But insight into suffering in this triple world lacks anything it might seek after. Thus it is called wishless. A concentration with such an object is referred to as the deliverance gate of the wishless. Because one enters the Pure Land through these three deliverance gates of emptiness, imagelessness, and wishlessness, they are called its entrance gates. The meaning of the word great is as explained above.

These paths, vehicles, gates, and so forth, which are associated with and located in the Pure Land, serve the purpose of leading sentient beings to enjoyment and delight in the true merits [of the mind of wisdom]. This is our interpretation of their function. Such is the perfection of entrance gates in the Pure Land.

The Eighteenth Perfection: Foundation

Like other palaces, this one also must be supported. Thus the Scripture next explains the perfection of its foundation. The line "it rests on a kingly collection of great jeweled lotus flowers, ornamented with innumerable collections of good qualities" means that, just as the earth rests on the wind-wheel and just as a palace in this world rests on that earth, just so that great palace rests on that kingly collection of great jeweled lotus flowers, ornamented with innumerable collections of good qualities. This means that that palace is constructed from lotus flowers and great gems and thus arises from the collected goodness of innumerable good qualities. Because these gems are the best among gems, they are called great and because these flowers are the best among all flowers, they are called kings of flowers. Or perhaps because these flowers are the best of the lotuses that arise from the good roots of bodhisattvas, they are called great, while because they arise from the eminent good roots of Buddhas, the kings of Dharma, they are called the kings of flowers. Furthermore, since these gems and flowers are rare, they are said to be kings of flowers. Because there is more than just a single one and because their petals are many, they are said to be a collection. This Scripture explains that the Bhagavat dwells among this collection of flowers and there places his palace.

If that palace refers to that Pure Land which is grounded on the Tathāgata's true enjoyment body, then we say that such a

296a

palace is coterminous with the Dharma realm, and in such a Pure Land each and every enjoyment body of the Buddha would be able to preach this Scripture as his basic theme. But if that palace refers to the Pure Land which is grounded on the enjoyment body of a Tathāgata as it is manifested appropriately to the bodhisattvas, then its extent is undetermined, and in such a Pure Land all Buddhas in unison manifest a single body and preach this Scripture. The extent of that palace cannot be determined

Chapter III

The Buddha's Good Qualities

The Scripture says: "The Bhagavat's purest enlightenment does not elicit the two [obstacles]. He has arrived at the imageless Dharma. He dwells in the abode of awakening. He realizes the equality of all Buddhas. He reaches the place of no obstacle. His Dharma is unfailing. His activity is invincible. That which he has established is inconceivable. He attains equality in regard to the three times (past, present, and future). His bodies issue forth to all worlds. His wisdom is unperplexed in regard to all things. In all his actions he perfects great enlightenment. In all doctrines his wisdom lacks uncertainty. All the bodies he manifests cannot be separated. His is the wisdom well sought after by all bodhisattvas. He attains that victorious far shore of the Buddha's nondual abode. That undivided deliverance wisdom of the Tathāgata is brought 296b to full perfection. He has realized the equality of Buddha lands without limit. He reaches to the ultimate Dharma realm. He reaches to the limit of empty space and will never come to an end."

The Commentary explains: The Scripture next describes how a Buddha is different from other masters. This is why it explains that the Bhagavat's good qualities are preeminent. Also, so that others might engender pure faith, it explains the perfection of the Bhagavat's good qualities. Understand that these include twenty-one kinds of eminent good qualities.[17]

Introductory Section:
The Buddha's Complete Enlightenment

The phrase "the Bhagavat's purest enlightenment" means that the Buddha Bhagavat is completely enlightened as to all necessary objects of understanding, whether conditioned or unconditioned. It means that in pure and wondrous perfection he is completely enlightened to all necessary knowables, that he is completely enlightened to the universal nature of all just as it is and to the limits of its existence. This is what is called the Bhagavat's purest enlightenment.

The First Quality: Absence of Obstacles

The phrase that "[the purest enlightenment] does not elicit the two" refers to that preeminent quality whereby the Bhagavat completely lacks obstacles. This means that the Bhagavat lacks the two obstacles [of passion and to knowledge], which obtain among common worldlings and adherents of the lesser vehicles. Common worldlings elicit transmigration and bring about attachment to that transmigration. But the word-hearers and individually enlightened ones elicit cessation, delight in, and become attached to that cessation. In contrast, since the Bhagavat does not elicit these two obstacles, it is said that he does not elicit the two.

The Second Quality: Skillful Means in Converting Beings

The phrase "he has arrived at the imageless Dharma" refers to the preeminent quality of the Buddha's skillful means in converting. This means that the imageless Dharma is cessation. The Buddha well understands the skillful methods whereby sentient beings, according to their capacity, are made docile and converted, and in such a manner he comes to address them in order to lead them to enter and realize the imageless Dharma.

The Third Quality: Discernment

The phrase "he dwells in the abode of awakening" refers to the preeminent quality whereby the Bhagavat discerns [the dispositions of] those who are to be made docile and converted. This means that, dwelling in great compassion, day and night at the six times,[18] he discerns the world.

The Fourth Quality: Equality of Activity

The phrase "he realizes the equality of all Buddhas" refers to the preeminent quality whereby the Bhagavat attains an activity identical with that of all Buddhas. This means that he realizes that all Buddhas are identical in their activity in virtue of this equality.

The Fifth Quality: Elimination of Obstacles

The phrase "he reaches the place of no hindrance" refers to the preeminent quality whereby the Bhagavat eternally eliminates what must be eliminated. This means that he has already realized liberation from the two obstacles of passion and to knowledge and is constantly apart from any obstacle.

The Sixth Quality:
Unfailingness of the Teaching

The phrase "his Dharma is unfailing" refers to the preeminent quality whereby the Bhagavat subdues the teachings of non-Buddhists. This means that the true Dharma of the Buddha cannot be overturned by any teaching of the non-Buddhists, since it has already subdued them in the very manifestation of that true Dharma.

The Seventh Quality: Invincibility

The phrase "his activity is invincible" refers to the preeminent quality whereby the Bhagavat subdues inimical forces. All actions are directed toward material form and [the other aggregates] and, when they scatter the mind and hinder the good, they are termed inimical forces. But the minds of all Buddha Bhagavats are well set in concentration and well disposed, so they are not scattered. Because this quality has attained perfection, no evil 296c can hinder them. Thus they are able to subdue all objects and, in virtue of the fact that all their activity [is unimpeded, it is invincible].

The Eighth Quality:
Inconceivability of the Teaching

The phrase "that which he has established is inconceivable" refers to the preeminent quality whereby the Bhagavat establishes the Dharma. This means that the Dharma established by the Buddha transcends the sphere of rational inquiry.

The Ninth Quality: Equality of Time

The phrase "he attains equality in regard to the three times" refers to the preeminent quality whereby the Bhagavat makes declarations in the three times. This means that without any obstacle, he declares events of the past and future as if they were in the present.

The Tenth Quality:
Manifestation of Transformation Bodies

The phrase "his body issues forth to all world-realms" refers to that preeminent quality whereby the Bhagavat descends from the Tuṣita Heaven. This means that in all world-realms whatsoever he manifests transformation bodies, because at those times he enters his mother's womb.

The Eleventh Quality: Severance of Doubt

The phrase "his wisdom is unperplexed in regard to all things" refers to the preeminent quality whereby the Bhagavat is severed from all doubt. This means that in regard to all things he has attained the wisdom of certitude which is able to expel all doubt.

The Twelfth Quality:
Appropriate Manifestation of His Body

The phrase "in all his actions he perfects great enlightenment" refers to the preeminent quality whereby the Bhagavat is able to manifest his body, as appropriate, to sentient beings in any vehicle. This means that he completely understands the differences in the lineages and habits of all sentient beings and, as appropriate, manifests his body to them.

The Thirteenth Quality:
Absence of Uncertainty in Teaching

The phrase "in all doctrines his wisdom lacks uncertainty" refers to the preeminent quality whereby, in the wisdom that wondrously comprehends all doctrines, the Bhagavat is able appropriately and constantly to teach and admonish correctly. This means that whereas all those who cling to uncertainty regarding any teaching lack such a profound ability to teach and admonish appropriately, the Buddha Bhagavat alone, in the full certainty of his wisdom that understands all doctrines, is able to teach and admonish appropriately, unfailingly, and ceaselessly.

The Fourteenth Quality:
His Undefiled Body

The phrase "all the bodies which he manifests cannot be separated" refers to the preeminent quality whereby the Bhagavat is able to support his undefiled bodies. This means that all the Buddha bodies do not arise from unreal imagining, because they lack the defilements of passion, action, and birth. Thus the Tathāgata's bodies do not arise from defiled imaginings.

The Fifteenth Quality: Perfecting Bodhisattvas

The phrase "his is the wisdom that is well sought after by all bodhisattvas" refers to the preeminent quality of his uninterrupted skillful means whereby the Bhagavat brings those of Buddha lineage to perfection. This means that all bodhisattvas, in order to maintain their Buddha lineage without interruption, intensively cultivate practice. Such is not the case with the word-hearers. Thus that Buddha wisdom is well sought after only by the bodhisattvas.

The Sixteenth Quality:
Nonduality of the Dharma Body

The phrase "he attains that victorious far shore of the Buddha's nondual abode" refers to the preeminent quality of the Bhagavat's essence body. This means that because the Dharma body of awakening is characterized by nondiscrimination, it is said to be nondual. The Buddha's nondual abode is precisely that Dharma body. Its essence is suchness. Because it is characterized by nondiscrimination, the dichotomy of the two aspects [of subject and object] does not arise in it. With such a victorious concentration, he constantly dwells there [in that nonduality]. Such dwelling in nonduality is precisely that victorious far shore. Since the Buddha has already realized this, he is said to have attained it.

297a

The Seventeenth Quality:
Deliverance through the Enjoyment Body

The phrase "that undivided deliverance wisdom is brought to full perfection" refers to the preeminent quality whereby the Bhagavat's enjoyment body is differentiated. This means that the enjoyment body is not divided because these enjoyment bodies of the Tathāgata are each separate things. Because the wisdom of the Tathāgata is able to lead all sentient beings to engender deliverance, [the Scripture] speaks of the deliverance wisdom of the Tathāgata, for in this wisdom the Buddha has already attained full perfection. Thus the Scripture says that the wondrous wisdom of the Tathāgata is undivided, for the enjoyment bodies manifested in the pure Buddha land are undivided. In the great assembly he manifests various bodies, and thus the enjoyment of Dharma by all the bodhisattvas is also undivided. The Tathāgata, in the bodies manifested by his wisdom, has arrived at full perfection.

The Eighteenth Quality: Unlimited Suchness

The phrase "he has realized the equality of Buddha lands without limit" refers to the preeminent quality whereby the Tathāgata realizes the characteristic of suchness. This means that suchness has no limits because it is far removed from any limiting, descriptive marks, whether conditioned or unconditioned, and from any limiting marks of location. Thus suchness is precisely the reality nature of the equality of Buddha lands. Because he has realized the universal equality of these Buddha lands, he completely knows all conditioned and unconditioned things without confusion.

The Nineteenth Quality: The Pure Dharma Realm

The phrase "he reaches to the ultimate Dharma realm" refers to the preeminent quality whereby the Bhagavat attains the result. This means that he has attained to the ultimate Pure Dharma Realm. This Dharma realm is the result of cultivating the path.

The Twentieth and Twenty-First Qualities: Inexhaustibility

The next two kinds of preeminent good qualities refer to the inexhaustibility of the Bhagavat's good qualities. The phrases "he reaches to the limits of empty space" and "he will never come to an end" refer to the two inexhaustible, preeminent good qualities, whereby the Bhagavat's self-benefit benefits others. This means that just as empty space, in its passage through the successive formations and dissolutions of the eons, is constant and inexhaustible, so all the Tathāgata's true and good qualities are also constant, uninterrupted, and inexhaustible. Just as the future is not exhausted at any moment, so his good qualities, which benefit others, will never come to an end, for he constantly brings about benefit and joy for all sentient beings.

In the following section we are going to present another commentary [on these Buddha qualities], one which outlines the specific meaning of each of the scriptural phrases. The words of the Scripture are the standard, which are then explained in these interpretations. Therefore this will be a summary of the [same] doctrine, which has just been explained, on the twenty-one kinds of preeminent good qualities.

The First Quality:
Unimpeded Enlightenment

The phrase "his purest enlightenment does not elicit the two" refers to that quality, engendered from wisdom, whereby the Bhagavat is freed from all obstacles in all that he knows. This means that word-hearers do have obstacles to wisdom and do discriminate without limit as to time and place, because they lack the functioning of wisdom in the awakened state. The Tathāgata is not like them, for, in regard to time, place, and any discrimination at all, his omniscient wisdom evolves without obstacle in the awakened state and lacks the dichotomy of either knowing or not knowing in regard to everything. Thus the Scripture says that it does not engender the two. It is because of this that the Scripture next speaks of the purest enlightenment. Other interpretations should be consonant with this.

297b

The Second Quality: Nonduality

The phrase "he has arrived at the imageless state" refers to the preeminent quality whereby the Bhagavat is able to enter nonduality. This means that he is able to enter suchness, which itself is characterized by the constant absence of imagination, by freedom from the proclivities of all passion, and by purification from the descriptive marks of existence or nonexistence. Moreover, he is able to cause others so to enter.

The Third Quality: Effortless Activity

The phrase "he dwells in the Buddha abode" refers to the preeminent quality whereby the Bhagavat's effortless activity is never at rest. This means that that activity by which he effortlessly benefits sentient beings is never interrupted nor cut off, because he dwells in that noble heaven, that Brahmā abode.

The Fourth Quality: Impartial Activity

The phrase "he realizes the equality of all Buddhas" refers to the preeminent quality whereby the Bhagavat's bodies, thoughts, and actions are not discriminated, because they are supported on the essence body. This means that the activities whereby he benefits others are not discriminated one from the other, because of the pure suchness wisdom of all Buddhas, because of his thoughts that bring benefit and happiness to all sentient beings, and because of both his enjoyment and his transformation bodies.

The Fifth Quality:
Suppression of Obstacles

The phrase "he reaches the place of no obstacle" refers to the pre-eminent quality whereby the Bhagavat has already cultivated the suppression of all obstacles. This means that he has already cultivated the holy path, which suppresses all obstacles of passion and to knowledge, and has already arrived at that place which is freed from all obstacles. "Place" here means that on which he relies, that to which he has gone.

The Sixth Quality:
Unfailingness of the Teaching

The phrase "his Dharma is unfailing" refers to the preeminent quality whereby the Bhagavat is not vanquished by any unorthodox teaching. This means that the Dharma, witnessed in his teaching, cannot be overthrown by others.

The Seventh Quality: Invincibility

The phrase "his activity is invincible" refers to the preeminent quality whereby the Bhagavat cannot be overcome by the worldly factors of gain and so forth, although he appears in the world.

The Eighth Quality:
Inconceivability of the Teaching

The phrase "that which he has established is inconceivable" refers to the preeminent quality whereby the Bhagavat establishes the true Dharma. This means that that preeminent Dharma of twelve sections transcends the activities of all rational inquiry. It is not something that fools can comprehend. Because he proclaims all the individual and common descriptions [of this doctrine], the Scripture says that he establishes it.

The Ninth Quality: Nonduality

The phrase "he attains equality in regard to the three times" refers to the preeminent quality whereby he is able truly to make declarations. This means that he declares the past and the future as if they were present, because the meaning of his words, which encompasses the three times, produces declarations in regard to what has appeared [in the past] and in regard to what has yet to appear [in the future]. These declarations are unfailing. Because his insights into these three divisions [of time] are unfailing, the Scripture says that they are equal.

The Tenth Quality: Manifestation of Bodies

The phrase "his body issues forth to all world-realms" refers to the preeminent quality whereby the Bhagavat, at the same time and in all world-realms whatsoever, manifests enjoyment bodies and transformation bodies. This means that in all world-realms without limit, he manifests bodies as wondrously colored as precious gems as appropriate to those to be converted.

The Eleventh Quality: Severance of Doubt

The phrase "his wisdom is unperplexed in regard to all things" 297c refers to the preeminent quality whereby the Bhagavat severs all doubt. This means that he is firmly established [in wisdom] and can lead others to become so firmly established.

The Twelfth Quality: Appropriate Manifestation of Bodies

The phrase "in all his actions he perfects great enlightenment" refers to the preeminent quality whereby he leads [sentient beings] to undertake various practices. This means that, as appropriate for the sentient beings to be converted, he appears in bodies similar to theirs and leads them to undertake [those practices].

The Thirteenth Quality: Discernment

The phrase "in all doctrines his wisdom lacks uncertainty" refers to the preeminent quality of wondrous wisdom whereby the Bhagavat discerns the genesis of all future doctrines. This means that his complete awareness transcends the range of the word-hearers, and unfailingly knows the subtlest good seeds [that, on cultivation, will give rise to future good doctrines], just as one might recognize flecks of gold in stone pottery.

The Fourteenth Quality: Nondiscriminative Manifestation

The phrase "all the bodies he manifests cannot be separated" refers to the preeminent quality of the Bhagavat's manifestations, which flow from his perfect understanding. This means that the Buddha Bhagavat, just like a wish-fulfilling gem, renders visible the bodies of a Tathāgata of a golden hue through the enabling power of all Tathāgatas and the power of his own victorious understanding, although he lacks any discrimination. As the scriptures all explain, all Tathāgatas neither discriminate nor imagine [things] to be separate one from the other.

The Fifteenth Quality: Support of the Bodhisattva Mission

The phrase "his is the wisdom that is well sought after by all bodhisattvas" refers to the preeminent quality of the skillful means whereby he makes docile the sentient beings to be converted through his unlimited bodies. This means that his mission progresses in an uninterrupted continuity in conferring benefit on all the bodhisattvas, who, because of the Tathāgata's enabling assistance, have attained wondrous wisdom through the process of hearing, reflecting on, and practicing the true Dharma.

The Sixteenth Quality:
Nonduality Replete with Perfections

The phrase "he attains that victorious far shore of the Buddha's nondual abode" refers to the preeminent quality of the completion of the perfections (*pāramitās*) of giving and so forth, in the equality of the Dharma body. This means that in the nondual Dharma body of the Buddha land, all the perfections of giving and so forth are equally complete without confusion.

The Seventeenth Quality:
Manifestation of Buddha Lands

The phrase "that undivided, deliverance wisdom of the Tathāgata is brought to full perfection" refers to the preeminent quality whereby the Bhagavat manifests undivided, pure Buddha lands, according to his perfect understanding. This means that he discerns the differences in the understandings of sentient beings and [thus] manifests all kinds of undivided Buddha lands of gold and so forth.

The Eighteenth Quality: Limitless Equality

The phrase "he has realized the equality of Buddha lands without limit" refers to the preeminent quality whereby the Bhagavat's three bodies have no limit. This means that, having realized this universal equality without any division of before or after, the three bodies of Buddha have no limitations of place in that Buddha land, in that pure Buddha realm.

The Nineteenth Quality:
Unlimited Activity of the Dharma Realm

The phrase "he reaches to the ultimate Dharma realm" refers to the preeminent quality whereby the Bhagavat reaches to the limit of transmigration and constantly manifests and brings about benefit and happiness for sentient beings. This means that, because the Dharma realm is absolutely pure, it reaches to the limits of transmigration and constantly gives rise to the teachings of the scriptures, which flow from [that Dharma realm], in order constantly to manifest and bring benefit and happiness to sentient 298a beings who are to be converted in the future, as will be appropriate at that time.

The Twentieth and Twenty-First Good Qualities: Inexhaustibility

The phrases "he reaches to the limits of empty space" and "he will never come to an end" refer to the preeminent quality whereby the Bhagavat never comes to any end. This means that just as empty space is constant and never exhausted, so the good qualities that arise from the Dharma realm of all Buddhas are also [constant and never exhausted].

Just as the limit of the future has no final endpoint, so the good qualities of all Buddhas by their very nature are constant and inexhaustible, because their efforts in bringing benefit and happiness to all sentient beings will never come to rest. Their final limits cannot be specifically determined. Therefore, because the good qualities of the Dharma body, of the Pure Dharma Realm, of the true essence are eternal, so the good qualities of the enjoyment body and the transformation body also never will come to an end, although their nature is not eternal or uninterrupted.

However, [it might be objected that] all Tathāgatas originally elicit an encompassing vow to seek great wisdom for the sake of sentient beings. If all sentient beings then attain final cessation, at that time would not all the conditioned good qualities of the Buddhas also come to an end?

[We answer that] there will never be such a time when all sentient beings will attain final cessation, and thus the Buddha's good qualities will never come to an end.

This is so because of the basic nature of reality. From the beginningless beginning all sentient beings have been divided into five kinds of lineages (*gotra*). The first is the word-hearers' lineage, second is the lineage of the individually enlightened ones, third is the Tathāgata lineage, fourth is the undetermined lineage, and fifth is the lineage without transcendent potential. Their descriptions are as presented in the scriptures and the treatises. The first four of these will ultimately attain final cessation, due to the compassionate skillful means of all Buddhas, although they have no fixed time period [in which to do so]. But the fifth lineage, because it lacks the causal power of world-transcendent good potential, will never reach a time of final cessation. All the Buddhas are able to do for them is to manifest their supernatural powers by means of their skillful means and teach them the doctrine of avoiding evil destinies and being born into good destinies. But, even though they might rely on that teaching and be reborn in the human destiny, when they reach the place of no conceptualization and no non-conceptualization, they will inevitably fall back and sink into evil destinies. All the Buddhas will again manifest their powers by skillful means and teach them the transforming power of the Dharma, and they will again cultivate good and attain birth in good destinies. But later they will again fall back and experience suffering [in evil destinies]. Again, by their skillful means, the Buddhas will succor them. In such a fashion their transmigrations will never come to an end and [the Buddhas] will not be able to lead them to ultimate, final cessation.[19]

Although other scriptures do declare that all the different kinds of sentient beings possess Buddha-nature and all will become Buddhas, this refers to the Buddha lineage of the Dharma body, or it is said as a skillful means and refers [only] to a small part of sentient beings. Or again it is said in order to lead those of an undetermined lineage to decide quickly to arrive at the result of supreme awakening.

For these reasons the Buddha's good qualities, which benefit and bring happiness to sentient beings, will never come to an end. These good qualities, which benefit others, depend on the [Buddha's own] self-benefiting good qualities, and are therefore uninter-

298b rupted. Therefore, because the Tathāgata's conditioned good qualities arise from causes [in his self-benefiting good qualities], they will never come to an end, although from time to time they may be suspended. Because these good qualities of the Buddha do not come to an end, he perfects the purest enlightenment. All other interpretations must correspond to this one, point for point.

The reason why the text first treats the Pure Land of all Buddhas and then the Bhagavat's good qualities is because it thus shows that all the Buddha's good qualities depend on that Pure Land, and that the Bhagavat, in depending on the Pure Buddha Land, is so endowed with good qualities.

Chapter IV

The Good Qualities of the Bhagavat's Retinue

The Scripture next treats the perfection of the Bhagavat's retinue. This refers to the great word-hearers and the great bodhisattvas. Other scriptures say that they were his retinue because they were [respectively] completely docile and completely liberated. It is thus that they are referred to as the perfection of the Tathāgata's retinue.

This Scripture says that the immeasurable multitude of great word-hearers, together with the great bodhisattvas, being all docile sons of the Buddha, abide in the Great Vehicle, roam in the Great Vehicle, and so forth. Thus the word-hearers and the bodhisattvas, each in their turn, constitute the perfection of retinue.

There are five reasons why this Scripture first treats the word-hearers and only then the bodhisattvas. In the first place, it does so in order that those who have doubts about the Great Vehicle may abandon those doubts. In the second place, it does so to lead those bodhisattvas of undetermined lineage to engender a stable faith. In the third place, it does so to lead all those great word-hearers, who have already been purified, to discard the pride that puffs them up from being at the head of that multitude near the Bhagavat, from being personally converted by him, from being in constant attendance on the Buddha, from being similar to the Buddha in appearance, and from being within his inner retinue. In the fourth place, the Scripture describes the great word-hearers before the bodhisattvas in order to cause those bodhisattvas to have respect for that great multitude of word-hearers, for, as the scriptures teach, it is not proper for bodhisattvas to lack respect for word-hearers, and thus this Scripture praises the good qualities of the word-hearers. In the fifth place, it so describes them in

51

order to cause others to have pure confidence in that multitude of word-hearers.

There are also other multitudes gathered together in that assembly, but as the word-hearers and the bodhisattvas are pre-eminent, they are representive of these other multitudes. The Scripture says that "in this world a great multitude of gods, humans, *devas*, and so forth, heard what the Buddha said, were greatly elated, received it in faith, and put it into practice."

Earlier it was explained that the Pure Land is characterized by the pure conscious construction of the utmost mastery. How then, [it is objected], can word-hearers and their like be included in that assembly without contradiction?

[We answer that] there is no contradiction! If the word-hearers' understanding were just the same as that of the bodhisattvas, then there would be a contradiction. There would be a valid objection only if the capability of the word-hearers were identical with [that of the bodhisattvas]. But, although they dwelled in that same assembly, the word-hearers were like men born blind, because their karmic actions obstructed their [capability] to understand that pure wonder. Thus they were said to be completely unable to express the content of that pure wonder.

But, [it might be further objected], it is precisely because they were unable to understand that they should not have been included within that assembly!

[We answer that they were included] because, even though they did not understand that pure wonder just as it is, yet they did see the transformation body preaching on this earth. Although that gathering was brought together into one, yet, in virtue of the force of their karmic actions, what each one saw and understood was different.

298c   It is like somebody seeing real gold and calling it fire. Or it is like the four different kinds of sentient beings each seeing [the same object] differently. Or perhaps since they received the support of the Tathāgata's supernatural power, they were caused to attain the sight, hearing, and enunciation of that wondrous Dharma

for a short while. There is no error in admitting that such transformations [in their consciousnesses can occur], for the Tathāgata's
inconceivable power encounters no difficulty whatsoever in employ-
ing such states of meditation to deliver [sentient beings], since he
desires to adorn that assembly in which he preaches the Dharma.
Or perhaps [those word-hearers] were magical creations of the
Buddha himself, or of the bodhisattvas.

The Scripture says: "There was an unlimited community of
great word-hearers. They were all docile sons of the Buddha. Their
minds were completely liberated. Their wisdom was completely
liberated. Their moral discipline was completely purified. They
came to seek joy in the Dharma. They had heard much, retained,
and accumulated what they heard. They thought good thoughts,
spoke good words, did good deeds. Their wisdom was swift, quick,
incisive, salvific, penetrating, great, expansive, unequaled. They
had perfected that wisdom jewel. They had completed the three
insights. They had attained the happy abode of the highest state
of insight. [They dwelled] in that very pure, rich field. Their deportment was inspiring. The perfection of their great patience and gentleness was without decrease. Already good, they practiced the
sacred teachings of the Tathāgata."

The Commentary explains: The phrase "there was an unlimited community of great word-hearers" means that because their
number was difficult to count, they are said to be unlimited. Since
they heard the Buddha's voice and entered the holy path, they
were called word-hearers. Since they were monks (bhikṣus) who
had left their homes, they were called a community. Since all of
these word-hearers were of a lineage with extremely perceptive
senses and perfections, they were termed great.

Another opinion holds that they were called great because
they all dwelled at the result stage of no training.

However, the correct opinion holds that they were called great
because these word-hearers, although they had as yet attained but
meager results, were of undetermined lineage and were oriented
toward great wisdom, [that is, when determined, their lineage would

be that of the bodhisattvas]. Or perhaps they were termed great because of their large number.

The First Quality: Docility

Being such a great community, "they were all docile." One opinion holds that they were called docile because at the stage of training, they were free from the one hundred and twelve kinds of discriminative, gross passions that can be eliminated by insight, and so they were not obstinate, but [docile] like a tamed horse.

Another opinion holds that they were called docile because at the stage of no training they were free from the one hundred and twenty-eight kinds of passion that can be eliminated by the practice of meditation, were not unyielding, [but,] like pure gold, [were pliable].

The correct opinion holds that they were called docile because, being of a lineage that turned toward wisdom and having the capability to elicit great results, they evolved skillful wisdom images, in accord with the Buddha's intention.

The Second Quality: Sonship

The Scripture calls them "sons of the Buddha" because they are born of the true Dharma, as if they were born from the Bhagavat's mouth.

Another opinion holds that they are called sons of the Buddha because, having become great word-hearers, they are able to maintain the Buddha lineage without interruption.

The Third Quality: Liberation

The phrase "their minds were completely liberated" means that they were free from the covetousness of the triple world. As it has been taught, "Because they were free from covetousness, their minds had attained liberation." The phrase "their wisdom was 299a completely liberated" means that they were already free from all defiled ignorance. As it has been taught, "Because they were free from ignorance, their wisdom had attained liberation."

The Fourth Quality: Pure Morality

The phrase "their moral discipline was completely purified" means that, as a scripture teaches, "Those who have completed the six branches[20] [of the rules for liberation are said to be completely purified in their moral discipline (*śīla*)." This means that they dwelled in the complete self-protection of pure morality and had perfected all their actions by modeling them on the rules for liberation. They were most scrupulous in regard to even the smallest transgressions and received instruction in the path of training.

Or perhaps they were said to be completely purified because they had attained uncontaminated morality.

The correct opinion holds that they were said to have been completely purified because, dwelling in the stage of no training, they turned toward the Great Vehicle, because their own morality was pure, and because they practiced the bodhisattva precepts.

The Fifth Quality: Skillful Morality

The phrase "they came to seek joy in the Dharma" means that when they sought the true Dharma, they desired to reach great joy. This means that Buddha wisdom does not seek after other things.

Or perhaps when they sought the Dharma, they avoided seeking things that might be censured or any bad conduct, in order to lead others to that joy.

The correct opinion holds that these great word-hearers single-mindedly sought the joy of the Dharma and not fame, profit, or reputation.

The Sixth Quality: Scripture Learning

Because they were able to attentively listen to innumerable scriptures from beginning to end, they are said to "have heard much." Because they were able to keep in mind the meaning of what they had heard, it is said that "they retained what they had heard." Because they frequently cultivated in meditation these words and meanings, and even memorized them, it says that "they accumulated what they had heard."

The Seventh Quality: Goodness

The Scripture says that "they thought good thoughts, spoke good words, and did good deeds" because these world-transcending arhats surpassed and opposed those teachings whereby fools think evil thoughts, speak evil words, and do evil deeds.

The Eighth Quality: Wisdom

The Scripture speaks of "swift wisdom" because, since the three actions [of body, speech, and thought] were purified and they practiced in accord with wisdom, they quickly penetrated the meaning of the Dharma and the moral discipline (*śīla*) taught by the Buddha. For the same reason it speaks of "quick wisdom" since all their actions were said to have been quick. It speaks of "incisive wisdom" because they penetrated subtle meanings. It speaks of "salvific wisdom" because they attained that wondrous wisdom that is able to transcend transmigration. It speaks of "penetrating wisdom" because this wisdom is able to understand the cause for cessation. Because it arrives at certitude it is called penetrating, for it [penetrates] cessation inasmuch as it is able to understand its cause. It is called "great wisdom" because it responds to questions with a certitude that is never exhausted. It is called "expansive wisdom" because, with its deep and wide perfection, it reaches everywhere. Other scriptures also describe it as a deep, wondrous wisdom, which means that others are unable to exhaust its depths. It is called "unequaled wisdom" because it is superior to that of all those word-hearers of dull senses. It is called "the wisdom jewel" because this wisdom is able to elicit the highest meaning. They are said to "have perfected that wisdom jewel" because all these word-hearers were endowed with this wisdom.

The Ninth Quality: The Three Insights

The phrase "they had completed the three insights" means that they had attained the three insights of the stage of no training, which are the insight of the wisdom which recalls former lives, the insight of the wisdom that knows the [conditions of the] death and birth [of all sentient beings], and the insight of the wisdom that exhausts the contaminated outflows.

These three insights, which are attained by sharp faculties at the stage of no training, are called the three insights because they are free from foolish views on either defilement or nondefilement, or on the three times. 299b

One opinion holds that insight has wisdom as its nature and, since such wisdom is able to expel darkness, it comes to be called insight.

Another opinion holds that since undefiled good roots are its nature, [such insight] reverses ignorance.

The Tenth Quality: Concentration

The phrase "they attained that happy abode of the highest state of insight" means that they had realized the preeminent concentration that will not be reversed.

The Eleventh Quality: Fruitfulness

The phrase ["they dwelled in that] very pure, rich field" means that being free from passion, just like a good field, they were able quickly to give rise to extensive, great fruit.

The Twelfth Quality: Inspiring Conduct

The phrase "their deportment was inspiring" means that they dwelled in the correct knowledge of all-inspiring conduct.

The Thirteenth Quality: Patience

The phrase "the perfection of their great patience and gentleness was without decrease" means that they dwelled together at ease in the deep patience [that understands] suffering.

The Fourteenth Quality: Perfection of Practice

This means that all their practices had reached perfection.

Chapter V

The Distinction Between Wisdom and Cessation In Regard to the Great Word-hearers

The basic [intent] of the Tathāgata's sacred Dharma is that sentient beings escape the sufferings of transmigration. Now all these word-hearers, having ascended to the stage of no training, did escape from transmigration and thus [the intent of that] sacred Dharma was fulfilled. [It may be asked that] since this was so, why then did [the Buddha] again [in this Scripture] teach them the doctrine?

We answer that he did so in order to cause them to turn to great wisdom.

But, [it may be objected,] all these great word-hearers dwelled in the stage of no training and, when they had completed their last existence, they would certainly have entered eternally quiescent cessation. Furthermore, as other treatises explain, this place of quiescence is identical with awakening. Why then did he lead them to seek great wisdom, thereby experiencing suffering for such a long time?

We answer that in their transformed condition there is no experience of suffering. Therefore the objection [that they would experience suffering] is invalid.

But, [it is objected,] because [their transformed condition] does involve the suffering implicit in all karmic formations, this objection is certainly valid, [for they do experience these karmic formations]!

[We answer that] although they do pass through these sufferings [inasmuch as their transformed station of existence is karmically formed], yet there is no validity to the objection, because they are led to attain great joy and happiness in the Tathāgata's three bodies [and thus their transformed condition of existence is a manifestation of ultimate wisdom].

But, [it is further asked], all great happiness does not go beyond cessation, which they would have already attained [if they had entered cessation]. What then was lacking [in that cessation] that they should again seek after great wisdom?

[We answer that] although they did have the happiness of calm quiescence, yet they lacked the experience of that happiness, for the happiness of such an awakening would have eradicated innumerable good qualities, such as the happiness of experience.

Of what possible use is such a conditioned happiness, characterized by the suffering implicit in all karmic formations?

[We answer that] the state of being both conditioned and uncontaminated is similar to cessation. Because it is uncontaminated, it is not included in the suffering implicit in all karmic formations. Moreover, they attained awakening in order to be able to convert the multitudes of sentient beings who have to be converted and to lead them to escape transmigration.

But, [the objection continues,] having already realized Buddhahood, would they have lacked this ability [to convert beings]?

[We answer that] from the beginningless beginning, the basic nature of the reality of sentient beings is that the different lineages of those who convert and those who are to be converted are interrelated. The absence of such an interrelationship implies the impossibility of conversion. Thus, by means of various kinds of skillful means, the Tathāgata converts all sentient beings and leads them to attain the result of awakening. He converts those whom he is to convert, [with whom he has a karmic relationship. Thus, if the great word-hearers were to have entered cessation, having no karmic relationship with any sentient beings, they could not convert those whom they were to convert].

If this be the case, then [it can be objected that] those word-hearers, whether they have eliminated seven rebirths or [only] one rebirth, whether they have eliminated rebirth in any superior world or whether they have just one remaining rebirth, whether they have attained a totally nonreflective cessation in any of these stages or in all their births, how could they once again cultivate wisdom causes for the duration of three incalculable eons?

[We answer that] although they do attain total nonreflective cessation in all the stages imbued with passion, nevertheless, because of the power of their vows, they experience magical births and thus are able to cultivate wisdom causes for the duration of three incalculable eons. Therefore the objection is invalid.

The state of total nonreflective cessation is not characterized by a multitude of causes and, when it occurs, there is a final cessation of rebirth. But this is not an eternal state of nonbirth, for while, in virtue of the power of their vows taken in concentration, dwelling for a long time within transmigration, they do have causes which engender birth, and thus their efforts are able to engender results for a long time. In their present bodies they develop and grow until they finally realize Buddhahood. Just like those arhats who conserve their energies for a long life, they do not experience rebirth. This is as explained in the *Treatise on the Stages of Yogic Meditation (Yogācārabhūmi)*: 299c

> In such a case, do these word-hearers who turn toward wisdom abide in cessation without remainder and therein elicit the aspiration for supreme awakening (*bodhicitta*)? Or do they abide in cessation with remainder?
>
> We answer that they abide only in cessation with remainder, [that is, in their bodies]. If they were to abide in cessation without remainder, it would be impossible for them to engender any activity and all their endeavors would cease.
>
> But, [it is asked,] if they abide only in cessation with remainder and therein elicit the aspiration for supreme awakening, how is it possible for them to realize that supreme awakening in just one lifetime? The arhats certainly do not have any remaining support for another rebirth. How much less could they have a continuity of many rebirths? [But we know that many rebirths are necessary for the many practices requisite for the realization of

supreme awakening. Therefore, these word-hearers could not possibly attain awakening in cessation with the remaining support of their present bodies.]

We respond that they are able to accomplish this because they increase their lifespans. In many ways the Bhagavat depends on these word-hearers who have turned toward wisdom. With a deep meaning he said: "Whoever has well cultivated the four supernatural powers, he will be able to remain [in his body] for one eon, or again for another eon." This "another eon" can mean more than just one additional eon. But, although they expand their lifespans and elicit the aspiration for supreme awakening, their practice is extremely halting because they have a predilection for cessation. They are not the equals of those bodhisattvas who have just elicited the aspiration [for wisdom] and are beginning their practices. But, by increasing their lifespans, they maintain their sense bodies, although each creates a transformation body and, in the presence of their brethren, they skillfully manifest final cessation in [entering into] a cessation without any remainder [and they seem to die]. It is for this reason that all think: "Venerable So-and-so has passed into cessation without remainder and has entered final cessation." But in fact, because they maintain their sense bodies, they go to distant places in this world-realm of Jambudvīpa at will and dwell there. Even the gods are unable to identify them. How then could other sentient beings be able to identify them? Because they do delight in cessation, they journey to various world-realms and approach Buddhas and bodhisattvas in order to honor them. Being equipped with the practices of wisdom, they are on the sacred path. But when they become negligent, then various Buddhas and bodhisattvas exhort them and, being so exhorted, they are able to be more careful in their practices.

Furthermore, these word-hearers who turn toward wisdom, whether in the stage of training or of no training, are able to renounce their vows as word-hearers, [for in fact they are of undetermined lineage. They are in these stages] because their sense natures have differences and because their supporting causes have differences.

If they are in the stage of no training, they will turn toward wisdom because of the force of their vows taken in concentration and, because they manifest a body which has previously been cre-   300a ated and variously equipped, they will engender a continuity of results for a very long time indeed. They will gradually increase their eminence until they realize awakening and their abilities will then become exhausted. Although such results are directly produced by the contaminated causes [of their imperfect practices], yet they are assisted by their uncontaminated vows taken in concentration. This is what is termed the inconceivable transformation of transmigration.

If, however, they turn toward wisdom in the stage of training, either their remaining passions have yet the force to produce rebirth, and then, in that last rebirth, they will suppress passion, because that last body will be equipped with the power to elicit vows in concentration and, as explained above, they will then reach awakening; or, since they have already turned their minds toward wisdom, they have already suppressed all passion because the body they manifest is equipped with the power to elicit vows in concentration. As above explained, they will reach the realization of awakening. But in either case they employ the assistance of uncontaminated concentration vows. Those who have no passion are supported on the inconceivable bodies of transformation, while those who are yet influenced by the force of passion are supported on the fragmented bodies of karmic maturation. But when we speak of the transformations created by these word-hearers, it is not [always] necessary to make such fine distinctions.

Chapter VI

The Good Qualities
of the Bodhisattvas

The Scripture says: "There were also present there an unlimited number of bodhisattva-great beings (*māhasattva*s) who had assembled from all Buddha lands. They all dwelled in the Great Vehicle. They traversed that Dharma of the Great Vehicle. Their minds were equal in regard to all beings. They were free from all discrimination of *kalpa* and non-*kalpa*. They had suppressed all inimical forces. They were far removed from the thought-binding discrimination of all the word-hearers and individually enlightened ones. They were sustained by enjoyment and delight in that expansive great taste of the Dharma. They rose above the five dreads. They had assuredly entered the state of no returning. They mitigated the oppressive lands that torment sentient beings and appeared before them. These wondrously born bodhisattvas were of the highest order."

The Commentary explains: They are called bodhisattva-great beings because, in seeking wisdom, they understood all three vehicles (i.e., of word-hearers, of individually enlightened ones, and the Great Vehicle) so as to select the greatest. Because their object was wisdom (*bodhi*), they are called bodhisattvas (wisdom-beings). They have perfected their great vows whereby self-benefit benefits others, for they have sought great wisdom in order to benefit sentient beings. Also the term "being" [in the phrase great being] has the meaning of courage and thus they are called *bodhi*-beings, since they have progressed courageously in their quest for great wisdom. Again, they are called great beings because they completely understood all states of existence in order to select that of supramundane bodhisattvas.

The Scripture praises the good qualities of these bodhisattvas in order to dispel any contemptuous feelings on the part of sentient beings. Other [texts] say that all the multitude of word-hearers must respect all those bodhisattvas who for a long time have practiced celibacy. Furthermore, these bodhisattvas are honored in order to lead sentient beings to engender pure faith. How much more then [should they have faith] in the Tathāgatas. In praising the good qualities of these bodhisattvas, the Scripture explains that they have three greatnesses in virtue of which they are called great beings. The first is the greatness of their numbers, in that 300b they are immeasurable. The second is the greatness of their good qualities, in that they abide in the Great Vehicle, roam in the Great Vehicle, and so forth, [as explained in the Scripture]. The third is the greatness of their action, in that they mitigate the passions of all sentient beings. Such a benefiting and gladdening of sentient beings is the action of these bodhisattvas.

The phrase "they assembled from all Buddha lands" means that they came and assembled to hear the Dharma from all kinds of Buddha lands in the ten directions. There must have been some bodhisattvas from this lower world-realm among those bodhisattvas who assembled there, but the Scripture says only that bodhisattvas from different places assembled there. They did not come to that assembly just because they wanted to control indolence and pride, rather they came from their world-realms because they wanted to hear the Dharma and they were not led there by others. They were all endowed with great supernatural powers and had each come from their far-distant realms.

But how do we know that those other [word-hearers] did not come to that assembly? Above, the Scripture did not say that the multitude of word-hearers came to that assembly because they remained where they were. When it says that they came to that assembly from different places, this refers to the bodhisattvas. The Scripture, however, speaks in general terms and so does not make this distinction.

In regard to the greatness of their good qualities, we must recognize nine kinds of qualities.

The First Quality:
The Greatness of Their Zeal

This means that "they all dwelled in the Great Vehicle" because of the force of their zeal. Being firmly established in that Great Vehicle, they save sentient beings, cause them to escape transmigration, and lead them to elicit the aspiration for supreme wisdom.

The Second Quality:
The Greatness of Their Cause

This means that "they traversed the Dharma of that Great Vehicle," that is, the ten stages, in order to successively hear, reflect on, and meditate on [that Dharma].

The Third Quality:
The Greatness of Their Object

This means that "their minds were equal in regard to all beings" [who are the objects of their compassionate actions], for in virtue of their great compassion and impartial, skillful means, they had attained equality between self and others in regard to all sentient beings.

The Fourth Quality:
The Greatness of Their Time

This means that "they were free from all discrimination of *kalpa* and non-*kalpa*" in that they were impartial to all time (*kalpa*) as if it were all one single instant. [In the above sentence] *kalpa* is called *vikalpa*, discrimination. It is because they were free from all such discrimination in regard to all *kalpas*, eons, or all non-*kalpas*, non-eons, that they did not discriminate *kalpa* from non-*kalpa*. [Not discriminating any time periods], they were able to practice for a long time without becoming weary.

The Fifth Quality:
The Greatness of Their Nondefilement

This means that "they had suppressed all inimical forces" in that, because they had abandoned all acquisitions, they were able to suppress inimical forces. As it is said, "When a bodhisattva knows that all acquisitions have no enduring reality and he does not covet them in his mind, then he is able to suppress all inimical forces."

The Sixth Quality:
The Greatness of Their Attention

This means that "they were far removed from the thought-binding discrimination of all word-hearers and individually enlightened ones" in that they had severed and were far apart from that kind of attention which occurs in the two vehicles.

The Seventh Quality:
The Greatness of Their Sustenance

This means that "they were sustained by enjoyment and delight in that expansive, great taste of Dharma" in that they took as their sustenance joy in the taste of the Dharma of the Great Vehicle.

The Eighth Quality:
The Greatness of Their Purity

This means that "they rose above the five dreads" in that the purity of all their [three] actions of body, speech, and thought delivered them from all dread. They did not transgress the precepts (*śīla*), nor have any reason to dread falling into evil destinies. The five dreads are insecurity, the dread of evil spells, the dread of dying, the dread of evil destinies, and the dread of going before crowds. When they had realized the land of pure thought and happiness, 300c all these five dreads were removed.

The Ninth Quality:
The Greatness of Their Attainment

This means that "they had assuredly entered the state of no returning" in that they single-mindedly had attained the prediction of omniscience, for in this stage they assuredly would not retrogress. In the first seven stages they still were involved in the work of intensified effort and therefore had not yet attained the effortless path of no returning. But in the other stages, in virtue of the fact that they were not so involved in the work of intensified effort, they had assuredly entered the stage of no returning. Because the stage of no returning is an effortless path, an assured entry, the Scripture says that they assuredly entered the stage of no returning.

Then in the greatness of their action, "they mitigate the oppressive lands that torment sentient beings and appear before them." This phrase means that all bodhisattvas are able to mitigate the oppressive lands of internal and external suffering that afflict sentient beings and for this purpose they render themselves visible to them. Since their land is one of great mercy and compassion, they are able to mitigate the sufferings of all internal ills and the oppression that comes from the coveting of externals. Because these two [actions] bring benefit and happiness to sentient beings, those who have attained such are said to have come to the perfection of action.

Again [there is a further commentary on these nine good qualities, which is presented below].

The First Quality:
The Greatness of Their Abiding

The phrase "they all dwelled in the Great Vehicle" means that in virtue of dwelling in the stage of joy they had realized the all-pervasive Dharma realm of ultimate truth, for then they first realized the ultimate truth of the doctrine of the Great Vehicle and are therefore said to abide in the Great Vehicle.

The Second Quality:
The Greatness of Their Moral Discipline

The phrase "they traversed the Dharma of that Great Vehicle" means that in the stage of purification they practiced the three kinds of bodhisattva moral discipline. The doctrine of the practice of the Great Vehicle is identical with the three kinds of moral discipline.

The Third Quality:
The Greatness of Their Concentration

The phrase "their minds were equal in regard to all beings" means that in the stage of illumination they had attained all preeminent concentrations, elicited the four immeasurables, and impartially brought benefit and happiness to all sentient beings.

The Fourth Quality:
The Greatness of Their Nondiscrimination

The phrase "they were free from all discrimination" and so forth means that in the stage of radiance they had attained the thirty-seven factors favorable to wisdom, were apart from all kinds of discrimination, and did not distinguish discrimination from nondiscrimination. Discrimination means the discrimination of the view of self, which is abandoned by insight. This is already severed in the stage of joy. Nondiscrimination means the innate view of self, which is abandoned [only] by the practice of meditation. In this stage it is severed. All the states associated with these two kinds of self-view are called all the kinds of discrimination here, for one differentiates them in terms of their operation. Although they are progressively eliminated [in the course of the stages], yet this explanation, [in saying that they are abandoned at this fourth stage], gives a general description of them, just as the fourth meditation is said to be apart from both suffering and joy, or the result of the third [meditation] is said to be apart from the five lower obstacles, [when in fact these things are also abandoned progressively over the course of the stages].

[But there are differences of opinion as to just which self-view is severed at this stage of radiance.] One opinion holds that at this stage the innate passions of the thinking consciousness are completely severed.

A second opinion holds that at this stage the innate self-view of the perceiving consciousness is completely severed, not of the thinking consciousness, because in the seventh stage of far-reaching there is yet some subtle functioning of subtle passion. If such were lacking there, then the thinking consciousness would have no support for defilement and consequently would not be similar in support to the five sense consciousnesses. If these subtle delusions of the thinking consciousness were already severed, then the gross delusions of the perceiving consciousness would not function in the fifth, sixth, and seventh stages. Such, however, would contradict the teaching of the *Treatise on the Stages of Yogic Meditation* and the *Scripture on the Explication of Underlying Meaning*. Then such a state would be similar to the diamond-like concentration as it occurs in the two vehicles since, if the delusions of the thinking consciousness together with the subtle passion of the perceiving consciousness were both severed at the same moment, then [it would be the same as the case of the arhat where] the subtle passions of the thinking consciousness were first severed and the gross passion of the perceiving consciousness was severed later. 301a

Therefore, in this fourth stage [of radiance] one attains the wisdom cessation of no-self in the perceiving consciousness, but the innate self-view is not yet severed and the subtle passion of the thinking consciousness, in addition to some delusion in the perceiving consciousness, remains to be severed by the practice of meditation. Thus when the Scripture speaks of suppressing and being freed [from all kinds of discrimination], this is not to be understood as an absolute cessation. When one reaches the diamond-like mind in the tenth stage of the Dharma cloud, then all is instantaneously severed and annihilated, because their seeds are uprooted by the practice of meditation.

The Fifth Quality:
The Greatness of Their Equality

The phrase "they suppress all inimical forces" means that at the stage of invincibility they see that the Four Noble Truths are all of an equal nature, and they suppress the inimical force that makes distinctions between appropriating transmigration and cessation.

The Sixth Quality:
The Greatness of Their Insight

The phrase "they were far removed from the thought-binding discrimination of all word-hearers and individually enlightened ones" means that in the stage of presence they gain the insight that the twelve conditions which give rise to both defilement and purification are all of an equal nature, and they are thus far removed from the thought-binding discrimination of the two vehicles, which does distinguish between the defilement of oppression and the purification of joy.

The Seventh Quality:
The Greatness of Their Realization

The phrase "they were sustained by enjoyment and delight in that expansive, great taste of the Dharma" means that in the stage of far-reaching they had realized the imageless truth, and in the wisdom of emptiness they gave rise to preeminent practice and enjoyed the great Dharma.

The Eighth Quality:
The Greatness of Their Liberation

The phrase "they rose above the five dreads" means that in the stage of steadfastness all passion no longer functioned for them. It was because they had been liberated from the causes for the five dreads that they are said to have risen above these five dreads. The results of these five dreads had already been severed in the stage of joy.

The Ninth Quality:
The Greatness of Their Attainment

The phrase "they had assuredly entered the state of no returning" means that in the stage of unerring judgment they had certainly entered the state of no returning, replete with all the ten bodhisattva practices.

The Tenth Quality:
The Greatness of Their Compassion

The phrase "they mitigated the oppressive lands that torment sentient beings" means that in the stage of the Dharma cloud they had attained the great Dharma body, had engendered a cloud of great compassion, had poured down the great rain of the Dharma, and had eradicated all the oppressive elements that torment sentient beings.

Furthermore, these ten phrases from the Scripture could also be interpreted according to the ten perfections, the ten great vows, and so forth, since from the stage of joy on, each successive stage supports these practices of all the stages.

The phrase "these wondrously born bodhisattvas were all of the highest order" means that they were able to elicit a state of concentration replete with good qualities. They are said to be "wondrously born" because these bodhisattvas had attained this state of concentration. Because the names of these bodhisattvas were all expressive of Dharma, just as Maitreya [is so called after the doctrine of friendliness (*maitrī*)], these bodhisattvas are foremost among that multitude and thus they are said to be of the highest order.

Below, the Scripture will only speak of bodhisattvas, because it summarizes what has been here explained [as comprising that multitude], and thus employs but one term [in referring to them]. But the rest of that multitude should be understood also to be included in their number. The intent of the transmitter of this doctrine was simply to summarize [and not to exclude the others from that multitude].

Part Two

The Content of the Teaching

Chapter VII

An Analysis of the Five Wisdom Factors

The Scripture says: "At that time the Bhagavat addressed the wondrously born bodhisattvas as follows: 'You wondrously born ones should understand that there are five factors which comprise the land of great wisdom. They are the Pure Dharma Realm, mirror wisdom, equality wisdom, discernment wisdom, and duty-fulfillment wisdom.'"

The Commentary explains: We have now explained the first part and dealt with the cause for the arising of this teaching. This second part will explain the content of this sacred teaching. [There are fourteen points to discuss in considering these five factors.]

The First Theme:
The Intended Audience for This Teaching

The Scripture says that [the Bhagavat] addressed himself only to the wondrously born bodhisattvas, for they were the recipients of this preeminent teaching. Why did he not address himself [also] to the multitude of word-hearers?

This is because the minds of the bodhisattvas were set on seeking the entirety of wisdom and only they, having heard much Dharma, would give rise to a preeminent understanding. Only they, having given rise to such a preeminent understanding, would be able to penetrate [its depths]. Only they, having penetrated [its depths], would be able correctly to put it into practice. Only they, having correctly put it into practice, would be able quickly to carry it to completion. Word-hearers are unable to seek the entirety of wisdom. Even if they were able to seek to hear such a doctrine, they would not give rise to a preeminent understanding. Even if they were to give rise to a preeminent understanding, they would be unable correctly to put it into practice. Even if they were correctly to put it into practice, they would be unable to bring it to completion. Thus he did not address them.

[But, it is objected,] if this be so, then, when he preached this Scripture, why did he include [those word-hearers] in the assembly [in the first place]?

[We answer that] he did so in order that the multitude would be extremely large. Consequently he changed their lineage so that he could lead those word-hearers who had turned toward wisdom to elicit the aspiration for great wisdom, and thus he drew them into that great multitude. Or perhaps there is no contradiction here because it was actually bodhisattvas who manifested themselves in the visible appearance [of those word-hearers].

In sum, there are four characteristics that establish the Buddha's Pure Land: number, support, names, and the meaning of penetrating differentiations. We now turn our attention to these themes.

The Second Theme:
The Number of Factors Comprising Wisdom

In number there are five factors [that comprise wisdom]. Later we will explain their specific natures. Their number is really self-apparent [from the Scripture text], and it is here mentioned only to be perfectly clear about it, for there are only five factors, no more and no less. Although factor (*dharma*) here means that which supports an individual descriptive mark, this does not mean that these [factors] generate a maturation that is imagined.

The Third Theme:
How These Factors Support Wisdom

Support means that these five factors support the land of great wisdom. Great wisdom is awakening, which is endowed with the three bodies of essence, enjoyment, and transformation. These will afterward be explained in detail. That land of great wisdom is the entire range of the practice embodied on the ground of great wisdom. We establish a differentiation in the individual descriptions [of these five factors] because all things fall within the range [of great wisdom]. Because everything that is included within the words that describe the content [of that great wisdom] and the essence [of that great wisdom], which includes only its given description, is unified here, there are unlimited good qualities of two kinds in that land of great wisdom. In general, there are two, the conditioned and the unconditioned. Unconditioned qualities are supported on the Pure Dharma Realm. That Pure Dharma Realm is the unconditioned quality of suchness. All [these good qualities] are [but the mental] differentiations of the essence of suchness. Conditioned qualities are supported by the four wisdoms, because, being uncontaminated, the activity of these wisdoms is strong. It is thus that wisdom is visibly manifested.

301c

In ultimate truth, in all consciousnesses and conscious states in all their varieties, each wisdom singly comprises within itself all good qualities and aspects. But in their perceptible aspects, discernment wisdom includes the four meditations and gains deep insight into all bodies. Equality wisdom includes the four correct efforts and the four immeasurables. The four correct efforts, although they are constituted by zeal, are yet included within the Tathāgata's equality wisdom and have no gradations. The four immeasurables, because their action is impartial and equal, are included within equality wisdom. The steps to supernatural powers are included within discernment wisdom because they are constituted by concentration, for this [equality wisdom] is the support of all prayer formulae (*dhāraṇis*) and concentrations, as will be explained below in the Scripture. Therefore, the prayer formulae and concentration practices of other meditations, recollections, understandings, and concentrations, the wisdom of peaceful resolve, penetrating, unobstructed understandings, the powers of the Tathāgata's exclusive eighty Buddha qualities, the powers of fearlessness, and so forth—all these in their various aspects are included within discernment wisdom. The many aspects of wisdom insight of the supernatural powers are included within duty-fulfillment wisdom. The supernatural powers and the Buddha powers of the wisdom that exhausts contamination are included within all four of these wisdoms, inasmuch as they continuously destroy contamination. But, inasmuch as they are directed toward cessation, which exhausts contamination, they are included within mirror wisdom and equality wisdom. The wisdom powers of the seven all-pervading practices are included within all four wisdoms. All the powers of wisdom and all basic wisdoms in their many aspects are included within mirror wisdom and equality wisdom. The seven factors of wisdom in their many aspects are included within equality wisdom. The true, uncontaminated state of the ten wisdoms regarding suffering and so forth in their many aspects are included within mirror wisdom and equality wisdom. Mindfulness of Dharma in its many aspects is included within mirror wisdom. Severance from continuous karmic maturation in its many aspects is included within the Pure Dharma Realm and mirror wisdom. The perfections, whether they be uncontaminated or appear as contaminated, in their many aspects are included within the Pure Dharma Realm and mirror wisdom, but if they are really contaminated, they are included within the last two wisdoms. All the major and minor marks [of a Buddha] in their many aspects are included within duty-fulfillment wisdom. All other Buddha qualities or their associated characteristics are also so included.

Thus these four wisdoms completely include all Buddha lands, all uncontaminated consciousnesses and conscious states, whether they be taken together or distinguished into the varieties of their

manifestation. The Pure Dharma Realm includes the quality above   302a
all qualities, which is suchness. Thus these five factors together
include the good qualities of all Buddha lands.[21]

The Fourth Theme:
The Meaning of the Five Factors

The names [of these factors] refer to [the factors from] the Pure
Dharma Realm to duty-fulfillment wisdom. The Pure Dharma Realm
[has ten meanings]. First, it is separated from the adventitious obstacles of passion and to knowledge. Second, it is the true, indefectible
nature of all conditioned and unconditioned things. Third, it is the
cause from which all sacred doctrines arise. Fourth, it is the true
essence of all Tathāgatas. Fifth, it is essentially pure from the beginningless beginning. Sixth, it is endowed with all kinds of essential
qualities surpassing the number of atomic particles in all the ten
directions. Seventh, just like empty space, it is neither produced nor
destroyed. Eighth, it is universally present and common to all things
and all sentient beings. Ninth, it is neither identical with nor different
from all things and it is neither existence or nonexistence. And,
tenth, being separated from all images, from all discriminations,
and from all names, it is entirely unobtainable and is realized only
through the wisdom of purified arhats. Suchness, which is revealed
by the no-self of the two emptinesses [of one's own self and the self
of other things] is the essence [of the Pure Dharma Realm]. All the
arhats realize it in part and all Buddhas realize it in full. Therefore
it is called the Pure Dharma Realm.

Mirror wisdom [has eleven meanings]. First, it is separated from
clinging to "I" and "mine," from all subject-object dichotomies. Second, its object and mode of functioning are difficult to know. Third,
it is never confused nor forgetful in regard to all knowables. Fourth,
it does not imagine differences in knowables. Fifth, it is uninterrupted and unceasing at all times and in all places. Sixth, it is
absolutely separated from the contaminated seeds of the obstacle
of passion. Seventh, it is replete with all seeds of all pure, uncontaminated good qualities. Eighth, it is able to manifest and engender

all wisdom images in all realms. Ninth, it is the support for the images of all bodies and lands. Tenth, it upholds the good qualities of all Buddha lands. And eleventh, it will never come to an end and has no point of termination. Therefore it is named mirror wisdom.

Equality wisdom [has six meanings]. First, it has deep insight into the universal equality of self and others. Second, it is associated constantly with great mercy and compassion. Third, it constantly and uninterruptedly establishes the nonabiding cessation of Buddha lands. Fourth, at will it confers happiness on all sentient beings. Fifth, it manifests all kinds of images of enjoyment bodies and transformation bodies. Sixth, it is the specific support for discernment wisdom. Therefore it is named equality wisdom.

Discernment wisdom [has five meanings]. First, it has deep, unhindered insight into the differentiations of all knowables. Second, it retains and remembers all prayer formulae and concentration practices, and all wondrous concentrations. Third, it is able to manifest all masterful activity in the great assemblies. Fourth, it is able to cut off all doubts. Fifth, it is able to pour down the rain of Dharma. Therefore it is named discernment wisdom.

Duty-fulfillment wisdom [has two meanings]. First, it is able to manifest the various, immeasurable, innumerable, inconceivable Buddha transformations in all world-realms whatsoever, as they are appropriate to the sentient beings to be converted and matured. Second, its skillful means constantly and uninterruptedly bring benefit and happiness to all sentient beings. Therefore it is named duty-fulfillment wisdom.

302b

The Fifth Theme:
The Five Factors as Cause and Result

Here we will treat these five factors from the standpoint of cause, result, and the distinctions of those results. The cause is the Pure Dharma Realm because it is the enabling cause for engendering and increasing sacred Dharma. The result is those sacred wisdoms which are engendered with it as their knowable content because it supports them. There are four kinds of these sacred wisdom results, which are distinguished according to their function. This means that, having the Pure Dharma Realm as their knowable content, they support all doctrines as heard, they realize the equality of self and others among all sentient beings, they manifest the preeminent skillful means of the true Dharma, and they bring about benefit to others.

Now we will treat these five factors from the standpoint of the essence, cause, and result of awakening. The essence of awakening is pure suchness. The essence of [mirror wisdom] is that nondiscriminative wisdom which has [suchness] as its knowable content. The essence of [equality wisdom] is its constant and continuous causation of the wisdom of equality among all sentient beings, the result of which is benefit for all sentient beings. The essence of [discernment wisdom and duty-fulfillment wisdom] is the discernment of who can be converted and who cannot and, as appropriate, the fulfillment of that task [of converting].

Now we treat these five factors from the standpoint of their differences as the results of Buddha lands. The result of wisdom and abandonment is the essence of Buddha lands. The result of abandonment is the Pure Dharma Realm because it is absolutely severed from all obstacles. Wisdom is the four above wisdoms of mirror wisdom and so forth, for these are manifestations of consciousnesses and conscious states in the lands of the result of awakening. Among all good qualities, wisdom is most eminent, and it is named wisdom because in general it supports all conditioned good qualities.

Now we treat these five factors by summarizing what has been explained above. In general they include all factors of awakening in Buddha lands. The hearing of Dharma nurtures and supports all the good qualities which comprise those Buddha lands. They constantly give rise to equality in bringing about benefit and happiness for all sentient beings. They are accompanied by the adornments of prayer formulae and concentration practices, by unlimited, immeasurable, rich understandings, and they are able to bring about benefit and happiness for all sentient beings.

The Sixth Theme:
The Consciousness Converted by Each Wisdom

Now we treat the question of which consciousnesses are converted by each of the four wisdoms. The *Summary of the Great Vehicle* teaches that "they convert the aggregate of consciousness."

[It may, however, be objected that] since [these wisdoms] are states of consciousness, they are unable to convert consciousness.

[We answer that] it is because these four are associated with the wisdom of the uncontaminated mind that we conventionally term them wisdoms [and thus they are not karmic states of consciousness at all].

[But, the objection continues,] the words of that *Summary of the Great Vehicle* treat the highest wisdom. Is it proper then to say that [such supreme wisdom] is ultimately existent, or [only, as you seem to have just done,] that it is conventionally existent?

We answer that we should say both. If we are talking about wisdom itself, then it does ultimately exist. But if we are talking about wisdom as the consciousness and conscious states that accompany wisdom, then we say that it is conventional. One must make this distinction. Since wisdom is the principal factor in this uncontaminated consciousness and these conscious states, they are called wisdom.

By the conversion of the aggregate of consciousness, one attains the mind associated with the four uncontaminated wisdoms. This refers to the mind of mirror wisdom and so forth. By the conversion of the container consciousness, one attains the mind associated with mirror wisdom because it is able to support the seeds of all good qualities and to engender images of all bodies and lands. By the conversion of the thinking consciousness (*manas*), one attains the mind associated with equality wisdom because it is free of discrimination regarding self and others and has realized universal equality [between self and others]. By the conversion of the perceiving consciousness (*manovijñāna*), one attains the mind associated with discernment wisdom because it is able to discern all things without obstacle. By the conversion of the five sense consciousnesses, one

302c

attains the mind associated with duty-fulfillment wisdom because it is able to manifest and bring to completion external tasks.

Another opinion, however, holds that it is by the conversion of the perceiving consciousness that one attains duty-fulfillment wisdom, and by the conversion of the five sense consciousnesses that one attains discernment wisdom. But this opinion is not valid because it inverts the proper order and because discernment wisdom, which enunciates Dharma and dispels doubts, is not a function proper to the five sense consciousnesses.

Therefore in the stages of conversion of transmigratory consciousness, the consciousnesses and conscious states associated with these four [wisdoms] attain the consciousnesses and conscious states associated with these four results of awakening through their [respective] conversions.

The Seventh Theme:
The Knowable Content of the Four Wisdoms

Next we treat the knowable content of the consciousnesses and the conscious states associated with these four wisdoms. According to the theory of a "single image," the consciousnesses and conscious states associated with mirror wisdom are nondiscriminative and have as their knowable content only suchness. This is not a subsequently attained [wisdom] because its knowable content and mode of functioning are unknowable.

According to the theory of "an ensemble of images," mirror wisdom has as its knowable content all things. As the *Ornament of the Scriptures of the Great Vehicle* teaches, "mirror wisdom is not fooled in regard to all knowable content." And this *Scripture on the Buddha Land* teaches, "Just as a multitude of images appear in a great mirror, just so a multitude of images from all the [six] internal organs, the [six] external objects of those organs, and all the [six] sense consciousnesses [resultant on that sense perception] do appear in the wisdom mirror of the Tathāgata." The phrase "all the organs" refers to the six sense organs. "All the objects" refers to the six sense objects. And the phrase "all the consciousnesses" refers to the six sense consciousnesses [of seeing, hearing, smelling, tasting, touching, and perceiving]. Therefore the multitude of images from the eighteen realms [of perception] do appear in this wisdom. Therefore this wisdom has all things as its knowable content. It is because this mirror wisdom always has all things as its knowable content that we say that the Tathāgata is omniscient. If this were not so, then since the other wisdoms certainly do not know all things, the Tathāgata would not be called omniscient.

Therefore, [this second theory continues,] internally mirror wisdom has as its knowable content the seed of its own essence, [which is suchness,] but externally it has as its knowable content all knowable things, whether ultimate or conventional, and it manifests all images of bodies, lands, and so forth. When it takes as its content the limit of ultimate truth, it is called nondiscriminative wisdom, and when it takes as its content the limit of conventional truth, it is called subsequently attained wisdom. Although it does indeed have all things as its knowable content, yet its mode of functioning is subtle and difficult to know, just as the knowable content and the mode of functioning of the container consciousness, because subtle, are also difficult to know, although it has as its knowable content the triple world. It is not then the case that this wisdom, because it is difficult to know and realize, has as its content only suchness in nondiscriminative wisdom. Although its essence is one, yet its activities of [manifesting] truth are many and it is thus distinguished according to these activities and divided into the two wisdoms [of nondiscriminative and subsequently attained]. There is no contradiction here. Moreover, it is only when it reaches to the truth of ultimate meaning that it can understand conventional truth. Therefore, although it is one mind, its truth is said to have a before and an after. Or perhaps what is designated as subsequently attained wisdom [only] appears to be subsequently attained. The other wisdoms are also to be interpreted in this manner.

[There are three opinions on the knowable content of] the consciousnesses and conscious states associated with equality wisdom.

303a

One opinion holds that it has as its knowable content only mirror wisdom, just as the defiled thinking consciousness has only the container consciousness as its content.

Another opinion holds that it has as its content only suchness, the limit of reality, because it has equality as its knowable content.

The correct opinion holds that this equality wisdom also has as its knowable content all things because it has as its content the equality [between all things]. The *Ornament of the Scriptures of the Great Vehicle* teaches that equality wisdom has all sentient beings as its knowable content because its content is the equality between self and others and "it manifests images of Buddhas according to the prayer and aspiration of sentient beings." This *Scripture on the Buddha Land* teaches that equality wisdom discerns both ultimate and conventional truth because it realizes the ten descriptive marks of equality. Therefore it has as its knowable content all things. There is no contradiction in this! If it did not have conventional truth as its content, then it would be unable to manifest images of Buddha according to the prayers and aspirations of sentient beings. Thus it is not correct to consider equality wisdom as having only mirror wisdom as its content on the analogy with the defiled thinking consciousness, since this would disagree with the above quoted sacred doctrines as well as with other scriptures.

The consciousnesses and conscious states associated with discernment wisdom have as their knowable content all common and individual marks without obstacle. Therefore it has as its content the entire range of the knowable.

[Again there are two opinions] in regard to the knowable content of duty-fulfillment wisdom. One opinion holds that the consciousnesses and conscious states associated with duty-fulfillment wisdom have as their knowable content the five sense objects because the *Ornament of the Scriptures of the Great Vehicle* teaches that the five senses of a Tathāgata are each "transformed in regard to these five sense objects."

The correct opinion holds that duty-fulfillment wisdom also has as its knowable content all objects without any obstacle. The

Ornament of the Scriptures of the Great Vehicle also teaches that "duty-fulfillment wisdom gives rise to various transformations which are immeasurable and inconceivable in all object realms, and thus brings benefit to all sentient beings." Also this *Scripture on the Buddha Land* teaches that duty-fulfillment wisdom gives rise to all the transformations of the three actions of body, speech, and thought, and discerns "the differences in the eighty-four thousand states of mind of sentient beings," and that "it proclaims the antidote," implements the four methods of discourse, and "experiences all the meaning of the past, future, and present." If this wisdom did not have as its knowable content all knowable objects, it would have no such abilities.

Furthermore, it is said that the unobstructed mastery of the Buddha mind is able to illumine each and every knowable object. The force of attention is sometimes focused on one thing and sometimes on all things. The above passage from the *Ornament of the Scriptures of the Great Vehicle* on the transformation of the senses is not conclusive proof [that this wisdom has as its content only the five sense objects], for it does not state that it is related only to these [sense objects].

The Eighth Theme: Wisdom Awareness

[Dignāga's] *Collection of Remarks on the Means of Valid Cognition (Pramāṇasamuccaya)* says that all consciousnesses and conscious states which are conscious of their own essence are called direct awareness. If this were not so, there would be no memory or recollection [of things perceived in the past], just as if they have never been perceived at all. Therefore the consciousnesses and conscious states associated with the four wisdoms are able to illumine and know their own essence.

[But it is objected that] this is contrary to the way things function in this world. A knife does not cut itself! The tip of one's finger does not touch itself! [How then can consciousness know itself?]

303b   [We answer by asking] if [the objector] has ever noticed that lamps, [which are also in this world,] are able to illumine themselves.

But, [the objector continues,] how do you know that lamps illumine themselves?

[We answer that] in the direct awareness of the absence of darkness, it is apparent [that the lamps illumine themselves]. If they did not illumine themselves, they would still be enveloped in darkness and would not then be directly perceptible at all. Therefore we know that lamps illumine themselves.

[But, the objector says,] since lamps are not themselves darkness, why must they illumine [themselves]? [Being of the nature of light, lamps do not have to illumine themselves, for, as lamps, they are never dark.]

[We answer that] the essence of such things as a pitcher or a piece of cloth is not itself darkness, but, when they are not illumined by lamps, they are enveloped in darkness and are not directly perceptible. When lamps illumine them, those lamps expel the darkness and cause them to be directly perceptible. And so we say that they are illumined. It is just the same with the lamps themselves. When they are lighted, the enveloping darkness is expelled and they themselves become directly perceptible. This is why we say that the lamps illumine themselves.

Therefore, all consciousnesses and conscious states, whether eminent or weak, are able externally to know objects and internally to know themselves. Just like the light [from lamps], they are able to both illumine other things and to illumine themselves. They are not like knives at all and cannot be compared to such things.

The Ninth Theme:
The Structure of the Luminous Mind

Each and every defiled consciousness and conscious state has the two aspects of image and insight. The *Collection of Remarks on the Means of Valid Cognition* additionally explains that consciousness and conscious states have three aspects. The first is that which is apprehended. The second is that which apprehends. And the third is the self-awareness [that is aware of apprehending]. These three aspects are neither identical nor different, [for they constitute aspects of the same structure]. The first is that which is known. The second is that which knows. And the third is the result of knowing, [the self-awareness of knowing what is known].[22]

If one analyzes the matter more carefully, there must also be a fourth aspect to complete this explanation. The first three are as above and the fourth is an awareness of the awareness of the very [act of being aware]. The first two aspects are external, [inasmuch as insight is into an image which appears as if external,] while the last two are internal [inasmuch as both are awarenesses of the functioning of consciousness]. The first [image-aspect] is simply the knowable object, while the other three are both [knowable objects and acts of knowing]. This means that the second insight-aspect knows only the first image-aspect, whether it be through an act of true knowing or not, whether it be through an act of direct awareness or an act of inference. The third, the self-awareness aspect, is aware of the second insight-aspect and the fourth awareness of self-awareness, [for it knows that insight into an image occurs and that one can be aware of this awareness]. The fourth awareness of self-awareness is aware of the third self-awareness aspect, [for it knows the process of subjective knowing]. The third and fourth aspects are both direct perception, [for they occur simply by paying attention and being aware and are not the results of inference].

From this reasoning, although [consciousness] is one, yet it is a unified composite of many aspects. Since these aspects are neither identical nor different from one another and since both the internal and external [functioning of consciousness] is accounted for, this explanation avoids the fallacy of an infinite regress.

As a scripture teaches, "the mind of sentient beings is twofold. Internally and externally all its aspects are entangled in what is apprehended and the act of apprehending. Its insights are of different varieties." This verse means that the mind of sentient beings is a unified composite of two aspects. Whether internally or externally, all are entangled in [these aspects] of what is apprehended and the act of apprehending. The insights [of this mind] are of different varieties, for some are true acts of knowing, some are mistaken acts of knowing, some are direct awareness, and some are acts of inference.

Although the consciousnesses and the conscious states of the four wisdoms have all these different aspects, yet they consist in uncontaminated direct awareness. This interpretation is all-inclusive, as has been explained in other treatises. In this interpretation, although the functions [of the mind of wisdom] are many, yet its essence is one, just as in the one Dharma there are many different meanings, such as [the truth of] suffering, of impermanence, and so forth, and yet the essence of that Dharma is one.

The Tenth Theme:
The Aspects of the Mind of Wisdom

Now we treat the question of the dependently arisen image- and insight-aspects of the consciousnesses and conscious states associated with these four wisdoms. Clearly they have the insight- 303c aspect which illumines the content of those wisdoms. It is also clear that they have the self-awareness aspect which fully illumines both the insights they have and the awareness of their self-awareness. Furthermore, they also have the aspect of the awareness of that self-awareness which illumines that self-awareness. If they lacked these aspects, then such could not be termed wisdom at all [because one would not be aware of anything].

But there is some uncertainty in regard to the image-aspect [of the wisdom mind]. [There are three opinions.] The first opinion holds that the true, uncontaminated consciousnesses and conscious states [of the mind of wisdom], in virtue of the absence of obstacles, immediately illumine objects present before them without [the mediation of] any image that, having issued from the evolutions of consciousness, might appear [to them]. Therefore, this uncontaminated mind is said to be imageless, because it does not imagine. Furthermore, it is also said that the objects [of the wisdom mind] are inconceivable. [And this implies that there is no image, for what is imaginable is conceivable.]

The second opinion holds that the true, uncontaminated consciousnesses and conscious states [of wisdom] do have the image-
aspect. The objects which appear to all consciousnesses and conscious states are indeed knowable objects, [and in this the mind of
wisdom does not differ from the mind of transmigration. The
difference between them is that the mind of wisdom] does not latch
onto those images as if the mind were a set of pincers. Wisdom
does not project its light on objects as do lamps. Rather it reflects
the images of things, as do bright mirrors. It is said to be without
obstacle because its insight illumines these objects which appear
[in images] within consciousness. Wisdom is said to be imageless
because it does not grasp at those images. It is said to be inconceivable because its wondrous nondiscriminative functioning is
difficult to fathom, not because it does not manifest images. If one
were to claim that it has no images, then it would have no image-
aspect. If being nondiscriminative meant that it had no insight-
aspect, then, entirely lacking both image- and insight-aspects, it
would be like empty space or the [imaginary] horns of a hare and,
[being entirely nonexistent,] not be termed wisdom at all. It is
rather because it does not cling to images that it is said to lack the
images of things apprehended and the act of so apprehending, and
not because wisdom lacks the function of illumining objects that
appear before it. If the uncontaminated mind entirely lacked this
image-aspect, then the Buddhas would not manifest the various
images of bodies and lands. But this contradicts the scriptures and
treatises in many places. If the conversion of the support of the
aggregate of material form were itself completely unrelated to
material form [and thus to material images], then likewise the
conversion of the other four aggregates would be unrelated to sensation, conceptualization, volition, and consciousness. [But such a
view] is a serious error [because it negates the nature of consciousness as other-dependent].

The third and correct opinion holds that the consciousnesses
and conscious states associated with uncontaminated, nondiscriminative wisdom illumine [only] its own essence and therefore have

no distinct image-aspect because they are nondiscriminative and because their object, suchness, is not separated from its essence. But images of objects do appear and are directly present and illumined in the consciousnesses and conscious states associated with subsequently attained wisdom, just as they are in the contaminated mind, because it is discriminative and because its objects are separate from its essence.[23]

[An objection is posed that] if the uncontaminated mind understands objects that are separate from its essence, then is it not the case that even though it lacks any images that appear as those objects, yet it does take them as objects?

[We answer that in its discussion,] the *Collection of Remarks on the Means of Valid Cognition* does not state that because there are no images that appear as atoms in the five sense consciousnesses there are no objects [for consciousness] at all. Therefore the uncontaminated seeds in the uncontaminated mind, which in perception are identical with those objects, arise and, although as objects they appear to be contaminated, yet they are uncontaminated, just as the uncontaminated mind may appear to be contaminated while in fact it is not so. This concludes our discussion [on the aspects of the mind of wisdom].

Note that all this analytical argumentation is reasoning according to conventional truth and is not the truth of ultimate meaning, for the truth of ultimate meaning is beyond words and transcends thinking and thus lacks both an image-aspect and an insight-aspect, is unable to speak about consciousnesses and conscious states, is beyond fabrication, and is inconceivable.

The Eleventh Theme:
The Number of Wisdom's Conscious States

We now treat the question of how many conscious states are associated with the consciousnesses and the conscious states of the four wisdoms. There are twenty-one: the five universal states [of contact, attention, perception, conceptualization, and reflection], the five special conscious states [aspiration, resolve, recollection, 304a concentration, and wisdom], and the eleven good conscious states [of faith, the sense of shame, the sense of integrity, noncovetousness, non-anger, nondelusion, zeal, composure, vigilance, equanimity, and nonviolence]. In all places the Tathāgata has the five universal conscious states. With constant joy he understands all knowables and his aspiration is without decrease. His preeminent understanding, imaged forth in objects, is constantly without decrease. He understands objects already experienced and recalls them without increase. His mind is not scattered and he constantly discerns. He is constantly associated with pure faith and the other good conscious states. He has no defilement and is never drowsy. He has done no evil [that could cause remorse]. He has realized the state beyond logic and reasoning.

In contrast, the shallowness of the contaminated mind is unsettled and to some degree associated with conscious states in which objects are clung to and become obstacles. But uncontaminated consciousnesses and conscious states are characterized by mastery and the absence of obstacle. All such conscious states are equally without obstacle.

The Twelfth Theme:
The Sequence of Attaining the Four Wisdoms

Next we treat the question of the sequence in which these four wisdoms are attained. At what point does the uncontaminated seed [of wisdom], which from the beginningless beginning has depended on the transmigratory continuity of karmic maturation, become actually manifested?

Once the aspiration for the mind [of wisdom] has occurred, then one gradually progresses because of the external permeations [of hearing Dharma]. The consciousnesses and conscious states associated with mirror wisdom are converted at the moment of diamond-like concentration, when all contaminated seeds and karmically maturing consciousnesses are destroyed. At this moment one attains the first actual manifestation of the uncontaminated seed of the result of awakening. Supported on that fullness [of the uncontaminated seed, such consciousness] will never come to an end but will be constantly and uninterruptedly associated with equality wisdom.

When the bodhisattva at the first stage of joy initially attains insight, then this equality wisdom is first actually manifested. Thereafter in the successive stages, practice causes it to grow into its fullness. When uncontaminated insight becomes present this wisdom is completely manifested, but if the contaminated mind is yet present then it is at times interrupted. In this manner it develops up until the tenth stage of the Dharma cloud. After this last stage, it will continue without ever coming to an end, and be constant and uninterrupted. Just like the contaminated container consciousness, it always functions in synergy with thinking consciousness, so when uncontaminated mirror wisdom functions together with equality wisdom, this equality wisdom is also uninterrupted.

The consciousnesses and conscious states associated with discernment wisdom are also present in the first stage of joy. When insight is initially attained, this wisdom is first actually manifested. Due to subsequent cultivation, it gradually increases. However, when the contaminated mind is yet present, or when the mind is absorbed [in concentration, sleep, or coma], then it is interrupted. In this manner it develops until the stage of the result of awakening. But if one enters the concentration of destruction then it will not be actually manifested.

The consciousnesses and conscious states associated with duty-fulfillment wisdom, according to one opinion, are actually manifested in all the stages above the first stage of joy, because they are involved in disseminating the Dharma. But the correct opinion holds that they arise only at the stage of the result of awakening, because in the ten stages the five senses, which are evolutions of karmically maturing consciousness, are contaminated. Therefore, what relies on these five consciousnesses is also contaminated. It is impossible for these five contaminated sense organs to produce an uncontaminated consciousness. Even in the stage of 304b the result of awakening this wisdom is not always present, for it arises by a turning of attention [to the tasks to be done in order to benefit sentient beings] and is frequently interrupted.

The Thirteenth Theme:
The Seeds of These Four Wisdoms

Now we treat the question of the seeds of the consciousnesses and conscious states associated with these four wisdoms. The original, beginningless nature of reality does not arise from permeation. This original nature is innate in the five lineages [of sentient beings]. But immediately on the arising of the aspiration [for supreme wisdom], these seeds do develop and increase through the permeations of external objects, [as in the hearing of Dharma]. Thus the lineages [of sentient beings] are brought to completion through permeation. From the first stage on they follow their course and become manifest. By repeated permeations they increase and become eminent until the realization of diamond-like concentration. From that point, although they are frequently manifested, yet [these lineages] are not again influenced by permeation, nor are they again caused to increase, since the fullness of their merits cannot be increased in virtue of the fact that, being supported on pure consciousness, they are neither undetermined nor capable of being influenced by permeation, and in virtue of the fact that in this manner we avoid attributing gradations to the merits of earlier and later Buddhas.

The consciousnesses and conscious states associated with these four wisdoms are entirely good and are fully encompassed with in the truth of the uncontaminated path, for all Buddhas lack any contaminated seeds. Although they frequently manifest transformation bodies in transmigration, which [are encompassed within] the truth of the origin of suffering and appear to be characterized by passion, yet in fact they are encompassed within the truth of the uncontaminated path. According to conventional truth, their descriptive marks are said to be the five aggregates, the twelve bases, and the eighteen realms, but in the truth of ultimate meaning they are not supported on these aggregates, bases, or realms, because they are separated from all fabrication and from all descriptive marks. In this manner these five factors are both conventional and ultimate truth. Inasmuch as they do not rely on names and words, the objects of their faculties all ultimately exist. But inasmuch as they do rely on names and words, these objects all conventionally exist. Furthermore, the suchness of the Pure Dharma Realm is their essence, since this is ultimate existence. Because of suchness we establish the descriptive marks of the destruction of all insightful discrimination, for [that discrimination] has [only] a conventional existence. All these wisdoms of the mind [of wisdom], as all direct awareness, such as blue, yellow, and so forth, do ultimately exist, but conscious states, such as idleness and so forth, all [discriminated] forms, such as longness or shortness, conventionally exist. We now rest our explanations and must return to commenting on the text of the Scripture.

The Fourteenth Theme:
The Discernment of These Five Factors

The fourth characteristic of discernment, [treated under the First Theme before the above extended explanations,] is itself divided into three parts. The first is the discernment of the differences between the five factors. The second is the discernment of phenomenal wisdom, which is experienced as being all of one unified taste. The third is the discernment of all the good qualities which characterize the Pure Dharma Realm in the concluding verses [of the Scripture], and the relationship between the three bodies and the five factors.

Chapter VIII

The Pure Dharma Realm

The First Simile:
The Lack of Any Descriptive Mark

The Scripture says: "You wondrously born ones should realize that the Pure Dharma Realm is like empty space, which, although all kinds of descriptive marks of every color are present in it, yet cannot be said itself to have any descriptive mark of color at all, because its essence is of one taste only. Just so the Tathāgata's Pure Dharma Realm, although it too pervades all knowables with all their descriptive marks, yet cannot itself be said to have any kind of descriptive mark at all, because its essence is of one taste only."

The Commentary explains: Now we will explain the marks of the Pure Dharma Realm. We must be careful in analyzing the Pure Dharma Realm, for there are objections.

It may be objected that the Pure Dharma Realm of all Tathā- 304c gatas is of the essence of suchness and that suchness is the common mark of all things. But, since all things do have various distinctions, so should the Pure Dharma Realm. But if it has these various distinctions then how can it be pure?

[We answer that] it is like crystals, which support various kinds of common marks, yet in themselves have no marks at all. In order to respond to this objection, [the Scripture] gives the first simile of empty space. It says that "it is like empty space, in which all kinds of descriptive marks of every color are present." The words "all kinds" refer to all the different kinds, for worldly space pervades all similar and dissimilar descriptive marks by which material forms, being limited by their bodies, are differentiated. The term "descriptive mark" is defined as that whereby the essence of a thing is apprehended in acts of understanding and clearly appears [in the mind]. The phrase "yet [empty space] cannot be said to have any characteristics of color at all" means that no perceptible

97

descriptive marks of any kind of material limitation can be attributed to empty space. The words "cannot be said" mean that the nature of empty space does not correspond to words and is ineffable, for the nature of empty space is such that one cannot attribute to it any manifesting descriptive marks or any manifested descriptive marks.

But, [it is objected further,] if one looks up into empty space, there are various descriptive marks and one can indeed say that [in empty space] these various descriptive marks do exist.

[We answer that] this looking at the various perceptible, descriptive marks in space is not looking at space, and therefore only by convention does one say that [space] has these various perceptible, descriptive marks, just as [verbal expressions] of blue and yellow, of longness or shortness, do not [point to something that] ultimately exists. Now, if they did not conventionally exist then they would be ultimately existing phenomena, [which is patently absurd].

[The objection continues by asking,] why is it then that [space], which universally pervades all material forms without having any descriptive marks, is said "to have an essence of one taste only"?

[We answer that] it is of one unobstructed taste and has no descriptive marks whereby it might be differentiated because empty space is not associated with those various perceptible, descriptive marks and does not become identified with them. Rather it does not depart from its own essence.

The sentence "just so the Tathāgata's Pure Dharma Realm, although it too pervades all kinds of knowables with all their various descriptive marks, yet cannot be said to have any kind of descriptive mark at all, because its essence is of one taste only" means that the Dharma realm is just like empty space in that both, although they universally pervade all material, limited forms, cannot be said to have any perceptible form at all. Even though we say that empty space exists, this is said only by convention and does not mean that it ultimately exists, for empty space does not depart from its own essence and take on other descriptive marks.

Although by conventional meaning we speak of empty space as this or that, yet the true nature of empty space is ineffable. The Pure Dharma Realm is just like this, for although by conventional designation we say this and that about emptiness, yet the true nature of emptiness is ineffable. As noted above, the Pure Dharma Realm is like a crystal, because it is the cause which supports the various descriptive marks common to things. Therefore the objection that the Pure Dharma Realm is associated with various distinctions commits the fallacy of an uncertain reason.

Rather, although when one looks into empty space, it [appears] to be associated with the various perceptible, material forms, yet it does not have any kind of perceptible form at all. Just as space 305a at times is associated with smoke, mists, clouds, and so forth, and due to our own power of unreal imagining its forms are seen, [so it is with the Pure Dharma Realm]. When we are looking at these various descriptive marks of smoke, mists, and clouds, we are not looking at empty space, because empty space cannot be seen. We see these material forms and descriptive marks because of the enabling force of our own unreal imagining, and such is not the Pure Dharma Realm.

Although the Pure Dharma Realm has no real perceptible, descriptive marks nor any enunciation of Dharma, yet it does issue forth in the different identifiable presentations of the Dharma, which do have perceptible, descriptive marks. But it does not on that account itself have these various descriptive marks. They do not cause the Dharma realm to be identified with those descriptive marks, because the Pure Dharma Realm is apart from all names. All names are objects of that understanding that is engendered from discrimination. However, the Dharma is not in vain because it is the continual cause for the realization of the Pure Dharma Realm. It is just as one would understand the meaning of a letter only by looking at the words, [despite the fact that meaning is not identical with the words themselves]. Since the Dharma flows forth from the great compassion of all Tathāgatas, it is able continually to express meaning beyond speech. It would indeed be a wondrous sight to see the empty sky painted with a multitude of colors. Even if many words were used to describe it, its ineffable beauty would still surpass all those words. As it has been said, "Oh, Sāgaramati, if one [were to see] all kinds of colors painted on the imperceptible, invisible, unobstructed, unmanifested empty sky, he would stand immobile, rapt in wonder."[24]

All Buddha Bhagavats have realized this profound, ineffable Dharma and, by the use of words, they are able to proclaim and teach its profundities for the sake of all sentient beings, for this is why they preach. Because they have the crystal Dharma realm as their nature and are pure, the objection [that clouds obstruct the pure sky] commits the fallacy of a dissimilar example and such reasoning violates either the first or the other two rules of logic [in that either the reason in the premise does not apply to the other two members of the syllogism, or that it is neither necessarily present in the example nor absent in all dissimilar cases].

The Second Simile:
The Descriptive Mark of Purity

The Scripture says: "Just as empty space, although it pervades all material forms and is not apart from them, yet is not defiled by their imperfections, so the Tathāgata's Pure Dharma Realm, although it pervades the minds of all sentient beings, since it is their reality and is not apart from them, yet is not defiled by their imperfections."

The Commentary explains: Again there is an objection, for if the Pure Dharma Realm pervades all knowables, then it must also be associated with the defiled, descriptive marks common to all of them, such as covetousness and so forth. How then can it not itself become defiled, as the other contaminated consciousnesses and conscious states are?

[We answer that the Scripture] presents this second simile on empty space in order to respond to this objection. The phrase "just as empty space pervades all material forms and is not apart from them" means that there is no other place [for those material forms to be]. Thus it says that [empty space] is not apart from them. But they cannot be said to be either identical with it nor different from it, because they all function within space and cannot be seen apart from it. Only if there were no distinction between space and these material forms would that empty space itself have the material forms and therefore must, like them, be inconstant. The phrase "yet it is not defiled by their imperfections" means that although empty space contains within it all material forms, yet it is not defiled by the imperfections of those material forms. Imperfections of material form refer to all the different kinds of descriptive marks of blue, yellow, and so forth, which represent the causes that engender and increase covetousness, anger, and so forth. They are called imperfections because such dark rainclouds and fog can cause empty space to lose its pure appearance and hinder the vision of that purity. Alternately, it is consistent [with the Scripture passage] to interpret these imperfections of material form to refer to the descriptive marks of such objects as they increase within the mind. It is not the case, however, that empty space itself is defiled by these imperfections of material form. 305b

The phrase "just so the Tathāgata's Pure Dharma Realm pervades the minds of all sentient beings, since it is their reality and is not apart from them" means that just as the Buddha's own mind is ultimately pure because its original nature is luminous and pure, just so are the minds of sentient beings. The original nature is ultimate and pure. The original nature of the mind is suchness. The minds of all sentient beings are equally [ultimate and pure].[25]

How can it be stated that their minds are equally [ultimate and pure]? It is so stated in virtue of the nature of emptiness. This means that the original nature of the mind, its reality nature, pervades the minds of all sentient beings. Therefore we use the term equally [ultimate and pure] to express this reality nature of their minds.

The phrase "since it is their reality and is not apart from them" means that the originally pure minds of sentient beings, although originally pure, are firmly established as the Tathāgata's purity of mind only when far apart from adventitious obstacles and defilements. The equality of the minds of all sentient beings consists in the essence of the full perfection of ultimate meaning, because the mind of equality of all sentient beings is the descriptive mark of that ultimate meaning and is not therefore differentiated from it. Because the minds of all sentient beings are characterized as the ultimate meaning of mind, they manifest and move in nondifferentiation. Because they move in equality, [the minds of sentient beings] are not differentiated.

The phrase "and yet it is not defiled by their imperfections" means that it is originally pure. Imperfections refer to covetousness and so forth, all of which are able to lead the mind to commit faults and become defiled. Although such imperfections function by an adventitious discrimination, they are not the essence of the mind.[26] That essence cannot be completely lost and it is able to bring about purification. We are here dealing with a mystery. The pure luminous reality nature of the original mind is what is meant by mind. It is not true that apart from this mind there is any other nature of a pure mind.

How then, [it might be asked,] can it be that the minds of sentient beings have covetousness and so forth?

[We answer that] such [imperfections] are supported on the power of their own discrimination, for until the faults of the mind have been completely severed these [imperfections] do arise through the power of ignorance. This means that just as the original nature of empty space is pure, but appears to be impure through the presence of illusory descriptive marks that appear due to cataracts damaging the pupils of the eyes, just so the original nature of the Dharma realm is pure but appears to be impure through the illusory descriptive marks that appear due to the causal force of covetousness arising from one's own discrimination, because cataracts of ignorance damage the wisdom eye. But that universally pure wisdom eye is itself never defiled. Furthermore, inasmuch as the Pure Dharma Realm is nondiscriminative, such universal purity is termed the Dharma body of all Tathāgatas, their true essence,

305c

because it is constantly without change. Therefore, the minds of sentient beings are all equal because the Pure Dharma Realm is present in the continuity of their minds. Thus it is said that "all sentient beings have the seed of a Tathāgata" and that "all sentient beings have Buddha-nature."[27]

[This doctrine is here taught] in order to lead the minds [of sentient beings] to decide to enter the Great Vehicle. In fact it applies only to those sentient beings of the Tathāgata lineage. To say that all sentient beings will become awakened is like saying that everything is inconstant [when we know that the Pure Dharma Realm is not inconstant,] or like saying that everything is suffering [when we know that some things bring real joy]. If the word "all" did not here mean just a small part of all sentient beings and not the complete entirety, then it would contradict what has been explained above concerning the five lineages. It would then imply that the good qualities of all Buddhas would finally come to an end because there would be nobody left to save. And this contradicts what has been explained above concerning the Tathāgata's good qualities, for they will never come to an end, they are never of no benefit, and they abide [forever] in the world with the purpose of saving beings and [leading them] to seek wisdom.[28]

Although all sentient beings have the Pure Dharma Realm, [they do not realize it,] just as a man born blind does not see the sun or moon because he is held within the power of his obstacle [of blindness]. As the verse says, "It is due to the defilement of sentient beings that the Pure Dharma Realm does not appear [in them], just as the moon [does not appear] in a broken basin. But it pervades the entire world, for its Dharma shines like the sun."[29]

From this reasoning the above objection that the Pure Dharma Realm itself becomes defiled because it is associated with the defiled descriptive marks of all passions, such as covetousness and so forth, and is thus just like the other contaminated consciousnesses, falls into the fallacy of an uncertain reason. Although empty space is associated with the defilements of material forms, it is not itself defiled. And although consciousness and conscious states are associated with the passions of covetousness and so forth, they still have as their essence the Pure Dharma Realm and are still pure. The example [of the objector's reasoning] is thus inconsistent [with his premise]. It is rather the case that those whose dispositions are impure see their own minds as defiled and on that account say that the Dharma realm is defiled. But those whose dispositions are pure see that the Dharma realm is always pure because, although associated with the defilements of covetousness and so forth, it is originally pure and undefiled. Therefore it is clear that this objection is a logical fallacy. Because this Dharma realm pervades everything, it is like empty space and is not defiled by the imperfections of any sentient being. Those who say that the Dharma realm pervades everything [and is thus defiled], in virtue of the fact that emptiness is something that is clung to, have not demonstrated their thesis.

306a

The Third Simile:
The Descriptive Mark of Nonactivity

The Scripture says: "Again just as empty space encompasses all the [three] actions of body, speech, and thought, and yet itself has no arising activity, just so the Tathāgata's Pure Dharma Realm encompasses all the transformations of wisdom and all phenomenal activities, and yet that Pure Dharma Realm itself has no arising activity."

The Commentary explains: Again there is an objection, for if the Tathāgata's Pure Dharma Realm has suchness as its essence, then it has no fabrication and no arising activity. How then could it come to encompass the arising of wisdom, which is cause for those phenomenal activities that benefit sentient beings? On the other hand, if it does encompass the arising of wisdom then it would have an arising activity, and then how could the Tathāgata's suchness be its descriptive mark?

In order to respond to this objection [the Scripture] presents this third simile on empty space. The phrase "just as empty space encompasses all the [three] actions of the body, speech, and thought" means that, although empty space does not have any purposeful activity, yet it is able to encompass these three actions of sentient beings.

[But it is objected that] inasmuch as the two actions of body and speech have a solidity of shape, they indeed can be contained [within empty space]. But how can the action of thought, which has no such solidity, be so contained? It is because of their solidity that we designate things as being contained [in something else].

[We answer that] we say that those [actions of body and speech] are contained in empty space because they are not prevented [from being so contained], for all occurrences of solid objects are not prevented [from being contained]. The case of thought is analogous, for its occurrence is not prevented [from being contained in something else] and thus we can say that it also is encompassed within empty space.

Furthermore, we conventionally describe empty space on analogy with the case where solid objects, when not prevented, move about in something else. Why can we not then conventionally describe empty space by analogy with the case where, in a similar fashion, the action of thought, immediately after being destroyed, again arises from something else within which it is contained, [that is, the container consciousness]. If it were otherwise, then a really existent space would pervade all places and then how could it encompass [anything]?

If one were to hold that the substance of space were really existent but not solid, and that when other [solid] things arose they could thus be said to be contained within [that real empty space], then [with equal logical consistency] we could claim that the substance of all things of the world of no form (arūpadhātu), which have no solidity, really did exist and were able to contain [other things], and thus that they could also be called empty space, [all of which is patently absurd].

Other scriptures do say that that which is without matter is called empty space, but this is said from the defiled, descriptive marks of common worldly knowledge. Therefore empty space contains the three actions of the body, speech, and thought without any logical contradiction.

The phrase "and yet empty space has no arising activity" means that empty space does not discriminate, as if it were to include this, but not that. Although it has no purposeful activity it is able to include [all things]. It is just like the brightness of the sun, of the moon, or of lamps, which, although not discriminating this from that, yet, when they arise, are able to illumine all material forms. Or it is like the wish-fulfilling gem, which, although without purposeful activity, is yet able to fulfill the desires of sentient beings. Other examples could be adduced to the point that empty space is manifested in everything.[30]

The phrase "just so the Tathāgata's Pure Dharma Realm encompasses all transformations of wisdom and all phenomenal activities that benefit sentient beings" means that the Tathāgata's Pure Dharma Realm maintains and abides in its own essence and, without purposeful activity, establishes those activities that universally benefit sentient beings.

306b

The term "wisdom" means mirror wisdom and the other three wisdoms (discernment, duty-fulfillment, and equality wisdoms). The words "all transformations" refer to the transformations of bodies, words, and thoughts. The phrase "all activities that benefit sentient beings" means that these activities are able to bring supreme happiness and benefit to sentient beings. The Pure Dharma Realm is able to encompass all of these because, when it arises, it is their enabling cause.

The phrase "and yet the Pure Dharma Realm has no arising activity" is interpreted as follows. Arising activity refers to purposeful activity that is able to cause the mind to reject some objects and choose others. Activity means the movement of the mind, for the agitation that characterizes the mind's thinking has such activity. Therefore, the above passage means that the Pure Dharma Realm is able to encompass all wisdoms, all transformations, and all phenomenal activities that benefit sentient beings, although it lacks any purposeful activity or mental agitation.

An alternate reading says that "it encompasses the transformations of all wisdoms and the phenomenal activities that benefit sentient beings." This would mean that it encompasses all enjoyment and transformation bodies because, as the cause that benefits sentient beings, it is inexhaustible, because it is extremely great and extensive, and because it is unobstructed. Although it is nondiscriminative, the enabling power [of the Pure Dharma Realm] can give rise to these bodies. This means that just as empty space issues forth in the activities of the arising of the forms it encompasses in virtue of the fact that the reality nature has the power to produce all kinds of different activities, and yet empty space itself had no constructed nor fabricated discrimination of "I" and "mine," just so the Tathāgata, dwelling in the uncontaminated realm and lacking any purposeful or fabricated discrimination of "I" and "mine," yet, in virtue of the power of his great vow previously cultivated, is able to engender phenomenal activities that benefit sentient beings through the transformations of all wisdoms. Thus the Tathāgata, in a most inconceivable manner, abides in the Dharma body, and because he is supported by the force of his previous vow he is adorned with the good qualities of all the major and minor marks and continues throughout eons without end. Although he is nondiscriminative he engenders the phenomenal activities that benefit sentient beings through these transformations of all the wisdoms. The Tathāgata has no deliberation as to his proper course of action, yet by the force of his original vow he is able to engender everything. It is due to that previously elicited vow that even when asleep or in the concentration of destruction, he awakens and leaves that concentration at the appropriate moment, although he has no purposeful activity. As the *Ocean Wisdom Scripture* (*Sāgaramati-sūtra*) teaches, "It is just like a monk who resolves [to awaken] at the sound of the bell, and, [having so resolved,] then enters into the concentration of destruction. Although in that concentration he would not hear the sound of the bell, since he would have [destroyed] all discrimination, yet, due to the force of his resolve he would awaken from that concentration at the appropriate time."[31]

The Fourth Simile:
The Descriptive Mark of Being Unconditioned

306c The Scripture says: "Again it is like empty space in which all kinds of material forms and descriptive marks appear to be born and perish, and yet this empty space is not itself born nor does it perish. Just so is the Tathāgata's Pure Dharma Realm in which all wisdoms, transformations, and phenomenal activities that benefit sentient beings appear to be born and to perish, and yet that Pure Dharma Realm itself is not born and does not perish."

The Commentary explains: Again there is an objection, for if the Pure Dharma Realm pervades all knowables and is not free from following upon them, then that Pure Dharma Realm must have a birth and a destruction. On the other hand, if it does not have a birth or a destruction then it cannot pervade all knowables and be free from following upon them all.

In order to respond to this objection the Scripture presents this fourth simile on empty space. The phrase "again it is like empty space in which all kinds of material forms and descriptive marks appear to be born and to perish" means that just as empty space pervades all forms [as stated above], so it also includes these forms and descriptive marks and is not free from following upon them all. But although all these forms appear to be born and to perish, the nature of empty space itself is not born and does not perish.

Thus the Tathāgata's Pure Dharma Realm pervades all knowables and encompasses all wisdoms, all transformations, and phenomenal activities that benefit sentient beings and is not free from following upon them all. But although such wisdoms are successively born and perish, yet the Pure Dharma Realm is neither born nor does it perish. This profound meaning is expressed in a scripture, "Because Mañjuśrī is neither born nor perishes, he is called a Tathāgata."[32] In the truth of ultimate meaning all things neither are born nor do they perish; but in conventional truth we do affirm birth and death, and thus we say that things [only appear] to be born and to perish. This means that their conventional descriptive marks appear to be born and to perish, but it is not the case that in the truth of ultimate meaning any real things are ever born or ever perish. In the Pure Dharma Realm all wisdoms, transformations, and phenomenal activities that benefit sentient beings are also like this, [for they are conventional descriptive marks.]

The Fifth Simile:
The Descriptive Mark of No Increase Nor Decrease

The Scripture says: "Again just as in empty space all kinds of material forms and descriptive marks appear to increase and decrease, and yet empty space itself has no increase and no decrease, just so in the Tathāgata's Pure Dharma Realm the sweet dew of the Tathāgata's sacred Dharma, which has both increase and decrease, is manifested, and yet that Pure Dharma Realm has no increase and no decrease."

The Commentary explains: Again there is an objection, for if the Pure Dharma Realm pervades everything and is not apart from the appearance of the Tathāgata's sacred Dharma, which has both increase and then subsequent decrease and destruction, then that Pure Dharma Realm must likewise have increase and decrease. And if this is so, then the Pure Dharma Realm cannot be pure.

In order to respond to this objection, the Scripture presents 307a this fifth simile on empty space. The phrase "just as in empty space all kinds of material forms appear to increase and decrease" means that the Tathāgata's sacred Dharma is most truly eminent and pure when compared to the heterodox teachings of the non-Buddhists, because it is like a rich liquor or a sweet dew. It can lead others to cessation and the [sweet dew of] eternal life. Thus the holiness realized through the devout practices of this sacred Dharma attains the result of no training. Because the many divisions [of the doctrine] have already been present for a thousand years, it is said that the Buddha's true Dharma has lasted a thousand years. But this does not mean that the Buddha-Dharma is only a thousand years old. The tradition of the word-hearers was divided into many sections only a hundred years after the Buddha's passing, but the bodhisattva tradition remains the same for more than a thousand years, for the one taste of purity does not engage in crafty debates.[33] It was after that thousand-year period that there arose the two different interpretations of the Sarvāstivādins, [who claimed that all things were really existent,] and the Śūnyatāvādins, [who claimed that all things were empty]. Thus it is said that the Tathāgata's Dharma has lasted a thousand years.

The phrase "and yet the Pure Dharma Realm has no increase nor decrease" means that it is only by conventional truth that the Tathāgata's Dharma has increase or decrease, but in the truth of ultimate meaning the Pure Dharma Realm is its nature and it has no increase nor decrease, just as [in the truth of ultimate meaning] material forms [have no arising nor passing away]. Having the Pure Dharma Realm as its essence and lacking increase and decrease, in the truth of ultimate meaning it is like empty space, for it too is characterized as having no increase nor decrease. When it is said that it appears, this means that its transformations within conventional consciousness appear as having increase and decrease, but such is not its true nature in the Pure Dharma Realm, for it is apart from the characteristics of fabrication and discrimination.

The Sixth Simile:
The Descriptive Mark of No Movement

The Scripture says: "Just as in space material forms and descriptive marks in the ten directions are limitless and inexhaustible, because the realm of empty space is limitless and inexhaustible, and yet empty space itself has no going or coming, no moving or changing, just so is the Tathāgata's Pure Dharma Realm, in that although it establishes benefit and happiness for all sentient beings in the ten directions and its various kinds of activities are limitless and inexhaustible, because the Pure Dharma Realm is limitless and inexhaustible, yet that Pure Dharma Realm has no going or coming, no movement or changing."

The Commentary explains: Again there is an objection, for if the Tathāgata has the Dharma realm as his essence and also bestows benefit and happiness on all sentient beings, whether they are going or coming, the Dharma realm is not separated from this [going and coming] and, just as other things, it must also have going and coming, as, for example, being born and so forth. If this be so, then the Dharma realm cannot be pure. On the other hand, if the Dharma realm has no activity of going or coming then it cannot bestow that benefit and happiness on sentient beings in the ten directions.

In order to respond to this objection, the Scripture presents this sixth simile on empty space. The phrase "just as in space material forms and descriptive marks in the ten directions are limitless and inexhaustible, because the realm of empty space is limitless and inexhaustible" means that the world-realms in the ten directions are limitless and inexhaustible, and thus all the various material forms and descriptive marks in them are also limitless and inexhaustible. Lacking limits in any direction both as to time and as to place, they are said to be limitless and inexhaustible.

The phrase "and yet empty space itself has no going and coming, no moving or changing" means that empty space encompasses everything, pervades everything, and yet has no activity.

The phrase "just so is the Tathāgata's Pure Dharma Realm, in that although it establishes benefit and happiness for all sentient beings in the ten directions and its various kinds of activities are limitless and inexhaustible" means that those activities of bringing benefit and happiness are limitless and inexhaustible, as explained above.

The phrase "because the Pure Dharma Realm is limitless and inexhaustible" means that the Pure Dharma Realm is limitless and inexhaustible because, although it has no movement, its enabling force can issue in activities that bring benefit and happiness to limitless sentient beings in limitless world-realms in the ten directions.

The phrase "and yet the Pure Dharma Realm has no going or 307b coming, no moving or changing" is to be understood as follows. Going means to leave here and to arrive there. Coming means to leave there and arrive here. In the phrase "no moving and no changing" the first is the explanation [of going and coming], while the second is an interpretation [of that]. The phrase "the Pure Dharma Realm has no going or coming" and so forth means that it has no limitation nor any restrictions of material form. If it had any limitation or restriction of material form then, like all things, it could be said to go and to come, to move and to change from place to place, and then it would not be limitless and unrestricted. The Dharma realm is like empty space, but it can be said to have the activities of going and coming, of moving and changing. In general this means that in the truth of ultimate meaning, the Pure Dharma Realm is the essence of all Tathāgatas and is pervasively present in the conscious streams of all sentient beings. Due to the maturing force of their own good seeds and the enabling cause of the Pure Dharma Realm, when a consciousness [of that Pure Dharma Realm] arises, then the activities [of the Tathāgata's wisdom] become clearly manifested and expressed in words as the benefit and happiness which the Tathāgata brings to all sentient beings. Were it not for such activity, such an enabling cause, then it would not happen that the Tathāgata's Dharma body would be able to have any activity of bringing benefit and happiness to sentient beings. As a scripture teaches, "Good sons, the Tathāgata lacks any going or coming whatsoever."[34] We did say above that the Tathāgata does go and come, but this refers [only] to his enjoyment and transformation bodies. Thus there is no contradiction here.

The Seventh Simile:
The Descriptive Mark of Eternity

The Scripture says: "Again, just as in empty space the three thousand world-realms appear to be destroyed and created and yet the realm of empty space is neither destroyed nor created, just so in the Tathāgata's Pure Dharma Realm there appears the realization of supreme awakening, which has unlimited descriptive marks and there is manifested the entrance into final cessation, and yet that Pure Dharma Realm does not perfect supreme awakening nor does it enter cessation."

The Commentary explains: Again there is an objection, for, if the Pure Dharma Realm is apart from going and coming, then how can it reach to supreme awakening and final cessation, since it neither goes nor comes anywhere? On the other hand, if it does have going and coming, then this would contradict what is taught [in the last section].

This objection is not valid because of this Scripture passage above. Just as world-realms appear to be destroyed and created and yet empty space is neither destroyed nor created, just so in the Pure Dharma Realm, although all Buddhas appear to realize supreme awakening and final cessation, yet in the truth of ultimate meaning the Pure Dharma Realm does not realize any 307c supreme awakening nor final cessation. Only if it did realize these could it be said to have going and coming. Just as in empty space the appearances of the destructions and creations of all world-realms are conventional truths and not the truth of ultimate meaning, since in great emptiness such things have emptiness as their nature, just so the Tathāgata's Pure Dharma Realm manifests the realization of supreme awakening, which has unlimited descriptive marks, and final cessation, but this is said in conventional truth and not in the truth of ultimate meaning, for the realization of supreme awakening and the entrance into final cessation do not really exist because all dependently co-arisen aggregates have no essence. If the Pure Dharma Realm be considered in the truth of ultimate meaning, then the existence of these two (supreme awakening and final cessation) is not an ultimate existence, for that which ultimately exists does not cast off its own descriptive marks and take on other descriptive marks. If one allows that the Pure Dharma Realm casts off what is not supreme awakening to realize supreme awakening and casts off what is not final cessation to attain final cessation, then such is not the truth of ultimate meaning.

One might think that precisely because of this explanation these two should be said ultimately to exist, for supreme awakening has never had a time when it was not supreme awakening and final cessation has never had a time when it was not final cessation. Therefore they should ultimately exist.

But, if this be so, then other things would likewise [ultimately exist]. The destructions of world-ages would be constant destructions and at no time would they not be being destroyed. The creations of world-ages would be constant creations and at no time would they not be being created. Pots and pans at no time would not be pots and pans, for [in the above opinion] all these things would also ultimately exist.

And if this be so, then ascetics would not have to cross over a world filled everywhere with the flaming fire [of passion] and go to that other realm but would suffer the flames of that fire in this [world]. Those who had attained the power of eminent faith in the various stages would not experience any conversion unto mastery. Those who have not attained any preeminent concentration or powers of mastery would both realize supreme awakening and negate supreme awakening, would both attain final cessation and negate final cessation. Thus, although one first [realizes] the state of supreme awakening and then that of final cessation, yet, because pure suchness does not lose its own descriptive mark, so the Pure Dharma Realm neither realizes supreme awakening nor enters cessation.

It is because these two do have increase as their own descriptive mark that they do not ultimately exist. Both the practitioner and his practice, because they are characterized by clinging to what is entirely imagined, do not really exist, and yet, because practitioners do come to understand all things, they are said to be awakened. Theirs is a transcendental, nondiscriminative wisdom, a realization of supreme awakening. In this state, taking suchness as their content of understanding, they do not manifest any discrimination in regard to these two (supreme awakening and final cessation), and thus there is no supreme awakening or final cessation. This profound meaning is expressed as follows [in a scripture]: "Your Majesty should know that because all things are not born, all Buddhas manifest nonattainment and nonrealization."[35]

Because clinging to the imagined is nonexistent, so the discrimination of birth and so forth does not exist. It is by conventional truth that these two are established, for the transformation body does manifest them as appropriate to the level of understanding of those sentient beings to be converted. Therefore the Tathāgata manifests these two and in establishing these two actions, he manifests everything.

308a

The Eighth Simile:
The Descriptive Mark of No Suffering

The Scripture says: "Again, just as in regard to the various material forms that depend on empty space, changes such as destructions and conflagrations can occur and yet the realm of empty space is not changed thereby and suffers no affliction, just so in the realm of sentient beings, which depends on the Tathāgata's Pure Dharma Realm, sinful actions of body, speech, and thought against the various precepts can occur and yet the Pure Dharma Realm is not thereby changed and suffers no affliction."

The Commentary explains: Again there is an objection, for if the Pure Dharma Realm pervades all kinds of sentient beings then how can those sentient beings have any sin? In the Pure Dharma Realm there is no sin because its essence is pure. The establishment of precepts would then be useless, for no sentient being would have any sin. On the other hand, if they did have sin then they would be afflicted and, just like the adherents of the lower vehicles, would not attain utmost purification.

It is in order to respond to this objection that [the Scripture] presents this eighth simile on empty space. The phrase "just as in regard to the various material forms that depend on empty space" and so forth shows that this objection is invalid, for just as in regard to such material forms as grasses and trees, which depend on space, changes such as being destroyed and so forth can indeed occur and yet empty space is not changed thereby, since, although it encompasses them, it is neither afflicted nor oppressed by any of their sufferings, such as being destroyed and so forth, just so in the realm

115

of sentient beings, which depends on the Tathāgata's Pure Dharma Realm, all kinds of sins can occur and yet that Pure Dharma Realm is not changed thereby nor does it suffer any affliction. Although sentient beings are within the Pure Dharma Realm, it is apparent that in virtue of their own imagining, they do engender the two kinds of sins in their actions of body, speech, and thought, for householders can commit evil sins, such as injuring their parents, and monks can commit sins as appropriate to their station. It was in order to subdue and regulate [sinful sentient beings] that the precepts were established. But all sins have only a conventional existence and the Pure Dharma Realm is not changed by such transgressions, for its essence is not altered, afflicted, or oppressed. If due to such suffering it were to become inconstant, then it would have sin and be like [the ultimate state attained by] the word-hearers. Such, however, is not the Pure Dharma Realm. Since it is able to remain constant in the face of all suffering it has no sin and is like unto empty space.

Furthermore, it is only in their conventional existence that all the material things are destroyed in space and not in their ultimate existence. Likewise, although sin and the establishment of the precepts are present in the Tathāgata's Pure Dharma Realm, these are established conventionally and do not ultimately exist. They are so established by conventional naming. The three actions of body, speech, and thought become evil only because of the way in which they arise and not because their essence [is evil]. There is nothing that is established as really existing in virtue of its own arising force. Likewise, evil actions of the body [do not have their own arising force], for [the body] is a composite of the elements of the earth, and so on. The actions of speech, like the sound of a drum, are not themselves evil. Likewise, actions that are not externally indicated do not really exist, for nonactivity is their only nature. Actions of thought do not ultimately exist, for they are determined to be evil only by being associated with the power [of evil permeations]. The causes [of all these actions] do not exist; therefore the resultant [actions themselves] do not exist. Therefore in the Pure

308b

Dharma Realm neither karmic actions nor their results ultimately exist because they all arise from imagination, are engendered from the evolutions of conventional consciousness, and are established as so characterized.

The Ninth Simile:
The Descriptive Mark of Not Being an Aggregate

The Scripture says: "Again, just as, dependent on empty space, great earths, great mountains, bright lights, waters, fires, Indra's retinue of stars, and suns and moons of all kinds can occur, yet the realm of empty space is not characterized by these, just so, dependent on the Tathāgata's Pure Dharma Realm, the [purified] aggregates of discipline, concentration, wisdom, liberation, and liberation-wisdom can occur, and yet that Pure Dharma Realm is not characterized by them."

The Commentary explains: Again there is an objection, for, if the Pure Dharma Realm pervades all things, then it must be characterized by the uncontaminated aggregates of moral discipline (śīla), concentration (samādhi), wisdom (prājña), liberation (mokṣa), and liberation-wisdom (mokṣa-jñana). If it is not apart from them then, like empty space, it must be characterized as being an aggregate.

In order to respond to this objection the Scripture presents this ninth simile on empty space. The above passage from the Scripture shows that this objection is invalid, for [the uncontaminated aggregates are present in the Pure Dharma Realm,] just as [the great earth, mountains, and so forth] are present in empty space. Just as, dependent on space, the earth, [mountains], and so forth can occur, and yet empty space does not take on the marks of being an aggregate in virtue of being associated with the common marks of the earth and mountains, just so, although the aggregates of discipline and so forth can occur in dependency on the Tathāgata's Dharma realm yet that Dharma realm is not identical with these pure aggregates.

You should understand that uncontaminated pure discipline

is here called the aggregate of discipline. Uncontaminated concentration is called the aggregate of concentration. Uncontaminated wisdom is called the aggregate of wisdom. The eminent understanding of the stage of no training is called the aggregate of liberation. The correct insight of the stage of no training is called the aggregate of liberation-wisdom. The first three are causes for the last two.

One opinion holds that the wisdom that has as its content liberation at the stage of no training is called deliverance wisdom and the other wisdoms are simply called wisdom.

But another opinion holds that all five of these uncontaminated aggregates are present both in the stage of training and in the stage of no training, but whereas they are only partially realized in the stage of training, they are fully realized in that of no training, for all bodhisattvas and Buddhas are endowed with these five [uncontaminated aggregates]. Thus, although these five aggregates depend on the Dharma realm, yet that Dharma realm is not to be identified with their descriptive marks and they do not lose their own descriptive marks as the five [uncontaminated aggregates]. Note that the five clinging aggregates of material form, sensation, conceptualization, volition, and consciousness and these five uncontaminated [aggregates] are the same in regard to the Dharma realm, [for they all are aggregates and not to be identified with that Pure Dharma Realm].

In summary we do affirm that there are no phenomenal qualities, such as discipline and so forth, in that Pure Dharma Realm, and yet there are true approaches to those good qualities therein, for its enabling causality engenders and increases all conditioned good qualities, which are not identical with those true good qualities of empty Dharma realm since they are unconditioned. These conditioned qualities, being dependent on this Dharma realm, 308c engender and increase all good qualities, but they are comprised in the conditioned transmigratory aggregates. But since they are not interrupted nor exhausted they are said to be eternal. It is not true, however, that they will never come to an end for all eternity, for having been engendered they will inevitably perish, since they are comprised in aggregates. They are not unconditioned factors, for they have as their content of understanding the meanings produced by reflection, and thus [in this fashion] they are eminent. Therefore we can conclude that the Dharma realm is truly the support for these five aggregates in [engendering] good qualities in all of the three vehicles.

The Tenth Simile:
The Descriptive Mark of No "I" or "Mine"

The Scripture says: "Again, in empty space causes and conditions develop and arise and the spheres of the three thousand world-realms can occur, and yet the realm of empty space itself has no arising activity, just so, in the Tathāgata's Pure Dharma Realm immeasurable descriptive marks and the spheres of all the Buddha assemblies are encompassed and yet the Pure Dharma Realm has no arising activity."

The Commentary explains: Again there is an objection, for, if the Pure Dharma Realm of all Buddhas is its essence then there is no differentiation in the enjoyment of this and that. How then could [that Pure Dharma Realm] have any differences in assemblies? On the other hand, if there is a differentiation in what is enjoyed [in those assemblies], then how can it be the Pure Dharma Realm of all the Buddhas?

In order to respond to this objection, [the Scripture] presents this tenth simile on empty space. The above passage shows that this objection is invalid, for it is just like empty space. In empty space, causes and conditions arise and the encircling of the enveloping wind-wheel which [supports] the three thousand world-realms can occur. Even though empty space has no discriminative thought that might differentiate "I" and "mine," yet it is able to encompass all these spheres of the different world-realms. Just so, in the Tathāgata's Pure Dharma Realm there can occur the one unified sphere of the assembly of all initiated bodhisattvas, who in the fullness of their qualities have attained the universal wisdom engendered from the enabling power of their own good actions. Since this [assembly] arises from a variety of different causes and conditions, those causes and conditions do not result in only one Buddha assembly but in a number of such assemblies. Another scripture expresses this same idea: "There can be various Buddhas and Buddha lands and Buddha assemblies." Yet the Dharma realm is not differentiated in the enjoyment of "I" and "mine" nor does it have any potentiality for creating differentiation between subject and object.

Although the Tathāgata's Dharma body has no images of differentiation or fabrication, yet, due to the power of original vows and eminent practice, enjoyment and transformation bodies do give rise to all the Buddha lands replete with their various descriptive marks. Thus arise all the differentiations in Buddha assemblies, all of which are but evolutions of conscious construction. But all these differentiations do not really exist. Just as by the power of his previous vow to benefit all sentient beings a universal monarch might perform eminent actions and engender wondrous and varied differentiations, such as excellent women and so forth,[36] just so all Buddhas, because they desire to benefit all sentient beings, engender eminent actions and in the enabling power of these actions give rise to various Pure Lands, thus constituting the differences in the enjoyment of Dharma in all the assemblies. But there is no discrimination in regard to these differentiations [for they are all evolutions from the Dharma body].

From this we can understand that the descriptive marks of the Dharma realm are profound, that its places are profound, that its actions are profound. The profundity of its descriptive marks means that it is apart from the ten kinds of impure defects and thus has the ten descriptive marks of purity. The ten kinds of impure defects are discrimination, defilement, purposeful activity, being conditioned, increase and decrease, movement, being transitory, suffering affliction, being an aggregate, and being attached to assemblies. The ten descriptive marks of purity are nondiscrimination, nondefilement, no purposeful activity, not being

309a

conditional, no increase nor decrease, no movement, being eternal, having no affliction, not being an aggregate, and not distinguishing "I" and "mine."

The profundities of action refer to the actions of transformations. The profundity of place means that [these Buddha places] have no movement and are in fact fully replete assemblies in the Tathāgata's Pure Land. All these places are metaphorically expressed through analogy with empty space, for that [analogy] is employed to express all the descriptive marks of the Dharma realm. As a scripture teaches, "All the metaphors we rely on express the Tathāgata's qualities, such as discipline and so forth, analogically but they all slander the Tathāgata, except the metaphor that employs the analogy of empty space, because the immeasurable qualities of the Tathāgata, such as his discipline and so forth, are indeed analogous to empty space."[37]

Chapter IX

Mirror Wisdom

The First Simile:
The Characteristic of Enunciation

The Scripture says: "Next, wondrously born ones, is mirror wisdom, which reflects all kinds of images as in a great mirror. Thus, dependent on the Tathāgata's wisdom mirror, a multitude of images of all senses, objects, and consciousnesses are reflected. But you should understand this mirror to be only a simile and should recognize that the Tathāgata's wisdom mirror is entirely universal. It is thus that this mirror of wisdom is called mirror wisdom."

The Commentary explains: Next the Scripture says wondrously born ones, next is mirror wisdom, for wisdom is to be explained after abandonment [and we have just described that abandonment in the above treatment of the Pure Dharma Realm]. We interpret that mirror wisdom by analogy [with a mirror], which is an impartial cause of the arising and manifestation of images of all things. This means that the eighth consciousness of all Tathāgatas is able to manifest and engender all images of all wisdoms just as a great mirror is able to manifest all images of this world, for [that container consciousness] is associated with wisdom. By conventional meaning we term [such manifestations of the converted container consciousnesses of Tathāgatas] wisdom. The phrase "all senses" refers to the six internal sense organs of the eye, ear, and so forth. The word "objects" refers to the six objects of those sense organs, that is, material form and so forth. These six internal sense organs and their six external objects are the twelve bases [of perception].   309b
The term "all consciousnesses" refers to the mind and mental states of the last three wisdoms, which have as their content those twelve bases, that is, all these [six] consciousnesses [which together with the twelve bases constitute the eighteen realms]. [The Scripture] says "a multitude of images" because differences in the various

functionings [of these wisdoms] do appear. Later on this Scripture says that at all times mirror wisdom, being always supported on all objects, is elicited together with the perceptible appearances of the various wisdom images. Other passages are to be interpreted in accord with this, for it is termed mirror wisdom because it can cause the arising of wisdom images. Equality wisdom takes as its content [the images of] mirror wisdom, with all its dependently co-arisen [images of] things. Discernment wisdom takes as its content all common and individual descriptive marks [of things], as does duty-fulfillment wisdom. The mind and mental states of these three wisdoms, in all the objects they apprehend both internally and externally, appear in the likeness of all these individual and common things, and various images clearly appear distinctly [in these three wisdoms]. Therefore all those images arise with the Tathāgata's mirror wisdom as their cause.

They are said to appear because they are clearly and distinctly manifested and understood. They are appearances in the mind of the Tathāgata's wisdom and nothing more, for in the Tathāgata's result stage their essence is equality wisdom and the other two wisdoms. When these wisdoms arise they are able thoroughly to understand, each according to its proper mode of functioning. Although they are nothing but the [undifferentiated] understanding of a Tathāgata, yet for the sake of analysis we do explain their descriptive marks. Others [who have not attained awakening] lack such [wisdom] capacity, for it is [only] through mirror wisdom that one is designated as capable of manifesting [wisdom], inasmuch as it brings about images of dependently co-arisen things just as a bright mirror manifests all its images.

An alternate interpretation is that in the phrase "all senses, objects, and consciousnesses" we are dealing with three distinct items [and not the eighteen realms]. The senses are the six sense organs, the objects are their six spheres, but the consciousnesses are the first six consciousnesses [that is, the five sense consciousnesses and the perceiving consciousness]. These include all the multitudinous images of the eighteen realms, [that is, all knowables in the world]. All these images do appear as appropriate to the specific nature of the other three wisdoms [which depend on mirror wisdom]. Because discernment wisdom and the other wisdoms are all able to manifest the universal nature of reality just as it is and to the limits of its existence, they have as their content [all the images] in the pure conscious construction associated with the Tathāgata's mirror wisdom. Because these three wisdoms give rise to their respective wisdom images they are said to manifest them. In general, such a description applies only to the understanding of a Tathāgata, but for the sake of analysis we say they manifest their [own specific] characteristics. The rest of the interpretation is as above.

Furthermore, the eighteen realms are all present to the consciousnesses and the conscious states associated with the Tathāgata's mirror wisdom, and thus their images appear therein, since when the Tathāgata's mirror wisdom arises it is able entirely to illumine all objects. All senses, their objects, and the [resultant] consciousnesses clearly appear as images in this wisdom because it apprehends their descriptive marks and causes them to appear.[38] Although mirror wisdom has no discrimination of subject and object, yet all knowable images do appear in it just as in a mirror, for this is the mode of functioning of this wisdom. Although the Tathāgata has no discrimination between subject and object, between unity and difference, yet he is able to be aware of the images of things characterized either as individual or as common as they arise in his mind and, since he is thus aware, he can explain these individual and common marks of all things without failure. It is in virtue of these images that the Tathāgata is perfected in his never-failing memory of things, for due to this all knowables are at all times clearly apparent in his mirror wisdom and in the other three wisdoms. If this were not so then how could the Tathāgata be called omniscient? If there were no mirror wisdom or if there were not the other three wisdoms then he would not be able constantly to be aware of the individual and common marks of all things.

309c

One might proffer the opinion that [the Tathāgata] has such a profound ability for omniscience in virtue of his [temporal] continuity, for a verse says, "It is because of his continuity that [the Tathāgata] has such a profound ability and is omniscient, just as a fire consumes everything [piece by piece]. It is not the case that he knows everything simultaneously."

But these are untrue words, for when the minds of non-Buddhas apprehend one thing they do not apprehend other things or know other things, and therefore they are not omniscient. A temporally sequential continuity is unable to apprehend and know [all things in one] moment. In the above opinion [the Buddha] would at one moment know only one aspect of the common marks of all things. If, however, this were so then the Tathāgata would be termed omniscient only by conventional meaning. But this is not so, for then he would not truly be omniscient, as omniscience means to be all-knowing in ultimate meaning.

Furthermore, in virtue of the fact that mirror wisdom is their content, in the continuity of the minds of Tathāgatas there appear all the images of the senses, objects, and consciousnesses of other beings in both world-transcendent and good worldly states, for if there were no mirror wisdom then these images would not so appear. They arise and are understood because of the force [of this mirror wisdom]. This means that the Tathāgata's mirror wisdom is their enabling cause and that all the senses, objects, and consciousnesses of all world-transcendent and good worldly states arise because of it, just as a multitude of images appear in a bright mirror. Although each sentient being has his own causal force, yet only in virtue of the enabling power of mirror wisdom do these [images] appear [in the minds of the awakened]. It is just like seeds, which would not produce their sprouts without the earth and so forth, or the images of things, which would not be reflected without a mirror.

But, [it is objected,] if this be so then the Bhagavat would be just like Maheśvara, who in the false view [of the non-Buddhists] is thought to be the cause of the world. Can it really be held that [the Bhagavat] is the universal cause of all the results [of awakening] in the world?

We do not commit this error, because when [mirror wisdom] arises it is able only to be the enabling cause [for those results]. It is not an eternally creative agent. Rather [mirror wisdom] arises due to the joint accumulation of merit and wisdom which have been cultivated for immeasurable eons [by sentient beings, who are thus the direct causes of these results]. Therefore, although [mirror wisdom] is a cause whereby all kinds of good arises for sentient beings, it is not to be understood as the non-Buddhists understand Maheśvara, who is falsely thought to be the creative agent of the world and whose nature is held to be eternal.

If there were not any image in that mirror [of wisdom] then how could there be any analogies [for expressing ultimate truth]? It is from the union of the thing [reflected] and the mirror that there comes to be a content for understanding. It is because images do thus appear that we are able to use such analogies. It is because 310a of the maturation force of the permeation of the images that are perversely clung to by all sentient beings that images appear which seem to objectify the maturation of one's own consciousness. Thus in this world arrogant pride arises and people think that they see images on the mirror of the self, arguing that there is no other mirror in which they could arise. But this *Scripture on the Buddha Land* says only that those images appear and not that they are produced [by any self]. Understand that the descriptive marks of all objects are appearances of the evolutions of consciousness and so do not ultimately exist apart from conscious construction, for that [conscious construction] is their ultimate meaning.

However, the doctrine of conscious construction–only does not mean that there are no conscious states and does not teach that there is only one consciousness. Each sentient being has the eight consciousnesses and their accompanying conscious states. Although all material forms and so forth do have their specific classifications [as outlined in the Abhidharma tracts], they all arise from conscious construction through the permeations whereby consciousness matures, for it is the nature [of consciousness] to be so differentiated. But even when these changes appear they are still not apart from conscious construction. By conventional speech we differentiate the content of these conscious states but such is not ultimate truth, for in the truth of ultimate meaning all things have no separate essence. Even suchness, although it is not an evolution of consciousness, is not apart from conscious construction, for it is the real nature of consciousness and is revealed by the common mark of the essencelessness whereby both the self and things are empty. We do then refute [the separate existence of] material form and so forth as imagined by the ignorant to be external to conscious construction. But we do not reject material form and so forth of other-dependent (*paratantra*) and fully perfected (*pariṇispanna*) [consciousnesses], for, in virtue of the fact that these are not apart from consciousness and conscious states they do not lack existence and are not apart [from that conscious construction]. Because these two consciousnesses of other-dependency and full perfection are not distinct [from one another], the Scripture refers to them as equal.

Both worldly mirrors and the Tathāgata's wisdom are nondiscriminative and both are able to present images without discrimination. It is termed mirror wisdom because [that wisdom mirror] is the cause of [such images].

The Second Simile: Nondiscrimination

The Scripture says: "In a great mirror, suspended in some high unshakeable place by a fortunate rich man, limitless people passing by could see their virtues and imperfections and then might come to desire to hold onto their virtues and discard their imperfections. Just so the Tathāgata has suspended his mirror wisdom in the Pure Dharma Realm, which, being uninterrupted, is unshakeable, because he desires to lead limitless innumerable sentient beings to gaze upon purity and to come to desire to hold onto that purity and discard all defilements."

The Commentary explains: The phrase "in some high...place" means the pinnacle or the acme. The "Pure Dharma Realm" is undefiled suchness and its ground is called the ground of peace because, whether as support or as content, it is uninterrupted. The term "unshakeable" means that since that mirror wisdom is supported on and has as its content understanding the Pure Dharma Realm, it exhausts the limits of transmigration and follows along in a constant continuity without interruption. This means that mirror wisdom is eternally separated from the oscillations of discrimination. This first [mirror] wisdom has always been and always will be, and thus its continuity is uninterrupted. The other three wisdoms (equality, discernment, and duty-fulfillment wisdoms), although they have no imaginings, yet do have a kind of nonclinging and nonpurposeful discrimination. They are realized in a temporal sequence and may be activated or not. Thus they are not unshakeable.

[This might seem to imply that the consciousnesses of these other wisdoms can be lacking in the state of awakening.] Thus one opinion holds that at the concentration of destruction, equality wisdom is not manifested, for the treatises explain that in the concentration of destruction there is no thinking consciousness. It is further stated that in one aspect [that concentration of destruction] destroys the constantly active consciousnesses and conscious states.

But, if this were so, then those treatises would teach that in these states [of arhatship,] the concentration of destruction, and the transcendent path,] there is no thinking consciousness at all.[39] And if this were so, then from the first stage of joy, when uncontaminated insight occurs, to the tenth stage of the Dharma cloud, [even though insight into the equality of all things occurs, yet] this equality wisdom would be lacking. And this is a serious error because it contradicts the scriptures and treatises. When the treatises explain that thinking is absent [in these states], they refer to the absence of defiled thinking and do not mean that thinking consciousness is lacking altogether. As long as one has not yet attained the selfless wisdom that realizes the emptiness of things, this [defiled thinking] is the support for the constant manifestation of clinging to the discrimination of things. As long as one has not yet attained the selfless wisdom that realizes the emptiness of

310b

129

self, this clinging is constantly active, because it is supported on this [defiled thinking consciousness].

If we examined the matter thoroughly, we would say that the container consciousness functions in synergy with a thinking consciousness. If a perceiving consciousness arises, then at the same time the container consciousness functions in synergy with these two consciousnesses. When one of the five sense consciousnesses arises, then it functions in synergy with these three consciousnesses, and so forth, until, when all five of the sense consciousnesses arise at the same time, then simultaneously the container consciousness functions in synergy with all these seven consciousnesses.[40] Know then that in [the three states of the transcendent path, the concentration of destruction, and the state of no training, a consciousness of thinking] also exists, for its mode of functioning, joined together with equality wisdom and apart from any discriminative clinging to defiled things, is subtle and not opposed to that concentration of destruction. The concentration of destruction is the natural development of the uncontaminated path, for its essence is uncontaminated. It is the self-clinging of defiled thinking that is opposed to it. The above statement that [the concentration of destruction] in one aspect destroys [consciousnesses and conscious states] does not then mean that it destroys all consciousnesses. Therefore equality wisdom, [which is the conversion of the support for thinking,] is present in the state of the result of awakening and, although it is constantly manifested, yet in the ten stages it is realized in a temporal sequence. But when the contaminated mind arises, then this wisdom does not arise, for it is then interrupted. It is not thus unshakeable. Because the other two wisdoms are also not constantly active in the state of awakening, they also are not unshakeable.

Why then has the Tathāgata securely placed this mirror wisdom in the Pure Dharma Realm? In order "to lead limitless innumerable sentient beings to gaze upon purity." Why should they gaze upon purity? So that "they may come to desire to hold on to that purity and discard all defilements." Defilements here refer to the qualities of passion and karmic rebirth. To discard means to suppress and sever, for, whether on the worldly or transcendent path, one suppresses and severs them either for a time or finally. Purity refers to all the good which can cause the minds of sentient beings to become purified. To hold on to means to support, for [that purity] firmly establishes, nurtures, and matures the seeds [of wisdom] and seeks to realize deliverance according to one's commitment. This means that all Tathāgatas, when they were bodhisattvas, came to aspire after the perfection of all kinds of benefit for sentient beings and entertained the joyous thought of benefiting and gladdening all sentient beings. Supported on the Pure Dharma Realm, they subsequently amassed the spiritual equipment of happiness and wisdom by their practices and turned back [from cessation] to seek a continued presence [in this world of transmigration]. All this was due to the fact that the skillful methods of mirror wisdom were earnestly cultivated [by them]. Having realized this wisdom, which has as its content the Pure Dharma Realm, their continued presence was without movement and although they had no purposeful, discriminative fabrication, yet that continued presence [in transmigration] was an enabling cause for leading sentient beings, according to their dispositions, to establish, nurture, and mature the seeds of immeasurable good roots, to attain worldly joy and transcendent deliverance. 310c

Therefore [these Buddhas] arose from the Tathāgata's mirror wisdom; and their transformed existence functions to proclaim the essence of the Dharma to all sentient beings in order that they might know [the differences between] defilement and purity, hold on to purity, and discard defilement. Such is their support for bringing benefit and happiness to sentient beings.

The Third Simile: Purity from Obstacles

The Scripture says: "Again, just as when a mirror is shined to a luster, its surface, bright, pure, and free from dust, shines and clearly illuminates everywhere, just so is the Tathāgata's mirror wisdom because, being Buddha wisdom, it is eternally separated from the [two] obstacles of passion and to knowledge, and its well-polished luster is the support for concentration. Its mirror surface is pure and without dust, and brings happiness and benefit to all sentient beings, for its light illumines everywhere."

The Commentary explains: It is "bright" because its essence is extremely pure. It is "pure" because, being apart from differentiation, it is free from adventitious dust. The phrase "free from dust" means that it has been completely purified from dust inasmuch as it is separated from anything that obfuscates the above two (clarity and purity). The term "shines" is used because of the [luminous] surface of that mirror. The term "clearly" refers to that purity. The phrase "it illumines everywhere" is used because of that freedom. It is said that that mirror wisdom is "Buddha wisdom" because it is forever apart from the [two] obstacles of passion and to knowledge, which are termed dust, and thus it is said that it is "eternally separated" [from these]. It is "polished to a luster" because such Buddha wisdom is eternally transcendent to the dust of all obstacles. "Passion" refers to the bonds of all the passions of craving, anger, and so forth, which in the state of bondage and guilt keep people drowsy, for, whether outwardly manifested or not, they all have the force to obstruct the arising of the holy path and the attainment of cessation. "The obstacle of passion" means that they scatter the body and the mind. "The obstacle to knowledge" refers to ignorance in regard to all knowables which, while not being itself a defilement, obstructs the universal wisdom [of a Buddha]. But it does not obstruct cessation, for we see that the word-hearers do attain cessation even though they have this obstacle. These two obstacles are also termed defiled hindrances. They are rendered quiescent by pure wisdom since they would defile that pure wisdom. Thus [wisdom] comes to control this adventitious dust, these hindering obstacles. The phrase "it is eternally separated from them" means that they never arise again. Because it is eternally separated from these obstacles, mirror wisdom is always pure, and thus it is said that it has "a well-polished surface." The phrase "it is the support for concentration" means that [concentration] is supported on mirror wisdom because it arises in dependency on it. The term "support" is also applicable to concentration, for on the path of uninterrupted deliverance it is the support that engenders the utmost purification. Thus either concentration or wisdom may be termed a support.

The most basic concentration is the preeminent diamond-like concentration, for through its power obstacles are eternally severed. In this case wisdom is that which is supported, for it is upheld in the power of concentration. The term "support" means that this wisdom arises in virtue of the uninterrupted nature of that concentration, for in the power of that concentration the utmost purification becomes separated from all discrimination and has no discrimination in virtue of the arising of mirror wisdom. This wisdom then is that which is supported, because it is supported by concentration.

311a

It is "bright" because of its original purity, which is bright, pure, and without dust. It is "pure" because it is apart from the obstacle of passion. It is "without dust" because it is apart from the obstacle to knowledge. The phrase "it brings happiness and benefit to all sentient beings, for its light illumines everywhere" means that this wisdom is able to bring about all benefit and happiness for all sentient beings because it is supported on concentration. Because of its activity "its light illumines everywhere." Because its essence is the pure mirror, the text uses the term "light." It "clearly illumines everywhere" because it is free from the [two] obstacles of passion and to knowledge. Therefore mirror wisdom is originally pure, far apart from the two obstacles, is bright, pure, and without dust. Although it cannot be seen, it gives rise to the enjoyment and transformation bodies, is able to produce all wisdoms, and is able to perfect all benefit for sentient beings. Therefore it is said that "its light illumines everywhere."

The Fourth Simile:
The Cause of the Arising of Images

The Scripture says: "Again, just as the basic nature of a mirror is to depend on conditions whereby various images and appearances arise in it, just so the Tathāgata's mirror wisdom gives rise to various wisdom images and appearances because it always depends on conditions."

The Commentary explains: [There is an objection, for] if mirror wisdom is the cause whereby images of all wisdoms arise for all sentient beings, then how can it not become differentiated [in those images]? How can the essence of this wisdom not itself be differentiated? Moreover, if at all times it constantly is able to be the cause [of images], then how could it at some particular time all at once give rise to images of all sentient beings and of the other wisdoms?

The above passage from the Scripture is meant to respond to this objection. It is not true that the essence of a mirror is itself differentiated because its images are different. It is not true that it gives rise to its images either constantly or all at once, for it must wait on a host of conditions. Therefore mirror wisdom does give rise to various different images because at all times it waits on this host of conditions, but it itself does not become differentiated because those images are different, just as the shades of blue are not differentiated [in the state of totality]. It is not true that it gives rise to the images of all sentient beings and the other wisdoms either constantly or all at once because it must wait on the presence of the proper occasions and conditions to be able to give rise [to any image].

This means that the pure consciousness associated with mirror wisdom has two functions. The first is the function of being a direct cause, for innate in that pure consciousness are all the pure seeds of wisdom that are able to manifest and give rise to bodies and lands if they encounter the [proper] conditions. Only then will [these seeds] manifest the various bodies and lands that are the content [of wisdom]. Only then will it be able to give rise to the different modes of activity that characterize the consciousness and the conscious states associated with equality wisdom and the other 311b wisdoms. The second function is being the enabling cause, for if sentient beings are equipped with their own direct causes, then, in virtue of the arising of the vow power from the pure roots in the pure consciousness of a Buddha, that pure consciousness lends them assistance in order to lead them to attain an unhindered growth and maturity. Thus although the essence of mirror wisdom is one, yet it is able to manifest and give rise to all these images of Dharma, but it is not true that it arises all at once, for it must wait upon external conditions.

The Fifth Simile:
The Characteristic of Not Clinging
to "I" and "Mine"

The Scripture says: "As in a mirror not just one but a multitude of images arise, and yet there are no images at all within that mirror and it has no movement and no activity, just so in the Tathāgata's mirror wisdom not just one but a multitude of wisdom images arise, and yet there are no images at all within that mirror wisdom and mirror wisdom has no movement and no activity."

The Commentary explains: [There is another objection, for] if all these wisdom images are already essentially present in mirror wisdom, how then could mirror wisdom arise conditionally? On the other hand, if they are not essentially present, then how is it able to produce all these wisdom images, since it has no movement or activity? One never sees a potter who without any movement or activity is able to make a new pot!

The above passage from the Scripture is intended to respond to this objection. This means that mirror wisdom is able to give rise to images just like a mirror. It says that "there is not just one" because there are many images. "They are a multitude" because their varieties are innumerable. If a mirror were to rely on just one kind of image, there would be only one reflection, and thus the Scripture says "not just one" [to exclude that possibility]. There is rather a "multitude" [of images] because it does reflect numerous varieties. In this fashion, although there are at first no images in the mirror, yet it gives rise to many images without itself having any movement or activity of deliberation or discrimination. Just so is mirror wisdom, for, although at first it has no images of any wisdom, yet it is able to give rise to various images of wisdom. Since it depends on a variety [of conditions], those [images] are not just one but a multitude. Although it gives rise to these wisdom images, yet it has no movement or activity of deliberation of discrimination. This means that just as a mirror, although nondiscriminative, yet is able to give rise to many images, just so mirror wisdom, although it does not cling to "I" and "mine" nor purposefully discriminate subject from object, is able to give rise to the images of the various wisdoms.

The Sixth Simile:
The Characteristic of Nonforgetfulness

The Scripture says: "Again, just as a mirror is neither united to nor separated from all its images because it does not accumulate them and because it is the cause for their manifestation, just so the Tathāgata's mirror wisdom is neither united to nor separated from all its wisdom images because it does not accumulate them and because it does not lose them."

The Commentary explains: [There is an objection, for] if mirror wisdom is united to all its wisdom images, then how could it not itself become differentiated, since they are differentiated? On the other hand, if it is not united to them, then how can it be their cause? We never see seeds able to cause sprouts when they are not united with those results! If the rays of the sun were not absorbed by quicklime stones, they would not become luminous!

The Scripture presents the above passage in order to respond to this objection. A worldly mirror, although able to be the cause for the arising of a multitude of images, yet is not united to those images because before they arise they have no essence that might be accumulated. It is neither directly joined to them nor they to it and it cannot be said to be united with them. But neither is a mirror separated from them because it is the cause of their manifestation, and thus it is not un-united to them either. It is because of this [mirror wisdom] that those [images] exist at all. Although

311c

it is such a cause of the appearance of images, yet the mirror itself does not become differentiated because those images are different. Mirror wisdom is also like this inasmuch as, although it is able to cause the production of wisdom images, it is neither united to nor separated from those wisdom images because it neither accumulates nor disperses them. The phrase "it is not united" means that before they have arisen, they have nothing that could be accumulated. The phrase "it is not separated" means that there must be that mirror wisdom for these wisdom images to arise, for, were it lacking, they would not arise. The phrase "because it does not lose them" is to be understood as follows. The meaning of the word "lose" is to be separated from, to fall away from, to become absent, for its opposite is not to lose. Because [mirror wisdom] retains and does not forget the descriptive marks of the content mediated through the images it gives rise to, the Scripture says that "it does not lose them." Thus in mirror wisdom are manifested all knowables, all the wisdoms of this triple world, and all sentient beings. If there were no such universal knowledge, mirror wisdom would not arise, for it does arise only by knowing everything. Therefore the Scripture says that "it does not lose them" because this wisdom does not forget the descriptive marks of any object. Because it does not lose them, it is not apart from them. Although it can thus cause the arising of wisdom images, yet it does not become differentiated because those images are different, for they issue forth in a nondiscriminative manner as if from a mirror. Although a worldly mirror can cause the arising of many images, it is not to be identified as being either united to or separated from those images. Just so mirror wisdom is not to be identified as either joined to or separated from its wisdom images, although it is able to cause their arising.

Although seeds are able to cause sprouts, yet they cannot be said to be either joined to or separated from them. Even the finest parts of the rays [of the sun] are not identical with the material bodies [they illumine], but because their common characteristics are united and joined together, a unified image that seems to be identical with the material body appears in consciousness [and the eye perceives it as luminous]. Thus all the causes and results we see in the world are causes without thereby being either united to or separated from [their results]. Only if they were not related as cause and result would their characteristics be definitively united.

The Seventh Simile: Omnipresence

The Scripture says: "Again just as the lustrous surface of a mirror is the supporting cause for the arising of all images in all places, just so the Tathāgata's mirror wisdom does not cut off the luster of all [their] innumerable practices, and it is the supporting cause for the arising of all wisdom images, that is, the wisdom images of the word-hearers' vehicle, the individually enlightened ones' vehicle, and the Great Vehicle, because he desires to lead all word-hearers to attain deliverance through that word-hearers' vehicle, all the individually enlightened ones' lineage to attain deliverance through that individually enlightened ones' vehicle, and all those of the Great Vehicle to attain deliverance through that Great Vehicle."

The Commentary explains: [There is an objection, for] how can it be possible that this wisdom can be able at all times to give rise to all the images of Dharma in the three vehicles?

The Scripture gives the above passage to respond to this objection. In order that a worldly mirror might reflect all images on its surface, various efforts are undertaken to polish both sides of its surface so that it may become capable of causing the manifestation of all images in all places. Just so is mirror wisdom. All Tathāgatas, when they were yet bodhisattvas, were unable to give rise to the images of Dharma of all the wisdoms of the three vehicles because their lineage [as Tathāgatas] was yet covered over by obstacles. But through the intense cultivation of uninterrupted immeasurable practices they became lustrous, and at the moment of diamond-like concentration they eradicated all obstacles and were perfected in purification. Then they became capable of producing the wisdoms of the three vehicles and such images were not severed, for both the range and the time period of their unlimited [practices] were unlimited. This explains the cause whereby [mirror wisdom] pervades all places. Due to the intense cultivation of many practices for an immeasurable time, mirror wisdom is able to give rise to the wisdom images of the three vehicles.

Furthermore, this mirror wisdom is free from all defilement in all places and at all times, and its various practices are fully perfected because its adornments are most fully purified. Therefore at all times and in all places, it is able to produce all images, for, as already explained, that preeminent diamond-like concentration severs all obstacles and realizes the Tathāgata's mirror wisdom, and thus its various wonderful adornments at all places and times are able to produce the images of the three vehicles.

This is to be understood to mean that there are indeed differences in the maturation of the good roots of individuals. Individuals of a determined lineage realize deliverance through their respective vehicles. Those of an undetermined lineage attain deliverance either through the Great Vehicle or through one of the other vehicles. The term deliverance means cessation. All individuals of the three vehicles have their own seed-lineage as the direct cause [for that deliverance] and the Tathāgata's mirror wisdom as the enabling cause. By their own intense efforts and the Buddha's skillful assistance, they cultivate and amass good spiritual stores, elicit the path, sever the [two] obstacles of passion and to knowledge, and, as appropriate to each, realize cessation.

In the case of word-hearers and individually enlightened ones of determined lineage who abide in the state of no training, their bodies and minds, which had been influenced by previous actions of passion, are spontaneously destroyed because they delight in tranquility and cessation and have eternally severed all those obstacles of passion which might elicit actions and engender rebirths. They will never be reborn again because they have no remaining support [for such a rebirth]. Thus all their conditioned states, whether contaminated or uncontaminated, whether manifested or unmanifested, are accordingly severed and destroyed. There remains only the conversion of the support, unfabricated and undefiled

312b

suchness, the Pure Dharma Realm, the liberation body (*vimukti-kāya*). This is called cessation without remainder, eternal, beatific, ultimate, quiescent, unfathomable, inconceivable. They are identical with all Tathāgatas. But inasmuch as they lack the adornments of conditioned pure qualities and do not engender benefit or happiness for sentient beings, they are not like Tathāgatas at all.

Those word-hearers and individually enlightened ones of undetermined lineage who abide in the state of no training, although they have no passion [and thus might quickly enter final cessation without remainder], yet do delight in wisdom. By the power of their vows, they maintain their bodies in continuity and cultivate the practice of the Great Vehicle until they attain diamond-like concentration, wherein all obstacles are destroyed and they realize the three bodies of Buddha. Although they do have conditioned, uncontaminated qualities, they do not have an uncontaminated body or mind and therefore they do [finally] realize cessation without remainder. The term "remainder" here means the contaminated body and mind of [transmigration in] the triple world. If bodhisattvas also severed the two obstacles completely when they reached the Buddha result, then we would have to say that they also would enter cessation without remainder, [for they would have no ties of passion to this world at all].

Thus some of those in the two vehicles first enter cessation with remainder and afterward cessation without remainder. But when bodhisattvas first realize the Tathāgata realm, they immediately realize these two cessations, for, in virtue of the fact that their contaminated bodies and mind are completely exhausted, they are said to have no remaining support [for any continued presence in the world]. Yet because they create appearances of contaminated bodies and minds, they are said to have some remaining support. Because they have realized compassion and wisdom without interruption, they are also said to have entered nonabiding cessation, [that is, cessation that abides neither in the transcendence of no remainder or the immanence of maintaining a remaining support].

Cessation means the eternal destruction of obstacles in the essence of suchness. Inasmuch as when uncontaminated wisdom has penetrated truth one severs all impurity and realizes [cessation], it is called the cessation of penetrating discernment. This cessation of penetrating discernment exists as a designation for suchness.

The ultimate stage of not discriminating things as if they were real is termed cessation. It is cessation because it has no goal to achieve, no fetid impurity, and is free from bondage and confusion. 312c

How then can the word-hearers and the individually enlightened ones attain this ultimate cessation, for they have not yet destroyed the permeations from the obstacle to knowledge?

The obstacle to knowledge is a lack of understanding rather than a defilement, and thus it obstructs wisdom, not cessation. Not being a passion, it is not able to engender any rebirth. Since [those word-hearers and individually enlightened ones] have no vow power, they turn their minds toward the ultimate state of no training and, having exhausted the measure of their long lives, become eternally extinct.

The Eighth Simile:
The Source of Universal Wisdom

The Scripture says: "Just as in a mirror great images, such as the great earth, high mountains, large trees, and broad palaces and lodges, can occur and yet that mirror is not measured by them, just so in the Tathāgata's mirror wisdom, wisdom images from the stage of joy to the stage of awakening can occur, wisdom images of all worldly and transcendent doctrines can occur, and yet that mirror wisdom is not differentiated by these."

The Commentary explains: [There is an objection, for] if mirror wisdom is able to give rise to wisdom images, then in the same measure that they are differentiated, so it also would be differentiated.

The Scripture presents the above passage to respond to this objection. Although a worldly mirror is able to cause images of the

141

earth and so forth, yet that mirror itself is not measured by those [images]. Even in a small mirror such great images of mountain ranges and so forth occur, and in a large mirror images of small pebbles occur. Although these images are of material forms, yet the mirror is not measured by the size of its images. Similarly mirror wisdom, although it gives rise to the immaterial forms of all the wisdom images of the ten stages, of worldly and transcendent doctrines, is not measured by the size of those wisdom images. Therefore the wisdom mirror of all Buddhas is termed the storehouse of great wisdom, for it is the foundation for transcendent and worldly wisdoms. As explained, the Bhagavat perfects this mirror wisdom of the storehouse of great wisdom and is able to engender omniscience.

Understand that the term wisdom in this Scripture denotes all good qualities, for the pure consciousness associated with mirror wisdom is replete with all the good seeds whereby self-benefit benefits others. This wisdom is able directly to cause the arising of wisdom images in one's own body and to enable the arising of those images in the bodies of others. This is so because mirror wisdom is able to create and manifest bodies and give rise to the Dharma enunciated through wisdom, and, by these evolutions [from the mind of wisdom,] give rise to the images of the other wisdoms.

Alternatively it can be interpreted to mean that, perfected by the permeations of the power of the compassionate vow, [mirror wisdom] becomes the enabling cause for the good doctrine of the other wisdoms, and thus it brings it about that in the bodies of others the good doctrines of wisdom are easily attained, engendered, and increased. As a scripture says, "All good states of sentient beings arise from the enabling power of the Tathāgata's compassionate vow."[41]

The Ninth Simile:
Nonarising in Unfit Vessels

The Scripture says: "Just as a mirror is not a cause of images when there are obstacles placed in front of it, just so the Tathāgata's

mirror wisdom is not a cause of wisdom images for sentient beings 313a
who have the obstacle of hearing untrue doctrines under the
influence of bad teachers, for they are unfit vessels."

The Commentary explains: [There is an objection, for] since
mirror wisdom is the cause whereby those in the three vehicles
attain deliverance, it does give rise to all wisdom images. Moreover, [mirror wisdom,] perfected by the permeations from the compassionate vow, is the enabling cause for all worldly and transcendent wisdom images. Why then does not this true wisdom arise
among non-Buddhists, for if it is constantly present to them as the
cause for those [wisdom images], then it would never be ineffective,
even in the case of non-Buddhists.

In order to respond to this objection, the Scripture gives the
above passage. Although a worldly mirror is able to cause the manifestation of all images, yet when intervening obstacles, for example, a wall, are placed in front of it, it cannot cause those images
to arise. Just so is the Tathāgata's mirror wisdom, for although it
is able to cause the arising of wisdom images, yet it cannot cause
them to arise for those who have the obstacle of delighting in hearing perverted doctrine under the influence of bad teachers, for they
are vessels unfit for the reception of hearing the true Dharma.
Therefore [wisdom] does not arise among the non-Buddhists but
rather is always rejected and nullified.

This is because their good seeds are suppressed and their evil
seeds find opportunity to increase. From the beginningless beginning, the times when sentient beings have cultivated good have
been few, but the times when they have wrought evil have been
many. Therefore good states, even though they encounter favorable conditions, are yet difficult to nurture, and evil states, even
though they meet only the weakest opportunity, still prosper.

The Tenth Simile:
Unfit Vessels Who Delight in Evil

The Scripture says: "Just as a mirror cannot give rise to images
in darkened places, just so the Tathāgata's mirror wisdom cannot

give rise to wisdom images among those sentient beings who foolishly delight in the enjoyment of evil."

The Commentary explains: Just as wisdom images do not arise when external conditions [that block that mirror] are present, so also they do not arise when internal conditions are present whereby, in virtue of previous actions, people delight in the darkness of evil and ignorance.

Those who delight in evil are aflame with all the passions of covetousness, anger, and so forth, but even more so are they heavily inclined toward delusion, for they do not understand the relationships between the causes and results of good and evil. All the Buddha's doctrines that have appeared in this world do bring benefit and happiness to all sentient beings. The good field of the Three Jewels nurtures the immeasurable accumulation of bliss for all in the world and transcendent to the world. But instead of desiring to hear, receive, delight in, and base themselves on that Dharma, some stop up their ears and embrace the perverted teachings of non-Buddhists, which bring neither benefit nor happiness. They turn toward and base themselves on [such teachings] and thus nurture and bring about a multitude of sufferings, immeasurable evil actions, and various kinds of evil powers. Is this not the obstructing force of ignorant, deluded darkness? The pull of ignorance in obstructing good is heavy indeed. We must then earnestly cultivate the light of wisdom, for one weighed down by ignorance is not a fit vessel for good.

The Eleventh Simile:
Perpetually Unfit Vessels

313b

The Scripture says: "Again just as a mirror cannot give rise to images that are far distant, just so the Tathāgata's mirror wisdom cannot give rise to images in those sentient beings who, because of their actions, are defective in regard to the Dharma or who do not believe, for they are unfit vessels."

The Commentary explains: Wisdom images do not arise because of the force of both internal and external obstacles. The first refers to those who, due to actions in former lives, are defective in regard to Dharma and are thus unable to hear the true Dharma for a long time. This means that they will pass through immeasurable eons without hearing the Buddha-Dharma of any Buddha because they have slandered the true Dharma in a former life. This obstacle is a result of their own actions and so wisdom images do not arise for them and they do not hear true Dharma, for their bodies lack such [potential].

Why then do we say that they have slandered that true Dharma? Or that this is the result [of their former actions]?

[We answer that] their ability to obstruct wisdom images which might arise does not mean that their not hearing the true Dharma is itself the result or the obstruction. Rather the result [of their former actions] and the obstacle [they have engendered in regard to Dharma] are their defectiveness in regard to the Dharma and their unsound sense organs and obtuse bodies and minds, for this is the reason why they are unable to hear and accept the true Dharma. It is the natural outcome of their actions.

The second case [of external obstructions] refers to nonbelief, that is, those who do not have any lineage, who have no potential for cessation, who do not delight in cessation, and who have no seeds of the transcendent path. They have a perpetual obstacle against the realization of suchness. Upon hearing the transcendent Dharma, they do not believe or accept it and they will never attain cessation in any of the three vehicles. Because the continuity of their bodies and minds is impure, they are unfit vessels for the sacred Dharma. Both for a time and for all time they do not engender any transcendent, meritorious images. Just as polluted water is unable to reflect the image of the moon, so mirror wisdom is unable to engender any wisdom images for these sentient beings.[42]

[In summary] then, mirror wisdom has these nine kinds of preeminent characteristics: sure enunciation, nondiscrimination, purity from obstacles, being the cause of the arising of wisdom images, no clinging to "I" or "mine," not forgetting any knowable, giving rise to wisdom images at all times and in all places, being the source that is able to give rise to all wisdoms, and being unable to give rise to wisdom images in unfit vessels. There are three kinds of vessels unfit for the sacred Dharma: those who are vessels unfit for the sacred Dharma because they have the temporary obstacle of having heard untrue teaching due to the influence of bad teachers; those who are vessels unfit for the sacred Dharma because they have the obstacle of being hindered by passion and delusion; and those who are vessels unfit for the sacred Dharma because they have the perpetual obstacle of being hindered by extremely heavy karmic actions or who lack any seed of the transcendent path (*icchantikas*). These three are included in the ninth characteristic, for they all are unfit vessels in whom [wisdom] images cannot arise.

Chapter X

Equality Wisdom

The Scripture says: "Next, wondrously born ones, is equality wisdom, which is replete and perfected with ten kinds of descriptive marks."

The Commentary explains: equality wisdom is replete and perfected with ten kinds of descriptive marks. Understand that these [marks] are the results of the practices of the ten stages. We will consider them one by one. Each is realized in equality wisdom, cultivated to completion, and perfected in the equality wisdom of the Buddha land. This is why it is said above that "equality wisdom is replete and perfected with ten kinds of descriptive marks." In general terms, in each of the stages one realizes the immeasurable reality nature of equality, cultivates completion, and perfects the equality wisdom of the Buddha land.

313c

The First Mark: Highest Delight in Marks

The Scripture says: "It realizes the supreme delight in all its marks because the reality nature of equality is fully perfected."

The Commentary explains: The phrase "all its marks" refers to all the major and minor marks of a great personage. They are said to be "equal" because all these marks are far apart from the pattern of clinging to what is entirely imagined. Another scripture says, "Because the Tathāgata is said to have the marks of a great personage, he has no marks, and thus it is said that he has the marks of a great personage."[43] The term "supreme" implies regal mastery. None of the aggregates of material form and so forth are regally masterful because they are each differentiated. Even taken as a whole, they are not regally masterful because, even in unison, they do not lose their [differentiated] essence. But [equality wisdom] is regally masterful and apart from clinging to imagination, because it is apart from these aggregates and has no

147

real personal essence. Therefore it is said to be equal. Another scripture teaches, "Bhagavat, I now understand that because everything has no essence, there is no poverty and no wealth." The term "delight" [usually] refers to that delight which comes from the force of imagining, whereby one engenders delight in regard to agreeable things and sorrow in regard to disagreeable things. But [equality wisdom] is called the understanding of equality [between the agreeable and the disagreeable], because in it nothing is clung to by imagination and there is no delight in clinging to [such images]. The phrase "it takes supreme delight in all its marks because of the reality nature of equality" refers to the realization of the stage of joy. This is what bodhisattvas first realize, and then through progressive cultivation in the subsequent stages of skillful methods they cause it to grow until in the final stage of awakening they bring it to full perfection. After this last stage [equality wisdom] no longer increases, for they have then realized its full perfection. It should be understood that this is the full perfection of equality wisdom.

The phrase "because it is fully perfected" was in the ablative case [in the original Sanskrit grammar] but it expresses an instrumental meaning, that is, in virtue of its full perfection. The [original Sanskrit] text here used the ablative case with an instrumental meaning.

The Second Mark:
The Experience of Conditioned Arising

The Scripture says: "It realizes the conditioned arising of all experience because the reality nature of equality is fully perfected."

314a   The Commentary explains: There are two kinds of dependent co-arising: internal and external. Internal dependent co-arising refers to the twelve branches of ignorance and so forth. External dependent co-arising refers to [the dependent co-arising] of all things, such as seeds, sprouts, and so forth. The internal is examined by the harmony or disharmony of the two modalities of defilement and purification. The external is examined in ascertaining that this exists because that exists, that because this arises, that arises. This means that sprouts come to be because of seeds, for sprouts are born because seeds have been born. In these two kinds of dependent co-arising all things exist as results because their causes exist, for results arise only in virtue of the arising of their causes. The meaning of dependent co-arising is the meaning of no purposeful activity. It is the meaning of the essencelessness of emptiness. It is the meaning of no real personal essence. These meanings are the intrinsic descriptive marks of dependent co-arising. Because [equality wisdom] experiences these, the Scripture uses the term "experience." Or perhaps because sentient beings are able to experience, it uses the term "experience," for all dependently co-arisen things are the content of experience and therefore all experience arises conditionally. It is far removed from all clinging to imagination and is called the understanding of equality because it has no purposeful activity, is empty, has no essence, and no real personal essence. The term "it realizes" means that all things are experienced as dependently co-arising, as the reality nature of equality. This wisdom is "fully perfected" because, as explained above, its realization is cultivated unto that full perfection. Therefore the reality nature of the equality of dependent co-arising is identical with the reality nature of the equality of all things. As it has been taught, "Oh *bhikṣu,* the entire Dharma realm is the conditionally produced, conditionally arising reality nature. This understanding is what is termed wisdom. As seen by the Tathāgata, the entire Dharma realm is the dependently co-arisen Dharma realm." Again another scripture teaches, "One cannot see even the most insignificant thing that is not dependently co-arisen."[44]

In this Scripture dependent co-arising is termed the reality nature of the equality of dependent co-arising. According to this profound meaning it is said, "If one gains insight into dependent co-arising, he sees into the reality nature. If one gains insight into the reality nature, he sees all Buddhas."[45] The above passage was presented in this Scripture because the actual nature of dependent co-arising is the ultimate Dharma, the ultimate truth of awakening, because the equality [of all dependently co-arisen things] is not different from place to place.

The Third Mark: No Marks

The Scripture says: "It attains a state far removed from all differentiating marks and without marks because the reality nature of equality is fully perfected."

The Commentary explains: The term "differentiating marks" refers to the differences in the marks of all that is created and destroyed within material form and the other four aggregates. It is "far removed" from all these separate, differentiating marks because [equality wisdom] is the common descriptive mark [of all things]. Such a common mark is a descriptive mark because this mark is a no-mark. As a scripture teaches, "The reality nature has only one mark and that is a no-mark." This absence of any descriptive mark is precisely the equality of the reality nature. The term "realizes" is used because this [equality wisdom] understands the reality nature of equality whereby all states of clinging to imagination are seen to be absolutely and eternally nonexistent. As explained above, equality wisdom "is fully perfected" because this realization is cultivated unto full perfection.

314b

An alternate opinion holds that its being far removed from differentiating marks means that it has no marks. And its being far removed from no marks means that it is not the case that it has no marks. Because it does not have no marks, this Scripture terms it the equality [of marks]. The rest is as above.

The Fourth Mark: Compassion

The Scripture says: "A broad refuge is great compassion, because the reality nature of equality is fully perfected."

The Commentary explains: There are three kinds of compassion. The first is that which is focused on sentient beings as its object. The second is that which is focused on the Dharma as its object. The third is that which has no object at all. When bodhisattvas first elicit the aspiration for wisdom, in many ways they cultivate the compassion that is focused on sentient beings as its object. In sundry manners this compassion is contaminated because of its conventional, conditioned object. When they are cultivating true practice [in the stages of the path of cultivation] in many ways they cultivate the compassion that is focused on the Dharma as its object. This compassion is also contaminated because it has the Dharma of the Great Vehicle as its object. When they have attained the patience of no-birth, in many ways they cultivate the compassion that has no object at all because, although the Dharma realm is their object, they lack discrimination, just as the maturation of the states of sense perception [have no discrimination], for they all arise spontaneously without prior intention. Therefore their compassion is said to be without object at all, to be the great compassion associated with mirror wisdom.

Another opinion holds that the only object [of this compassion] is the Dharma realm because any discrimination of external objects is nonexistent. Therefore it is called compassion without an object because it does not focus on either sentient beings or the Dharma.

However, the correct opinion is that it does indeed have as its object sentient beings and yet is nondiscriminative. Its universally equal activity understands all that which is conventionally valid, for the nature of sentient beings is universally equal, because the dependently co-arisen universal reality nature is universally equal, because essenceless suchness is universally equal. Therefore it is termed equality wisdom. Thus the objects associated with this wisdom include all the three compassions. However, it is said to be objectless because its action is nondiscriminative and equal.

The great compassion associated with equality wisdom in the land of the Tathāgata is perfected by a multitude of descriptive marks and constantly appears. The Tathāgata certainly has objectless compassion and, even if the other two [kinds of compassion] are not specifically mentioned, they are also perfected by him. With universal equality the Tathāgata saves all sentient beings through these three [kinds of] compassion. It is not only that he confers some small happiness on them. Rather he constantly brings about salvation for all inasmuch as he moves in that equality whereby all sentient beings and all doctrines are essenceless suchness. Thus the Scripture uses the term "great compassion." He is not similar to word-hearers who can bring some small benefit to sentient beings for a short time but are unable to save all sentient beings. Being superior to all such word-hearers, he does deliver all sentient beings inasmuch as he has amassed over a long time the completed perfection of blessed wisdom and spiritual stores, and thus the Scripture uses the term "a broad refuge" [in his regard]. This broad refuge and great compassion pervade everywhere and are said to be equal, that is, the reality nature of equality, for they are nondiscriminative. Or perhaps this phrase is employed because that broad refuge and great compassion have as their content that reality nature of equality. As explained above, this equality wisdom is fully perfected because this great compassion is cultivated unto full perfection.

The Fifth Mark: Unrejecting Compassion

The Scripture says: "Unrejecting is its compassion because the reality nature of equality is fully perfected."

The Commentary explains: The compassion of the word-hearers is unable to save all sentient beings, for its activity includes only a limited number of sentient beings in this realm of desire (*kāmadhātu*) and arises only for a limited time period. But the great compassion of the Tathāgatas is universally able to save all sentient beings, for its activity includes all sentient beings in the triple world and arises constantly. The term "nonrejecting" means that, without refusal, [the Tathāgata] constantly saves and does not abandon [sentient beings]. His compassion always arises without fail to save suffering sentient beings from the three sufferings as appropriate to each. Just as an adult would take pity on a [suffering] child, [so his compassion] arises equally for all sentient beings. It does not fall away even for a single moment in its maturing of sentient beings because the realm of sentient beings is limitless. In fact it never passes away. The Tathāgata is always associated with great compassion, and one cannot say that this compassion arises or appears only at certain times. As a scripture teaches, "Good sons, you must not say that the great compassion of the Buddha Bhagavats arises or appears for all sentient beings only at certain times. The reason why it constantly and always appears is that if that great compassion of all Buddha Bhagavats was not grounded [on wisdom], then they could not have realized supreme awakening. But the Tathāgatas have already realized that great wisdom and constantly entertain the thought that they must establish all the good roots of sentient beings, that they must elucidate the Dharma for those who do not yet understand it. In this manner the Tathāgatas always give rise to great compassion for sentient beings." Again another scripture teaches: "Night and day at [all] the six times, the Tathāgata beholds the world."[46]

[But, it is objected,] how then can it be said that his compassion arises always, [if it arises only at the six times]?

[We answer that] the phrase "the six times" means a constant continuity without interruption [and not just at those particular moments]. Thus there is no contradiction here.

Great mercy and compassion have benevolence, nonviolence, and nondelusion as their essence. In their conferral of happiness and deliverance from suffering, the mode of functioning [of mercy and compassion] does differ, but both include the three kinds of [compassion focused on] sentient beings and so forth. Mercy is benevolent, while compassion is nonviolent. Mercy directs its attention to the absence of happiness and desires to confer that happiness. Compassion directs its attention to the presence of suffering and desires to alleviate that suffering. Since this nonrejecting great compassion arises without discriminating [sentient beings one from the other], it is termed equal. Either this is itself the reality nature or it takes as its content that "reality nature of equality." As 315a explained above, equality wisdom "is fully perfected" because this compassion is cultivated unto full perfection.

The Sixth Mark: Transformation Bodies

The Scripture says: "It manifests itself according to the dispositions of all sentient beings because the reality nature of equality is fully perfected."

The Commentary explains: According to the earnest desires of sentient beings, they see different transformation bodies of the Tathāgata, for that is the manner in which the Tathāgata manifests his transformation bodies. Although the Tathāgata abides in a state of no fabrication, yet his pure consciousness associated with mirror wisdom manifests gem-like wondrous transformation bodies in virtue of the enabling power of equality wisdom.

Sentient beings say that they see these bodies exterior to their minds because he causes their good roots to mature so that images of these bodies appear in their minds. As a scripture teaches, "There are such manifestations because of the compassionate good roots of all Tathāgatas, for they cause the minds of gods, humans, and so forth to be transformed in various ways and to see the bodies of those Tathāgatas as if they were colored golden."[47] Again another scripture teaches: "If the sentient beings to be converted, as appropriate to each, see the colors of the *vaiḍūrya* or *maṇi*-gem [on the Tathāgata's body], this is because he is able to manifest these various gem colors and thus cause their own minds to be so transformed." He manifests the universal equality of the appearances of all Tathāgatas. The Scripture uses the phrase "the reality nature of equality" because in this way it identifies universal equality with that reality nature. This means that in accord with the earnest desires of sentient beings to be converted in common [by many Buddhas], all Tathāgatas make visible the appearances of transformation bodies, for each manifests the same appearance at the same place and at the same time, thus causing the mind of sentient beings to be transformed and thus bringing benefit and happiness to them. It is just like the descriptive marks of the container consciousness which are common to all sentient beings. When they mature, then each sentient being individually perceives the descriptive marks of the world [as common to all], and yet there is no contradiction here [between that common nature of those descriptive marks and the individual perceptions of beings], for these descriptive marks occur at the same place and time [for all individuals]. It is similar to the descriptive marks of the transformation bodies. Thus, as explained above, equality wisdom "is fully perfected" because it is cultivated unto perfection.

The Seventh Mark: The Tathāgata's Words

The Scripture says: "Its words are to be respectfully received by all sentient beings because the reality nature of equality is fully perfected."

The Commentary explains: When sentient beings hear words that are able to mature their good roots, they will be delighted and realize the happiness of pure faith. The Tathāgata manifests such words, for although he has no fabrication, yet, in virtue of the power of his compassionate vow, he does manifest such words. And those sentient beings to be converted are variously transformed in this fashion because of their own eminent powers of understanding.

This means that they hear the Buddha's voice coming from outside their own minds because all the words uttered by the Tathāgata are in accord with the functioning [of their minds].

The Scripture says that [those words] "are to be respectfully received" because all gods, humans, and so forth should not oppose them. It is taught furthermore that the Buddha's words are not in vain because if these words were not addressed to the mental functioning [of sentient beings], they would not be manifested. 315b

Although there are sentient beings who do not follow the Buddha's words, yet, because [those words] do transform and bring benefit, in the future they will certainly come to believe in and accept them. The Scripture says that "his words are to be respectfully received by all sentient beings" because his universal intention is embodied in those words. Those words are all equal because, by the above explanation, such enunciated words are manifested by all Buddhas in common. It is precisely this equality that is called the reality nature. Equality wisdom "is fully perfected" because, as explained above, this manifestation is cultivated unto perfection.

The Eighth Mark:
The One Taste of Tranquility

The Scripture says: "Tranquility in the world is all of one taste because the reality nature of equality is fully perfected."

The Commentary explains: The term "world" here refers to the five contaminated aggregates. The term "tranquility" is used because from moment to moment [equality wisdom] controls [these aggregates] through the two destructions whereby they are rendered quiescent and brought to cessation. The cause of tranquility is the holy path which is grounded on the other-dependent nature (*paratantra*) of cessation. Tranquility in the world is identical in meaning to suchness and, since this is full perfection, the Scripture says that it is "of one taste."

Furthermore, the term "world" means that since the pattern of clinging to what is entirely imagined is absent from the original nature, it is called "tranquility." Because suchness is manifested in this tranquility, it is said to be "of one taste." And this is the "reality nature of equality." As explained above, equality wisdom is "fully perfected" because this one taste is cultivated unto perfection.

The Ninth Characteristic:
Suffering and Happiness as One Taste

The Scripture says: "The suffering and happiness in all worldly states is of one taste because the reality nature of equality is fully perfected."

The Commentary explains: All worldly states are of eight kinds: gain, loss, defamation, eulogy, flattery, ridicule, sorrow, and pleasure. Gain is the thought of acquiring things. Loss is the thought of losing things. Defamation is insulting somebody behind his back. Eulogy is praising somebody behind his back. Flattery is praising somebody to his face. Ridicule is insulting somebody to his face.

Suffering is that which oppresses body or mind. Pleasure is that which delights body or mind. In general these eight are of two kinds: the four disagreeable ones, which are suffering, and the four agreeable ones, which are pleasure inasmuch as they produce delight. These eight are also explained as constituting the antagonism between suffering and happiness. The arhat dwells constantly in one taste, for when he attains gain, he is not delighted; when he encounters loss, he is not downcast; when he finds happiness, he is not covetous; when he is suffering, he is not cantankerous. As a scripture teaches, "The world of the arhat is of the one taste of equality, just as if it were empty space." The fool imagines that there are distinctions in the world, but the eight worldly states are everywhere the same for the arhat because he is far removed from such imaginings. And this is the "reality nature of equality." As explained above, equality wisdom is fully "perfected" 315c because this one taste is cultivated unto perfection.

The Tenth Mark:
The Nurture of Good Qualities

The Scripture says: "It cultivates the final stage of immeasurable good qualities because the reality nature of equality is fully perfected."

The Commentary explains: "Good qualities" here refers to the meritorious states of the virtues favorable to wisdom. The Scripture uses the term "cultivates" because equality wisdom permeates, nourishes, and matures deliverance. Although equality wisdom is nondiscriminative, like the *maṇi*-gem it causes the good qualities of different individuals to increase and mature unto deliverance through the enabling power of Buddhas and bodhisattvas. The phrase "the final stage" means that it causes deliverance, for it is able to attain final cessation in the three vehicles. One cannot say, however, that it causes worldly pleasure.

Such august wisdom is termed the "reality nature of equality" because it is far removed from the pattern of clinging to the imagined. Or perhaps this Scripture uses the phrase "reality nature of equality" because all the bodhisattvas cultivate the preeminent qualities of the virtues favorable to wisdom and come to that final stage. As explained above, equality wisdom "is fully perfected because these good qualities are cultivated unto perfection."

Chapter XI

Discernment Wisdom

The Scripture says: "Next, wondrously born ones, is discernment wisdom."

The Commentary explains: Know that we differentiate discernment wisdom in virtue of its causality, for [it exercises that causality] in ten manners as the cause of supporting, of engendering, of delighting, of examining, of experiencing, of differentiating destinies, of examining world-realms, of pouring down the rain of Dharma, of suppressing inimical forces, and of severing all doubt.

The First Cause: Supporting Recollective Formulae and Concentrations

The Scripture says: "Just as the realm of the physical world supports the realm of sentient beings, just so the Tathāgata's discernment wisdom supports the approaches of all recollective formulae (*dhāraṇīs*) and concentrations, and without obstacle expounds the wondrous Dharma of the Buddha."

The Commentary explains: This passage explains discernment wisdom as the cause for supporting. The phrase "just as the physical world supports the realm of sentient beings" means that the physical world, which consists of the wind-wheel at the base, and which is an evolution from the individual minds of sentient beings, is able to support the realm of sentient beings, the world of sensation, which is also an evolution from the individual minds of sentient beings. In like fashion, the Tathāgata's discernment wisdom is able to support all the approaches of recollective formulae and, more broadly, of all the wondrous doctrines of the Buddha, for it is associated with them and is able to elicit them. "Recollective formulae" refer to those superior recollective wisdoms which are able to support immeasurable Buddha qualities and hold them without failure. In one teaching it can support all teachings. In one expression it can support all expressions. In one meaning it can support all meanings.

316a

~ Because it supports and stores up immeasurable good qualities it is called an inexhaustible treasury. There are four kinds of recollective formulae: the support for doctrine, the support for its meaning, the support for mystic prayer, and the support for attaining bodhisattva patience. These are described in the *Treatise on the Stages of Yogic Meditation.*[48]

[It may be asked,] how is it possible that in but one teaching it can support all teachings?

[We answer that] this means that the inconceivable power of the superior recollective wisdom of Buddhas and bodhisattvas manifests the simple meaning of all doctrinal expression in the image-aspect of their own minds. It is also able to manifest the approaches to inconceivable, inexhaustible good qualities, for their insight-aspect and self-awareness aspect both have such an unlimited, preeminent potential, and both support everything and cause things not to be forgotten. Such is the inconceivable power called recollective formulae.

"Concentration" refers to those superior contemplations which include all the various concentrations, such as the concentration of the heroic journey, and which are able to bring to victory all transcendent and worldly concentrations. Since the other [concentrations] are incapable of leading one to victory, the above concentration is called that of the heroic journey. Or perhaps because such is the action of that heroic land of Buddhas and bodhisattvas, [all its concentrations] are called heroic journeys, for only Buddhas and bodhisattvas at the stage of the Dharma cloud attain these concentrations. All other concentrations are to be interpreted in accord with the explanation of this Scripture, that is, both recollective formulae and concentrations are to be explained as approaches because, just like the three approaches of emptiness, wishlessness, and imagelessness, they are able to engender all kinds of good qualities.

The phrase "without obstacle it expounds" refers to the four absences of obstacles in regard to the Dharma, its meaning, its explanation, and its interpretation. Due to these four, [this wisdom] is able to expound, as stated in this Scripture. All the words of the wondrous Dharma of all Buddhas, all the unlimited Buddha qualities of the Tathāgata's ten powers and fearlessnesses, must be similarly explained.

Discernment wisdom is able to support all these qualities because it converts the perceiving consciousness and attains a dynamic energy, for the purified perceiving consciousness associated with this wisdom is associated with and able to engender all good qualities and is thus said in the Scripture to be able to "support" them.

The Second Cause: Engendering

The Scripture says: "Again just as the world is the direct cause for consciousnesses that spontaneously engenders all kinds of immeasurable images, just so the Tathāgata's discernment wisdom is the direct cause for consciousness that simultaneously engenders immeasurable images of all knowables of wondrous wisdoms without obstacle."

The Commentary explains: This passage explains discernment wisdom as the cause for engendering. Discernment wisdom is able simultaneously to know all knowables because it is the cause whereby consciousness engenders the images of all knowables. The term "world" here means the entire receptacle world. Just as the receptacle world is able to be generative cause for the consciousness of sentient beings with all the various images in unlimited space, just so the Tathāgata's discernment wisdom is able unobstructedly to understand at one time and in one place all knowable realms, which are like empty space, because it is the generative cause for consciousness with its images of all the unlimited worldly and transcendent object realms.

This means that the discernment wisdom of all Tathāgatas is able to understand all objects and has a multitude of images that 316b appear as those knowable objects, just as a multicolored painting has a multitude of images. In its insight-aspect the nature of this wisdom is to be the generative cause for consciousness with these images; and it is said to be their generative cause precisely because it can manifest them. It is not, however, their direct cause, for [those images] arise [directly] from the seeds [in the converted container consciousness].

Here the term "cause" refers to a conditional cause, because insight engenders images, or because the essence [of consciousness] engenders activity. Although that essence is undifferentiated in itself, inasmuch as [the aspects of consciousness] are differentiated, [insight] can be regarded as a cause. This is similar to the engendering of that insight-aspect from the image-aspect [in transmigratory consciousness, only in wisdom the direction is reversed since a Tathāgata does not wait upon images of sensation in order to gain insight].[49]

The Third Cause: Delighting

The Scripture says: "Just as in the world there are various things to play with and the adornments of parks, groves, pools, and so forth can be deeply enjoyed, just so in the Tathāgata's discernment wisdom there are various things to play with and the adornments of the perfections, the virtues favorable to awakening, the ten powers, the fearlessnesses, and the exclusive Buddha qualities can be deeply enjoyed."

The Commentary explains: This passage explains discernment wisdom as the cause for delight. Just as in the physical world there are many things to play with and the beautifully adorned, brilliant splendor of parks, groves, pools, and so forth bring joy and delight to sentient beings, just so the Tathāgata's discernment wisdom in many ways is able to play upon the perfections, the virtues favorable to awakening, and so forth, and their beautifully adorned, brilliant splendor brings joy and delight to all bodhisattvas.

The "perfections" (pāramitās) refer to the six perfections. When expanded through analysis they become ten, for the last four are stages of skillful method. Alternately, when analyzed, they number eighty-four thousand, for as a scripture teaches, "If one analyzes their distinctions, their number is immeasurable." "The virtues favorable to awakening" number thirty-seven, but by extension they also are immeasurable. The "ten powers" are the wisdom powers of knowing the possible and so forth, which are all comprised in the wisdom faculties of the Tathāgata as the faculties of his knowledge. "The fearlessnesses" refers to the absences of the four dreads which are comprised in his five supernatural faculties and are the faculties of his knowledge, that is, faith, zeal, recollection, concentration, and wisdom. There are eighteen "exclusive Buddha qualities." As a scripture teaches, "The many aspects of these qualities are comprised in this wisdom and, being associated with them, it can bring them to completion." Thus this wisdom has all adornments.

The Fourth Cause: Examining

The Scripture says: "Just as the world is completely arrayed with the wondrous adornments of the continents, the islands, the sun and the moon, the Heaven of the Four Celestial Emperors, the Thirty-threefold Heaven, the Suyāma Heaven, the Tuṣita Heaven, the Nirmāṇarati Heaven, the Paranirmitavaśavartin Heaven, the Brahmakāya Heaven, and so forth, just so the Tathāgata's discernment wisdom examines the complete array of the wondrous adornments of the causes and results of both worldly and transcendent degeneration and prospering, as well as the full realization of word-hearers, individually enlightened ones, and bodhisattvas without exception."

The Commentary explains: This passage explains discernment wisdom as the cause of examining. It is just as in the physical world, the immeasurable continents are wondrously adorned and arrayed without being confused with one another. The term "continents" refers to the four great continents of Jambudvīpa, [Pūrva- 316c videha, Aparagodānīya, and Uttarakuru]. The term "islands" refers to the eight small islands of Cāmara, [which in pairs surround those four continents]. The mention of "the sun and the moon" includes all the heavenly constellations. "The Heaven of the Four Celestial Emperors" refers to those gods who dwell on each of the four sides of the fourth level of Mount Sumeru. "The Thirty-three-fold Heaven" means that because each of these four sides of that mountain peak has eight emperor gods, with [the addition of] Indra at their center, we arrive at this number [of thirty-three]. "The Suyāma Heaven" means that because these gods, having come of age (yāma), experience pleasure, it is called the coming of age (yāma). "The Tuṣita Heaven" is where those bodhisattvas who will become embodied [as Buddhas] in the future are transformed through the Dharma. Because they cultivate the fullness of joy (tuṣṭi), it is called Tuṣita. "The Nirmāṇarati Heaven" is where gods take pleasure in all the pleasures that they themselves bring about, for they are narcissistic. "The Paranirmitavaśavartin Heaven" is where they take pleasure in pleasures that they cause others to bring about and, when these pleasures are present, they control them. "The Brahmakāya Heaven" is called brahma because it is apart from desire and tranquil. The word kāya here means [not Brahmā's body, but] his multitude. The phrase "and so forth" refers to all the heavens above these mentioned here.

[Just as these heavens are discerned and examined], so the Tathāgata's discernment wisdom examines the causes and results of all worldly and transcendent degeneration and prospering, and all the full arrangement of the wondrous adornments of the three vehicles, without confusing one with another. "Worldly degeneration" refers to the causes and results of evil destinies. "Worldly prospering" refers to the causes and results of good destinies. Inasmuch as they are worldly devolution or evolution, they are respectively called degeneration and prospering. Degeneration also refers to loss and destruction, while prospering refers to increase and growth. The causes and results of the two vehicles are termed "transcendent degeneration." The causes and results of the Great Vehicle are termed "transcendent prospering." Degeneration means falling back, while prospering means forging ahead. The term "full realizations" refers to the result state [of enlightenment] as it occurs upon the manifestation of the causal issue of the three vehicles. Only at this full realization is one said to have attained the result of awakening.

Because discernment wisdom examines the differences in these states and their marks, this wisdom does resemble them and yet, with no confusion in its mode of functioning it clearly manifests [them]. Therefore this Scripture uses the phrase "the complete arrayment of wondrous adornments."

The Fifth Cause: Experiencing

The Scripture says: "Just as the world is extensively experienced by sentient beings, just so the Tathāgata's discernment wisdom manifests itself to all Buddha assemblies and pours down the rain of the Dharma to lead sentient beings to experience the joy of that great Dharma."

The Commentary explains: This passage explains discernment 317a wisdom as the cause for experiencing. Due to the enabling power of the karmic actions of sentient beings, the seeds common to their [individual] container consciousnesses evolve and engender the various prerequisites that make them able extensively to experience the physical world. In like fashion, the purified consciousness of the Tathāgata's discernment wisdom, assisted by equality wisdom as its enabling cause and evolving in synergy with mirror wisdom, manifests enjoyment bodies to various assemblies, warms them with its flaming ardor, and pours down the rain of the great Dharma in order to lead all world-transcendent bodhisattvas to experience joy in that great Dharma. Furthermore, with the assistance of the Tathāgata's duty-fulfillment wisdom, this purified consciousness also manifests transformation bodies to various assemblies, warms them with its flaming ardor, and pours down the rain of the great Dharma in order to lead those sentient beings who are to be converted to experience the joy in that Dharma here on this earth.

The Sixth Cause: Examining Destinies

The Scripture says: "Just as in the world the five destinies of the hells, hungry ghosts (*pretas*), animals, humans, and gods are all possible, just so in the Tathāgata's discernment wisdom the examining of the unlimited causes and results associated with these five destinies comes to be fully manifested."

The Commentary explains: This passage explains discernment wisdom as the cause of the examination of the destinies. Due to the enabling power of the karmic actions of sentient beings, the patterns of their own container consciousnesses evolve and engender the possibilities of differences in the causes and results of the five destinies. In a like fashion, the Tathāgata's discernment wisdom, because it has as its content the causes and results of these five destinies, distinguishes and reveals the two characteristics that resemble the causes and results of these five destinies. Yet it does not speak discriminately because it itself does not engender any of those undetermined states of the *devas*, the gods, the hungry ghosts, or the animals.

"The causes of the five destinies" means that those in the intermediate state between death and rebirth have these five destinies as the means [of being reborn]. Destiny means that to which one goes. Because those in the intermediate state are able to go, they are not yet included within the destinies. It is in virtue of the four kinds of birth established by the differences in the ways of being born that those in the intermediate state become included among those who are born.

An alternate opinion holds that those in the intermediate state are not included within the destinies because they have the means [for rebirth]. Thus the causes referred to in this Scripture are their karmic actions of passion and so forth, and their results are the five destinies.

The Seventh Cause: Examining Realms

The Scripture says: "Just as in the world all the realms of desire (*kāmadhātu*), form (*rūpadhātu*), and no form (*arūpadhātu*) are all possible, just so in the Tathāgata's discernment wisdom the differences associated with the unlimited causes and results of these three realms come to be manifested."

The Commentary explains: This passage explains discernment wisdom as the cause of examining realms. Due to the enabling power of their actions in the world, the common and individual patterns of the container consciousnesses of sentient beings evolve and engender the possibilities of differences in the causes and results of the three realms.

Included within the world are both the sentient realm and the nonsentient realm, that is, the realm of sentient beings and the physical world. If this were not so, then [the world] would not include those in the intermediate state [who are not sentient], nor those in the formless realm who have only a form engendered from concentration and no form produced by karmic action or physical location. These three realms are established within the world with their respective [meanings]. This means that in the physical world there are only the realms of desire and of form, of the sentient and the nonsentient. But in the realm of sentient beings there are all three realms, [including the formless realm]. These three only exist in the realm of sentient beings, for the physical world only supports the realms of the sentient and the nonsentient, while the world of sentient beings can support the [entire three] realms of sentient beings.

317b

In a like fashion, the Tathāgata's discernment wisdom has as its content the causes and results of all three realms, and in it are manifested the differences in their patterns. It is not that this wisdom engenders these causes and results, but, as explained above, they are examined by it. This means that, in virtue of the fact that discernment wisdom is universally able to examine all objects, the images of all realms, destinies, and births, the causes and results of the consciousnesses and conscious states supported on the maturation of all karmic actions and influenced by the actions of passion do indeed appear [in this wisdom consciousness].

This means that discernment wisdom, which arises from the

enabling power of the mirror wisdom of all Tathāgatas, although it does not cling to subject or object and is far removed from all the obstacles of passion and to knowledge, yet, in virtue of its examination of the elements of all causes and results, it is able to enunciate them and reflect their images, just as a pure mirror reflects a multitude of images. However, it does not issue in the nondiscrimination of that mirror wisdom. Although mirror wisdom is unconfused about all objects and is able to manifest all images without exerting any effort, yet it is nondiscriminative. But this wisdom is able to discriminately manifest all the images of objects. If it also were nondiscriminative, then it would be unable to examine the elements of the causes and results or to enunciate the Dharma without doubt for the various assemblies.

This passage definitely establishes that uncontaminated mind and mental states do have the image-aspect, [a question treated above as Theme Ten, in Chapter Two, Part Two,] for the unlimited causes and results of the five destinies and the three realms do come to be manifested in this wisdom of the Tathāgata.

There is an opinion that because the Tathāgata's wisdom is bright and pure, although the images of all objects do appear in it, yet those images are not evolutions of that wisdom, because they are not pure.

[We answer that] this opinion is invalid because all images of things are evolutions of the mind and mental states of sentient beings, [and thus there is no dichotomy between pure consciousness and impure images].

But, [it is further objected], if these images are evolutions of the mind and mental states of sentient beings, how can they be manifested in Buddha wisdom at all? It is impossible for one kind of cause to engender another kind of consciousness, for such contradicts sound reasoning. But then these images are the same as images in other minds [and cannot be manifested in the mind of wisdom].

[We answer that] these images of objects are manifested by the Tathāgata's uncontaminated mind, just as the image of defecation might appear in a bright mirror. Although it might appear to be impure, yet it is not so. That mind and mental states have as their content the reality nature, and even if they have other content they still do not act like pincers [which grasp things] nor like lamps [which project their light on things], for they have no movement at all. Rather, just as the nature of a bright mirror is originally pure, wisdom [is originally pure and yet] manifests images that appear like [defiled] objects, and is thus able to consider them. If the images of these things did not appear in this consciousness, then, although they had the power to engender mind and mental states, they could not be called the content [of consciousness], just as the five sense organs and so forth [are not called the content of consciousness, although they also have the power, in the presence of the images of objects, to engender consciousness].

As said elsewhere, "Is nondiscriminative wisdom limited in any way? Since its content is suchness and it is not apart from the essence of wisdom, it cannot be limited in any way." But the conventional wisdom that is subsequently attained, although not apart from suchness, in virtue of the fact that it is discriminative does not realize the essence of suchness, for it has as its content an image of suchness brought about through its own evolutions. One cannot then object that the uncontaminated images of objects in the uncontaminated mind are similar to the objects in the minds of common worldlings, or that although they appear to be uncontaminated, in fact they are contaminated. 317c

The basic principle of conscious construction–only is established to mean that, although the images evolved by conscious construction seem to imply a [real, external] existence, in reality there is no [corresponding] essence. If this were not so, then material form and so forth would exist just the same as mind and mental states. And this would invalidate the principle of conscious construction–only. This principle means that their real existence is not apart from consciousness. If consciousness and conscious states were not distinct from material form and so forth, but instead were yoked to them, then that would be [a theory of] objects only. That would be a grave mistake indeed!

The Eighth Cause: The Rain of Dharma

The Scripture says: "Just as in the world Mount Sumeru and the other great jeweled, lofty peaks can appear, just so in the Tathāgata's discernment wisdom the broad, deep Dharma which draws upon the power of all Buddhas and bodhisattvas can appear."

The Commentary explains: This passage explains discernment wisdom as the cause of pouring down the rain of Dharma. In this world there arise all the jeweled mountains because of the enabling power of the karmic actions of sentient beings. In like fashion, the Tathāgata's discernment wisdom gives rise to all deep doctrines because of the enabling power of the action of that true Dharma which influences all sentient beings, for it draws upon the might of all Buddhas and bodhisattvas. The Scripture says that "it draws upon the power of all Buddhas and bodhisattvas" because this doctrine reveals the power of the mastery of all Buddhas and bodhisattvas and is able to draw upon their august powers.

This means that the Tathāgata's discernment wisdom is able to engender the images of the Dharma in the consciousnesses associated with mirror wisdom, or that it itself is able to manifest these images of the Dharma. Since its objective is the maturation of good roots, [these images] are manifested in the minds of the sentient beings to be converted.

The Ninth Cause: Suppressing Inimical Forces

The Scripture says: "Just as in the world the broad, deep, unperturbed sea can appear, just so in the Tathāgata's discernment wisdom the doctrine of the deep Dharma realm, which is unperturbed by inimical forces, non-Buddhists, or false teachers, can appear."

The Commentary explains: This passage explains discernment wisdom as the cause for suppressing inimical forces. In the world there arises the unperturbed great sea because of the enabling power of the karmic actions of sentient beings. In a like fashion the Tathāgata's discernment wisdom gives rise to the doctrine of the Dharma realm, which doctrine is unperturbed, due to the enabling power of the action of the true Dharma in influencing sentient beings. "The Dharma realm" is the imageless truth of emptiness. The Scripture refers to this Dharma realm as "the doctrine of the Dharma realm." All non-Buddhists depend on their own opinions, but the truth of the emptiness of the Dharma realm controls such opinions and is apart from all such opinions. Therefore the doctrine of emptiness cannot be fathomed by them and they cannot 318a disturb such a powerful doctrine, as has been explained in the preceding section, where it was compared to a jeweled mountain in virtue of being high and vast. It is here compared to the deep sea inasmuch as the Dharma realm is deep. Discernment wisdom can engender the enunciation of all doctrines because it can illumine the causes of all things. Thus the phrase "in the Tathāgata's discernment wisdom" is in the locative case [in the original Sanskrit, but expresses a causal relationship]. As a scripture teaches, "The Buddha Bhagavat is called the sun of great wisdom because he is universally able to illumine and understand everything."

The Tenth Cause: Severing Doubt

The Scripture says: "Just as the world is surrounded by large and small mountain ranges, so the Tathāgata's discernment wisdom is surrounded by all the individual and common marks, in regard to which it is unconfused."

The Commentary explains: This passage explains discernment wisdom as the cause of severing doubt. This world of Mount Sumeru, its seven surrounding mountain ranges, the eight great seas, and the four continents are encircled and surrounded by an outer small range of mountains whose total number reaches a thousand. Again all this is encircled and surrounded by the next mountain range. Such a total is termed a small chiliocosm, [that is, one thousand such worlds all surrounded by their respective mountain ranges,] because its number reaches a thousand. Furthermore, all these [small chiliocosms] are again encircled and surrounded by the next mountain range, and such is termed a medium chiliocosm, [that is, a thousand small chiliocosms all together], for their number reaches yet another thousand. All these are yet once more encircled and surrounded by a great mountain range, which is itself supported below on the great wind-wheel. Such is termed a great chiliocosm, [that is, one thousand of the medium chiliocosms, which contain one thousand of the small chiliocosms, which contain one thousand worlds]. This is what the Scripture refers to in the phrase "it is surrounded by large and small mountain ranges."

In a like fashion, the Tathāgata's discernment wisdom universally knows all individual and common marks and is able to sever all worldly doubts. The cause of such doubts is confusion in regard to such individual or common marks, but, lacking any such confusion, this wisdom understands all these marks. It is able to sever the doubts of others because it itself has no doubt at all. Being apart from the [two] obstacles of passion and to knowledge, mirror wisdom is unconfused in regard to all individual and common marks, and is able to engender this wisdom. Because it supports and preserves this wisdom, this discernment wisdom is said to be "surrounded."

However, although mirror wisdom is able to know all individual and common marks, yet, being nondiscriminative, it is unable to enunciate the Dharma for others or to sever their doubts. But this discernment wisdom is both able to know all and can enunciate the Dharma and sever all the doubts of others because it is discriminative. Furthermore, it is the very essence of this wisdom to know the individual and common marks of all things, and it is surrounded by these two kinds of conditioned marks. "The individual marks" are like the mountains of the small range, while "the common marks" are like the mountains of the large range. Mirror wisdom is able to support [this discernment wisdom], just as from below the wind-wheel supports [the great chiliocosm].

[It is objected that] since [discernment wisdom] is supported by the direct insight of the Tathāgata's pure wisdom, [which as direct perception is directed only to individual marks,] how is it able to know the common marks of all things? If these common marks are known by direct insight [and not by inference], then how can the two means of cognition be held to be based on these two kinds of marks, [as is done by Dignāga in his *Collection of Remarks on the Means of Valid Cognition*]?

[There are three opinions.] The first holds that these two sources of true knowledge are established on these two marks only in the fragmented mind, but that that does not apply to the state of concentration. Even if the concentrated mind has all marks as its content [including the common marks], all are supported by direct insight [and there is no inference in the Tathāgata's wisdom].

The second opinion holds that the concentrated mind has as its content only the individual marks. But it also understands the common marks because it draws forth its skillful methods from those common marks. The truths manifested are then spoken by skillful method and are termed the knowledge of common marks. Otherwise, they would be termed knowledge of individual marks. It is from this reasoning that we say suchness is the common mark of all things, which are empty and selfless, and that suchness, as the manifestation of the two emptinesses [of self and things], is not their common mark.

318b

The correct, third opinion differs only slightly from [the above second opinion of] that treatise on Buddhist logic (Dignāga's *Collection of Remarks on the Means of Valid Cognition*), which accepts the existence of individual and common marks. That text says that in the truth of ultimate meaning, all things are termed individual marks because individual and common marks are each contained in their own nature and are not intermingled. If the discriminative mind establishes a general category and is able to express its meaning, it then penetrates through all things [in that category], just as one might string flowers together. Such [a category] is called a common mark [because it expresses the meaning common to many individuals]. Thus it is that the discrimination of the fragmented mind conventionally establishes the objects of inferential thinking. But all concentrated minds are far apart from such discrimination and [their understanding] is called direct perception. Although these minds do have as their content the suffering and impermanence of all things, yet, because each one of these things exists singly, they are said to be the individual marks [which are the contents of the direct perception of wisdom]. Therefore, suchness, although it is expressed as a common mark, is in fact the individual nature of all things, is their individual, existing mark. It is not a common mark [nor a general category] because one cannot say that it is either identical with nor different from all things, that is, with their common marks. This is why it is called both a common mark and an individual mark. Thus, when that treatise says that the truth of ultimate meaning of all things is termed their individual mark, although it expresses itself differently from this *Scripture on the Buddha Land,* yet there is no contradiction.

Chapter XII

Duty-Fulfillment Wisdom

The Scripture says: "Next, wondrously born ones, is duty-fulfillment wisdom."

The Commentary explains: Understand that duty-fulfillment wisdom brings about the transformation bodies of the Tathāgata. Furthermore, there are three kinds: the transformations of bodies, the transformations of speech, and the transformations of thought.[50] The first transformation is again of three kinds: the transformations manifested through supernatural powers, the transformations manifested through the experience of being born, and the transformations manifested as the results of actions. The transformations of speech also are of three kinds [of transformations]: the transformations of encouraging speech, the transformations of skillful speech, and the transformations of explanatory speech. The transformations of thought are of four kinds: the transformations of certain thinking, the transformations of constructive thinking, the transformations of emergent thinking, and the transformations of thinking about experience.

Duty-fulfillment wisdom is able to engender transforming activities in regard to the three actions [of body, speech, and thought], for the transformations of these three constitute the transformation body. You should understand that the essence of this [transformation body] is manifested in and through these three transformations and their activity. It is not that these three transformations are themselves the essence of wisdom. Rather they are the images that appear through wisdom. The pure consciousness associated with mirror wisdom, developing in synergy with the enabling power of duty-fulfillment wisdom, brings about the manifestation of the transforming activity of these three actions and is thus itself manifested.

Understand that each of the four wisdoms is able to engender all these activities. But, in their principal aspects, we say that equality wisdom engenders the enjoyment bodies; duty-fulfillment wisdom engenders the transformation bodies; discernment wis-318c dom examines all individual and common marks, all recollective formulae and concentration practices, and so forth; and mirror wisdom manifests all images of all things. Just as one by one the senses grasp all things, and yet none lacks a principal activity, so it is here.

The teaching of this Scripture definitely demonstrates that the mind and mental states of the three actions all have their transformations. All the qualities of this gross mind and these mental states, as they appear in the Tathāgata's wisdom, lead those in inferior positions to come to understanding. Otherwise, how could those in the two vehicles and common worldlings ever be enabled to understand?

[It is objected that] if the qualities of this mind and these mental states present to the Tathāgata are differentiated, then how can it be that the Tathāgata has long since realized awakening? How could he be able to manifest the various transformation bodies, which are themselves characterized by covetousness, anger, and so forth?

[We answer by noting that] another scripture does teach that "he transforms immeasurable kinds [of transformation bodies] in such a manner that they are conscious." And it is also taught that "transformation bodies are said to be both conscious and not conscious because they have a consciousness that is other-dependent, but not a consciousness that is self-dependent." This means that his transformation of mind is manifested in dependency on his ultimate mind. The image-aspect of his real mind appears as if it had the activities of thinking. It is just as in a mirror fire does not have a separate subsistence but arises in dependence on a multitude of causes.

Although we say that the mind and the mental states of others have no direct relationship with this transformed mind because they have no real function in its regard, yet in truth this transformed mind and transformed material form do have a real function in their regard because they function like actual material form, and thus we say that they have [such a real function]. Because the manifestations of the gross marks of such a transformation of mind are easy to understand, even apes and monkeys know the Tathāgata's mind. But if it were the real mind of the Buddha [that was manifested], then even the great bodhisattvas would be unable to understand it.

The First Transformation:
Supernatural Powers

The Scripture says: "Just as, because of the efficacious, physical actions of sentient beings, they seek various profitable endeavors, take up farming, enter a king's service, and so forth, just so, because of the actions of the efficacious transformations of the Tathāgata's duty-fulfillment wisdom, he manifests various skillful endeavors to suppress all cleverness and conceit among sentient beings and thus, because of his power in very skillful methods, he leads all sentient beings and causes them to enter the sacred Dharma and mature unto liberation."

The Commentary explains: This passage explains the actions of the transformation of the body, which consists of a transformation manifested through supernatural powers. They are called "efficacious" because they cause the mind to venture forth. Because of their ongoing, efficacious action, zeal is attained by those of good lineage, while diligent practice is attained by others. This is why such action is termed efficacious. In virtue of such an action of [transformed] bodies, sentient beings in the world practice the three correct actions [of body, speech, and thought]. The phrase "and so forth" indicates any kind of such endeavors. Duty-fulfillment wisdom, in synergy with zeal, engenders the action of transforming bodies. Because of this transforming action, when one becomes a bodhisattva he manifests various kinds of skillful endeavors, just as a craftsman might. In this wisdom, the descriptive marks of physical actions are manifested because he desires "to suppress cleverness and conceit." He manifests "very skillful methods" because in the path of awareness of the equality between compassion and wisdom, he first manifests supernatural powers. The Scripture says that "he leads beings and causes them to enter the sacred Dharma" because he first causes beings to elicit faith, just as by manifesting his supernatural powers, he saved Kāśyapa. The Scripture says that "he matures" them because he has the profound ability to make them docile. They are "liberated" because he leads both those of lineage and those of no lineage to be liberated respectively from the triple world and from evil destinies. Because of the transforming power of his Dharma, those of lineage are led to elicit the holy path and to be liberated from the triple world, while those of no lineage are led to cultivate worldly good and constantly to be reborn in good destinies. Being attentive to their good roots in order to preach the true Dharma to them, he leads [those of lineage] to be liberated from the triple world. Assuaging suffering by emitting his brilliant light, he establishes [those of no lineage] in good destinies.

319a

Another interpretation holds that the three actions of causing them to enter the sacred Dharma, to mature, and to be liberated mean that he causes them to give rise to the hearing of the Dharma, to reflecting on that Dharma, and to the cultivation of wisdom.

Another interpretation holds that these three actions mean that he causes them to engender the elements conducive to liberation and the elements conducive to insight, and then to engender the holy path.

Yet another interpretation holds that these three mean that he causes them to enter the path of insight, the path of practice, and the path of no training.

All three interpretations explain the descriptive marks of these three actions in their various functions.

The Second Transformation:
The Experience of Being Born

The Scripture says: "Just as, because sentient beings experience bodily actions they experience the objects of the various material forms and so forth, just so, because the Tathāgata's duty-fulfillment wisdom experiences transformed bodily actions, the Tathāgata goes to all the various places where sentient beings are born, adopts their life form, and dwells in an honored position among them. Because he thus adopts their lifestyle, he supports all kinds of sentient beings. Thus, because of his power in very skillful methods, he leads all sentient beings and causes them to enter the sacred Dharma and mature unto liberation."

The Commentary explains: This passage explains the action of the transformation of the body, which consists in the transformation manifested through the experience of being born. The Scripture uses the term "experience" because, wherever they are born in the world, sentient beings experience the objects of material form through their senses. The term "bodily action" is used because their bodies are constantly active. In all places of birth and at all times, duty-fulfillment wisdom manifests births and experiences objects. This means that it manifests transformation bodies in all places among gods and humans. It manifests a birth of the same kind as those among whom it dwells, whether they be of the *kṣatriya* or brahmin class. [In other births, the Buddha] supports all lower classes and brings benefit and happiness to them. The manifestation of the bodily action of this wisdom, whether in synergy with mirror wisdom or manifested under its own power, are all to be understood in this fashion.

The Third Transformation:
Manifesting the Results of Actions

The Scripture says: "Just as, because sentient beings experience bodily actions, they experience the good and evil results of what they do, just so, because the Tathāgata's duty-fulfillment wisdom experiences transformed bodily actions, the Tathāgata manifests and experiences all the practices that were difficult to cultivate in former times and in former births. Thus, because of his power in very skillful methods, he leads all sentient beings and causes them to enter the sacred Dharma and mature unto liberation."

The Commentary explains: This passage explains the action of the transformation of the body which consists of the transformation manifested as the results of actions. The term "bodily actions" is used because it is the body that acts. Because such [actions] are the results of previous actions, the word "results" implies the presence of a cause. Or perhaps when the body experiences the results of previous actions, because it has a constant activity, the Scripture uses the term "bodily actions." It is in virtue of these bodily actions that we experience the results of the craving and hatred that flow from those previous actions.

319b

Duty-fulfillment wisdom experiences bodily actions inasmuch as it manifests transformation bodies; and, in virtue of this action, it manifests and experiences everything. In the phrase "all the practices that were difficult to cultivate in former times and in former births," former times refer to all the affairs associated with former ages, while former births refer to the different births in those former ages. As the *Vessantarajātaka* and other *Jātaka*s explain, all former times depend upon those former births. The various practices of asceticism formerly cultivated are here termed "the practices that were difficult to cultivate." Or perhaps those practices refer to the practices whereby the transformation body of this present age (Śākyamuni) attained wisdom by first practicing asceticism and then abandoning such practices. This means that he first manifested and cultivated practices of asceticism to convert the sentient beings who imagined that such practices would put a stop to evil and give rise to good, and that this was the method to attain wisdom; but then he demonstrated the method of attaining wisdom by abandoning asceticism to show that it is not just by the practice of the precepts (*śīla*) that one attains purification, for that is attained through the cultivation of concentration and wisdom. As a scripture teaches, "At the time of the Buddha Kāśyapa, the Tathāgata Maitreya uttered this admonishment: 'O *bhikṣu*s, where is great wisdom in receiving the tonsure? Supreme wisdom is indeed difficult to attain!'" Because of this criticism [of asceticism], we now perceive what the result of asceticism is, for these words were meant to put a stop to asceticism and to manifest his transforming activity. If this were not so, then why would Maitreya, who had already shown reverence to immeasurable Tathāgatas and nurtured all his good roots, when he remembered the former births from the beginning, have uttered such a heavy and harsh criticism? You should understand that these words were intended to convert and save, for those who in virtue of listening to these words will attain salvation are led through them to abstain [from asceticism].

The Fourth Transformation: Encouraging Speech

The Scripture says: "Just as, because of the action of encouraging speech, sentient beings draw out their discussions and encourage one another, just so, because of the transformed action of the encouraging speech of the Tathāgata's duty-fulfillment wisdom, the Tathāgata pleasingly declares various kinds of doctrines that accord joy in the skillful wonders of his scriptures and their meaning. When those of little intelligence first hear, they respectfully believe. Thus, because of his power in very skillful methods, he leads all sentient beings and causes them to enter the sacred Dharma and to mature unto liberation."

The Commentary explains: This passage explains the action of the transformation of speech which consists in the transformation of encouraging speech. The term "encouraging" means that this speech, selected to bring about joy, is capable of doing so in virtue of the fact that, upon hearing such words, one develops and elicits great joy. This means that, because of the enabling power of the minds of sentient beings which develop speech, the images of speech appear in each of their individual consciousnesses as the enabling condition, and they then cause the minds of others also to elicit similar verbal images. Upon hearing such words from another, one engenders joy.

The transforming speech of duty-fulfillment wisdom must be understood in like fashion, for it manifests wondrous sounds and

319c

181

causes the minds of others to be converted. This means that upon hearing the Buddha's speech, they engender joy. The phrase "the Dharma that accords joy" means that gods, humans, and all those in the three vehicles joyfully hear in accord with the power of that cause and discern the Dharma. The phrase "the skillful wonders of his scriptures" means that his writings manifest beauty and bring about that joyful hearing. The phrase "the skillful wonders of its meaning" means that those meanings, being truly reasoned and clear, are easy to understand. The phrase "when sentient beings of little intelligence first hear, they respectfully believe" means that the Buddha's utterances are endowed with the sixty qualities [of inconceivable speech as explained in the *Ornament of the Scriptures of the Great Vehicle*].[51] Even those of foolish intelligence engender faith and understanding when they hear it. How much more would those of intelligence do so! This duty-fulfillment wisdom is able to manifest transformed speech and proclaim all skillful, wondrous scriptures and meanings. It is able to engender a joyful mind in sentient beings. It is able to confer good and manifest all things because the Buddha's voice proclaims the deep Dharma that is difficult to fathom. Thus this wisdom is able to confer other things as well, for through all treatises, through all material forms, and even through empty space, it is able to bring forth the enunciation of Dharma through this transformation of speech. Know then that his wisdom is inconceivable.[52]

The Fifth Transformation:
Speech of Skillful Methods

The Scripture says: "Just as, because of the skillful speech of sentient beings they indicate and attend to the task of summoning one another to destroy evil and praise good, just so, because of the transformed action of the speech of skillful method that arises from the Tathāgata's duty-fulfillment wisdom, the Tathāgata establishes the correct rules of training to destroy all madness and praise all sanity. Furthermore, he establishes some in the practice of faith and others in the practice of the Dharma. Thus, because of his power in very skillful methods, he leads all sentient beings and causes them to enter the sacred Dharma and mature unto liberation."

The Commentary explains: This passage explains the action of the transformation of speech which consists in the transformation of the speech of skillful method. It is just like the teachings associated with skillful speech in the world, which manifest all that must be done and all that must be left undone in order to benefit dear friends. It is because its efforts arise in regard to sentient beings who are crazed with passion that it is termed "skillful." In like fashion the Tathāgata from his great compassion establishes the rules of training for sentient beings in order to cause them to suppress all evil and cultivate all worldly good. By establishing differences in the stages of the holy path, he causes them to enter that correct path and transcend the triple world. Duty-fulfillment wisdom is able to engender such transformed speech and carry through to completion its tasks. This means that the stopping of evil and the development of all good is the function of this kind of speech.

The Sixth Transformation: Explanatory Speech

The Scripture says: "Just as, because of the explanatory speech of sentient beings, they develop explanations for meanings not understood and clarify all treatises, just so, because of the transformed explanatory speech of the Tathāgata's duty-fulfillment wisdom he severs the immeasurable doubts of all sentient beings. Thus, because of his power in very skillful methods, he leads all sentient beings and causes them to enter the sacred Dharma and mature 320a unto liberation."

The Commentary explains: This passage explains the action of the transformation of speech which consists in the transformation of explanatory speech. In accord with the differences in the thinking and dispositions of sentient beings, duty-fulfillment wisdom manifests the actions of its transformed speech. It enunciates various meanings and severs all doubt. This means that in uttering one sound, it expresses all meanings and all sentient beings attain benefit as appropriate to each. As a scripture teaches, "In one sound the Buddha explains all meanings and sentient beings attain understanding as appropriate to each, whether they be fearful or joyous, whether they are yet troubled or have severed their doubts."[53] This transformed speech, evolved from the inconceivable power of the Tathāgata's primal vow, in one sound is able to sever all doubt. The creating of transformation bodies is also able to enable sentient beings to see in the same image [meanings that] complete benefit and happiness [for them].

The Seventh Transformation:
The Thought of Certitude

The Scripture says: "Again, just as, because of the truly certain thinking of sentient beings they attain certitude as to what is possible and what is impossible, just so, because of the transformed thinking of certitude of the Tathāgata's duty-fulfillment wisdom he has certain knowledge of the eighty-four thousand different mental activities of sentient beings. Thus, because of his power in very skillful methods, he leads all sentient beings and causes them to enter the sacred Dharma and mature unto liberation."

The Commentary explains: This passage explains the transformation of thought which consists in the transformation of the thinking which attains certitude. Because the thinking associated with duty-fulfillment wisdom is able to engender this transformation, the Scripture says it is an action of "transformed thinking." This wisdom is able to attain certitude as to the differences in the eighty-four thousand mental activities of the sentient beings to be converted.

Alternately it is the images of that transformed thinking appearing in the image-aspect of this wisdom that are able to bring about certitude in regard to the eighty-four thousand mental activities, for these images lead one to understand and attain the benefit of the truth of ultimate meaning.

These eighty-four thousand mental activities are the different states of the seething minds of sentient beings in regard to the eighty-four thousand defiled objects in the wearisome functioning of their minds. These states are able to hinder the eighty-four thousand perfections, the recollective formulae, the concentrations, and so forth. The *Scripture of the Fortunate Eon (Bhadra-kalpika-sūtra)* elucidates their descriptive marks from the cultivation of the first perfection to the last that manifests the Buddha essence, explaining how each of the three hundred and fifty [concentrations and recollective formulae] are endowed with the six perfections.[54] Thus we arrive at two thousand and one hundred [perfections] which regulate the eighty-four hundred mental activities of craving, anger, delusion, and so forth of sentient beings. When we include the four great elements (earth, water, fire, and wind) and the six faults that arise from inadvertence, and thus multiply that above number by ten, we arrive at the number of eighty-four thousand [perfections]. By cultivating these one attains perfection in the eighty-four thousand recollective formulae and concentrations. But all this is simply a summary of what is immeasurable.

The Eighth Transformation: Constructive Thinking

320b

The Scripture says: "Just as, because of the constructive thinking of sentient beings they bring forth all kinds of emergent actions, just so, because of the transformed action of the transformed constructive thinking of the Tathāgata's duty-fulfillment wisdom he examines all the actions which sentient beings might do, what they should do and what they should not do, and he constructs rules to lead them to choose that which they should do and to abandon what they should not do. Thus, because of his power in very skillful methods, he leads all sentient beings and causes them to enter the sacred Dharma and mature unto liberation."

The Commentary explains: This passage explains the transformation of thinking that consists of the transformation of

185

constructive thinking. In examining all the actions of sentient beings, if evil actions are not done there will be benefit, but if they are done then loss ensues. If good actions are done there will be benefit, but if they are not done, loss ensues. He examines thus because he desires to lead them to choose benefit and abandon loss. For their benefit he constructs and supports the antidote, and he constructs the rules of abstinence so they will avoid loss. Because the thinking associated with duty-fulfillment wisdom is able to engender such transformations, it is called "the action of transformed thinking." Although all Tathāgatas in all things lack any purposeful effort, they cause the minds of sentient beings to evolve these transformed images that bring about [good moral behavior]. Therefore this thinking is termed "constructive."

Alternately, these transformed images appearing in the image-aspect of this wisdom enable sentient beings to examine the benefit or loss of all their actions and cause them to understand how to attain the benefit of the truth of ultimate meaning.

The Ninth Transformation:
Emergent Thinking

The Scripture says: "Again, because of the emergent thinking of sentient beings they bring about all their actions, just so, because of the action of the transformed thinking of the Tathāgata's duty-fulfillment wisdom and in virtue of his desire to proclaim the antidote he manifests that corpus of names, phrases, and words that bring about joy. Thus, because of his power in very skillful methods he leads all sentient beings and causes them to enter the sacred Dharma and mature unto liberation."

The Commentary explains: This passage explains the action of the transformation of thinking that consists in the transformation of emergent thinking. The thinking associated with duty-fulfillment wisdom is able to engender the two actions of the body and speech. Inasmuch as it employs such speech, the Scripture terms it "emergent thinking." Or perhaps it is so termed because this thinking emerges from wisdom, for it is that [wisdom] which is able to bring forth such transformations. Or again it may be that those images appearing in the image-aspect of this wisdom take on the appearance of speech. This wisdom transforms thinking because it desires to proclaim the antidote for sentient beings and to enunciate them for all actions. Since this enunciated doctrine consists of that corpus of names, phrases, and words, it manifests such a "corpus of names, phrases, and words." In speaking this corpus in accord with the dispositions of sentient beings, the Tathāgata leads them to desire to engender within themselves the antidote. Thus this transformed thinking appears in the image-aspect of the Tathāgata's duty-fulfillment wisdom, evolves that corpus, and proclaims to sentient beings the antidote for all actions. 320c In this power he causes the individual minds of all sentient beings themselves similarly to be transformed. The profundity of that Dharma enunciated by the Buddha engenders in them the desire to engender within themselves the antidote. Thus it is termed "emergent thinking."

The Tenth Transformation:
Thinking upon Experience

The Scripture says: "Just as, because sentient beings think upon their experiences they bring forth experiences of suffering and happiness, just so, because of the transformed action of thinking upon experience of the Tathāgata's duty-fulfillment wisdom, in virtue of the fact that he declares things in fixed and unfixed terms, in returning the question, and in maintaining silence, he manifests the meanings of the past, present, and future as appropriate at each instant. Thus, because of his power in very skillful methods he leads all sentient beings and causes them to enter the sacred Dharma and mature unto liberation."

The Commentary explains: This passage explains the action of the transformation of thinking which consists of the transformation of thinking upon experience. The term "thinking upon experience" means that thinking upon experience can move the mind to experience suffering or happiness. The term "the action of transformed thinking" means that the thinking associated with duty-fulfillment wisdom can engender the transformation of such thinking. The term "transformed action of thinking" refers to that transformed thinking manifested as the perfection of the image-aspect. It truly understands all questions and answers accordingly because it declares and answers through the four kinds of responses. It reveals the meanings of immeasurable doctrines in the three times and understands them as they really are. Since it already knows the essence of each thing as it really is, its declarations in regard to each thing are indefectible.

The four kinds of responses are the direct answer, the distinguishing answer, the returning of the question, and the silent answer. The direct answer is aimed at questions such as "Is it certain that all beings will be destroyed?" or "Why are the [Three] Jewels of Buddha, Dharma, and Sangha a rich field?" Such questions are answered directly and their meaning is fixed. The distinguishing answer is directed to such questions as "Will all that is destroyed certainly arise again?" or "Is it not true that there is only one jewel of Buddha, Dharma, and Sangha?" Such questions are answered by distinguishing, and their meaning is not fixed. The returning of the question is directed to such questions as "Are the bodhisattvas in the ten stages ranked in degree?" or "Are the [Three] Jewels of Buddha, Dharma, and Sangha eminent or inferior?" Such questions are answered by returning the question: "What is it that you expect from such a question?" The silent answer is directed to questions such as "Is the real essence of the self good or evil?" or "Is the color of the child of a sterile woman black or white?" Questions such as these receive a silent answer because they are the utmost of foolishness and deserve no answer.

You should understand that among these three kinds of transformations [of body, speech, and thought], the actions of the transformations of body and speech are either associated with one's own body or with the bodies of others, or they are unassociated with either. But the actions of the transformations of thinking are always associated with either one's own body or those of others.

Thus there are three kinds of supernatural transformations: the transformations [of material form] through supernatural powers, the transformations [of speech] through admonition and instruction, and the transformations [which adapt that] thought to the minds [of others]. These transformed actions of Buddhas in all their varieties are constantly and consistently inconceivable. Because these activities, their numbers, and their lands are inconceivable, his benefit to sentient beings is ceaseless and its emergence is inconceivable. These three transformed actions of all Tathā- 321a gatas [come about] because they place first their desire to mature sentient beings. Therefore they are called the utmost of skillful method. It is thus that a scripture teaches, "The Buddha Bhagavat is called the joy of great wisdom because he is able to uproot all the ills of passion."[55]

Part Three

The Practice Based on the Dharma

Chapter XIII

The Experience of Wisdom

The First Question:
Who Experiences Wisdom?

The Scripture says: "Then those wondrously born bodhisattvas spoke to the Buddha and said: 'Bhagavat, is it only the Tathāgata in the Pure Dharma Realm who experiences this phenomenal wisdom all of one taste? Or can bodhisattvas also be said to experience it?' The Buddha addressed those wondrously born bodhisattvas and said: 'You can also experience this phenomenal wisdom all of one taste.'"

The Commentary explains: This question is about the experience of that phenomenal wisdom all of one taste. When the Buddha realm was discussed earlier, it was said only that the essence of the Tathāgata's Pure Dharma Realm was all of one taste, that the Buddha's mirror wisdom and the other wisdoms in that realm all experience that one unified taste and are without movement or activity. Those wondrously born bodhisattvas doubt that it is only the Tathāgatas [who experience that one taste of wisdom], and thus they penetratingly raise this question.

Alternately, as explained above, these five factors constitute the realm of great wisdom. The essence of the Pure Dharma Realm is of one taste only. Mirror wisdom is also of one mark only because it depends upon this [Pure Dharma Realm] and takes it as its content, thus giving rise to nondiscriminative [wisdom]. Equality wisdom, which also has that suchness as its content and is apart from the discrimination of subject and object, is also of one taste only. The other two wisdoms are also of one mark only because in order to benefit others they also rely on suchness and have no discrimination of one thing from another. But if only Buddhas experienced this phenomenal wisdom all of one unified taste, then [wisdom] would have no relationship with anyone else. It was because they wanted to settle this question that those [bodhisattvas] asked: "Since [the Scripture states that] it is in the Pure Dharma Realm that this phenomenal wisdom all of one unified taste is realized, does this imply that others lack the experience of this wisdom all of one unified taste?"

The Scripture uses the term "experience" because [the bodhisattvas] are able to experience that which is to be experienced, that is, the content of suchness of one unified taste. It is "unified" because all its common [marks] come together into one. Although that unity may become differentiated so as to be manifested, yet in [the Pure Dharma Realm] it is always undifferentiated. Again it is said that because, being equal in regard to subject and object, it unites both, it is ultimately unified and undifferentiated. The term "taste" means the inner core, the one taste that takes as the content of its experience the suchness of the Dharma realm. The term "phenomenal" indicates phenomenal activity. The term "wisdom" means that wisdom which, being able to experience, correctly holds to mirror wisdom, equality wisdom, and the other two [wisdoms], for in various manners it has suchness as its content.

Alternately, the term "one taste" means the ability to experience the nondiscrimination of wisdom, while "phenomenal" refers to its result, because it arises by having as its content the Pure Dharma Realm.

Again perhaps the Scripture uses the term "one taste" because this ability to experience is indifferent to all sensations and remains equally the same in the face of either suffering or happiness, while the term "phenomenal" refers to its result, this state of indifference, which is associated with mirror wisdom and the other wisdoms.

Because that [phenomenal nature of wisdom] arises from this power [of indifference], we call it the result.

Again perhaps this wisdom is termed "phenomenal wisdom" because, characterized by an absence of purposefulness in indifference to all karmic activity, it emerges everywhere as able to experience that one taste. 321b

Or perhaps the term "experience" is used because wisdom in itself is able to experience its own essence, while it is of "one taste" because it lacks the two discriminations of self and others. It is "phenomenal" because that is the result constantly emerging apart from these two [discriminating] thoughts.

The Scripture explains that "bodhisattvas are also able to experience this wisdom." But, [it is objected,] if bodhisattvas are also able to experience it, then why does the Scripture say that these five factors constitute the realm of great wisdom, [which is the ultimate realm of Tathāgatas]?

[We answer that] the Scripture does say that the Buddha realm is constituted solely of these five factors, but it does not say that they constitute only that Buddha realm, for they are able to constitute also all the realms of the bodhisattvas.

The Second Question:
Which Bodhisattvas Experience Wisdom?

The Scripture says: "Then those wondrously born bodhisattvas addressed the Buddha and said: 'Which bodhisattvas experience this phenomenal wisdom all of one unified taste?' The Buddha addressed those wondrously born ones and said: 'Those bodhisattvas who have realized patience of the state of no arising and abide in the doctrine of no arising, when they attain the understanding of patience, they will gain mastery over the two conceptions. Inasmuch as they have banished these two conceptions of self and others, they will attain the mind of equality. From this point on the conceptions that differentiate between self and others will never again occur for those bodhisattvas and they will experience the phenomenal wisdom all of one unified taste.'"

The Commentary explains: The wondrously born bodhisattvas ask the question: "Which bodhisattvas experience this phenomenal wisdom all of one unified taste?" in order to show the difference between those bodhisattvas who have attained the patience of the state of no arising in the Great Vehicle and those bodhisattvas who in the stage of intensified effort have not yet experienced the phenomenal wisdom all of one unified taste.

The phrase "those bodhisattvas who have attained the patience of the state of no arising" refers to those bodhisattvas from the first stage of joy who have realized the suchness manifested through the two emptinesses [of self and things]. They have understood that the imagined pattern of all things neither arises nor is destroyed. They have understood the purity of the original nature and the cessation that is its essence. Thus they experience this phenomenal wisdom all of one unified taste.

This state differs from that in the path of insight of the two vehicles, which does realize the suchness manifested through the emptiness of arising [of the self], but does not realize the suchness manifested through the emptiness of things and is not yet able to see the equality of all things nor to experience the phenomenal wisdom all of one unified taste. Bodhisattvas who have not yet entered the ten stages are also unable to realize this wisdom because they have not yet gained insight into suchness, and that equality wisdom of one unified taste has not yet appeared to them.

According to one opinion there are three kinds of bodhisattvas in the ten stages. The first are those who have begun to elicit the aspiration for wisdom. These are those who in the first stage of joy have already entered the path of insight and understand that their true nature is unborn in virtue of the fact that their uncontaminated minds have engaged in the cultivation [of meditation]. The second are those who have already cultivated that practice. These are they who in the first six stages have already attained the path of cultivation in virtue of their progression in the cultivation [of meditation]. The third are those who have attained the state of no returning. These are they who above the first three stages have already perfected the path of the cultivation [of meditation], who no longer need to engage in effort and are beyond the path of intensified effort, for, because they abide effortlessly in the sixth stage of presence, all their passions will never arise again since from moment to moment their progress is irreversible. Among these only those who have attained the eighth stage of steadfastness realize that all things are originally unborn and do not arise. Only these attain the universal purification of this superior wisdom of patience. They constantly engender uncontaminated [purification] and abide effortlessly. Because they have attained this state the Scripture says that "they have realized the patience of the state of no arising." As a scripture teaches, "In the eighth stage all bodhisattvas are apart from conceptualizing things." Lacking "I" and "mine," they understand that all things are neither eternal nor transient, are not born, and do not arise. They understand the equality of self and others. This means that they attain the effortless control of these two conceptions and realize the mind of equality in regard to everything, for from this state they are free from these two conceptions, because they are free from effort and intense practice, and because they are entirely uncontaminated and extremely purified. Such nondiscriminative wisdom has attained mastery because it emerges effortlessly. Therefore they are said to "experience the phenomenal wisdom all of one unified taste." Bodhisattvas in the first stage, although they have already realized the equality of self and others, yet do have effort, intense practice, and purposeful activity, and inasmuch as they are not yet purified they are not yet established [in this patience of the state of no arising].

The Third Question:
The Request for Examples

The Scripture says: "Those wondrously born bodhisattvas again spoke to the Buddha and said: 'We request the Tathāgata to give some clear examples so that all we bodhisattvas might understand this profound meaning and might broadly proclaim and disseminate it

321c

in accord with such a purified understanding so that, when sentient beings hear, they will quickly understand this patience of the state of no arising.'"

The Commentary explains: Those wondrously born bodhisattvas present their request that [the Buddha] express this sublime meaning clearly in examples so that it might clearly be understood. Thus all those bodhisattvas, as well as others, on hearing this Dharma, might understand its profound meaning and understand that patience of the state of no arising.

The First Example:
The Grove of Unified Experience

The Scripture says: "The Buddha addressed those wondrously born ones and said: 'The gods of the Thirty-threefold Heaven, before they have entered the grove of unity, are entirely unable to have that unified experience which lacks "I" and "mine" in both its nature and its experience. But on entering that grove of unity they nondiscriminately experience [that unity] at will. Because of the good qualities of that grove of unity, it can cause those gods to enter and all their karmic actions, in both their nature and their experience, will become a unified experience without any deliberation. In like fashion, bodhisattvas before they have realized the patience of the state of no arising are entirely unable to attain the mind of equality which is totally equal and detached. They are nondiscriminative in the manner of the word-hearers and the individually enlightened ones because they yet have the two conceptions [that distinguish between self and other]. Thus they are unable to abide in the experience of the phenomenal wisdom all of one unified taste. But after they have realized that patience of the state of no arising, they banish these two conceptions and then attain the mind of equality, thereby becoming different from word-hearers and individually enlightened ones. Thus they are able to abide in detachment and experience this phenomenal wisdom all of one unified taste.'"[56]

The Commentary explains: These gods of the Thirty-threefold

Heaven have a grove of unity which has been formed from the unified, blissful power of all those gods. All the gods who are not in this grove are differentiated as superior and inferior in regard to the nature of their palaces and the experiences of their pleasures, and they have discriminative experiences of "I" and "mine." But on entering that grove they abandon all discrimination of superior and inferior "in both its nature and its experience." Being all equal, they lack "I" and "mine," and their unified experience is able to engender equality. This grove is said to be one of unity because its experience is a unification [of that of many gods].

322a

Because all these gods share in the enabling power of the unified, blissful action of equality, their container consciousnesses are changed and make this grove appear at the same place and time with the same, single image. Because of the enabling power of that grove of unity, their evolving consciousnesses are similarly changed; and, although individually each experiences, it is said that there is no differentiation [between those experiences]. In a similar fashion those bodhisattvas of the two vehicles who have not yet entered the ten stages have not yet realized suchness in the patience of the state of no arising manifested through the two emptinesses [of self and things], for they must yet sever their attachment to differentiation in the path of insight. They are not free from the two discriminative conceptions of self and other. They are thus unable to abide in the experience of the phenomenal wisdom all of one unified taste because they have not yet attained the equality and detachment associated with uncontaminated equality wisdom.

Another opinion holds that bodhisattvas below the eighth stage still must expend effort and are yet in the path of intensified effort. Subtle passion still emerges in them. They have not yet attained the patience of the state of no arising because they are not yet purified. They are thus unable to abide in the experience of the phenomenal wisdom all of one unified taste because they have not yet attained the equality associated with discernment wisdom in a mind of equality and detachment.

The Second Example: The Great Sea

The Scripture says: "Again, wondrously born ones, [consider this example]. The many large rivers and small streams, before they have entered the great sea, each have a different riverbed and their waters are different. Their amount of water is small and their water level increases and decreases. They each differ in the action of their flow. In small part they support the life of water creatures. But when they enter the great sea they have no differences in their beds and their waters do not differ. The amount of their waters is unlimited and their water level does not increase or decrease. The action of their flow is one. They are an extensive and great support for water creatures. In like fashion, bodhisattvas who have not yet realized the great sea of the Tathāgata's Dharma realm each have a different course, and their wisdoms differ. They have but little wisdom and that wisdom increases and decreases. They are each different in the action of the course of their wisdom. In small part they are a support for the maturation of the good roots of sentient beings. But when they have realized the great sea of the Tathāgata's Dharma realm they have no differences in their course. Their wisdoms are not differentiated and are unlimited. Their wisdom does not increase or decrease. They experience the phenomenal wisdom of one unified taste and are the support for the maturation of the good roots of immeasurable sentient beings."[57]

The Commentary explains: "The large rivers" refers to the Ganges and the other four great rivers. The "small streams" refers to all the other small rivers. The phrase "before they have entered the great sea each has a different riverbed" means that different terrains determined their respective courses. "Their waters are different" because, until they reach the sea, some are pure, some turbid, some muddy, and some beautiful. "The amount of their water is small" because they have not yet reached the sea. "Their water level increases and decreases" because there are variations in the amount of rainfall. "They each differ in the amount of their flow" because there are differences in velocity, power, and development.

322b

"In small measure they support the life of water creatures" because they are a support only for a small number of small aquatic sentient beings. The sentence "when they enter the great sea they have no differences in their bed" and so on indicates the direct opposite of the above. Understand that [the sea] is described as an "extensive and great support" because it supports a large number of enormous creatures.

The phrase "in like fashion, bodhisattvas who have not yet entered the great sea of the Tathāgata's Dharma realm" means that they have not yet realized the Buddha's Pure Dharma Realm. That "they each have a different support" means that they take different Tathāgatas as their respective supports. "Their wisdoms differ" because each differs in the meditational practices to which he is devoted. "They have but little wisdom" because they await the realization of Buddha wisdom. Their wisdom increases and decreases because the characteristics of all their lands are not preeminent, and because the characteristics of their respective concentrations are not preeminent. "They are each different in the action of the course of their wisdoms" because all these bodhisattvas differ in the number and extent of their respective concentrations. They thus differ in their actions and each, according to the enabling cause of his endeavors, is able to perform actions in the realm of sentient beings. But beyond this they do not progress, and thus they are different from one another. The sentence "in small part they are the support for the maturation of the good roots of sentient beings" means that they are a support for the maturation of good roots for a small section of sentient beings and in small measure. Because of the enabling power of all these bodhisattvas and in accord with their abilities, they do cause the good roots of others to mature. But, inasmuch as the concentration of these bodhisattvas is not yet that of a Tathāgata, being small in number and extent, the benefit and happiness which they bring to the sentient beings they convert is itself small. The sentence "when they have realized the great sea of the Tathāgata's Dharma realm" means that they realize the Pure Dharma Realm of awakening. That "they do not have any difference in their support" means that their support is purified suchness, for in the uncontaminated realm there are no differences between Buddhas. Neither are there such differences in the case of these bodhisattvas.[58]

"Their wisdoms are not differentiated" because their characteristics are similar to mirror wisdom and the other wisdoms, since they neither discriminate nor differentiate between themselves and others. "Their wisdom is unlimited" because they understand unlimited knowables. "Their wisdom neither increases nor decreases" because it is universally purified and because the objects of such universal wisdom are neither few nor many. "They experience the phenomenal wisdom all of one unified taste" because their characteristics are all similar to the actions of equality wisdom and the other wisdoms. "They are the support for the maturation of the good roots of immeasurable sentient beings" because the inexhaustible stores of their blissful wisdom are universal. Because they attain the Dharma body and exhaust the limits of transmigration, they are the support for the maturation of the good roots of all sentient beings whatsoever.

According to one opinion, the difference between these two examples is that the first describes the difference between those bodhisattvas who have not yet [attained the patience of the state of no arising, which some think occurs in] the first stage of joy [and others think occurs in] the eighth stage of steadfastness, and those bodhisattvas who have already attained that state. The second example of the great sea then treats the difference between those bodhisattvas who have not yet entered the eighth stage of steadfastness or the tenth stage of the Tathāgata realm, and those bodhisattvas who have already entered [those states].

But another opinion holds that both of these examples describe the differences between bodhisattvas who have not yet realized the patience of the state of no arising and those bodhisattvas who have already attained it. The first example explains that the meritorious qualities of these bodhisattvas are difficult to understand,

322c

just like that grove of unity, while the second example explains that the meritorious qualities of these bodhisattvas are inexhaustible, just like the great sea.

Chapter XIV

The Concluding Verses

The Scripture says: "Then the Bhagavat recited these verses."[59]

The Commentary explains: These four verses summarize what has been explained above. In outline they interpret the descriptive marks of the Buddha land, of the Pure Dharma Realm. In the Tathāgata's land, all conditioned and unconditioned qualities are comprised within the Pure Dharma Realm and all are the descriptive marks of that Pure Dharma Realm, for here descriptive marks refer both to that which is described (i.e., the Pure Dharma Realm) and to that which describes (i.e., the wisdom mind of mastery). Of these four verses, the first three and a half explain these descriptive marks, while the last half of the fourth verse presents the conclusion.

There are different [opinions] on the interpretation [of these verses]. The first holds that the first half of the first verse is specifically directed to the explanation of the Pure Dharma Realm, while the second half treats mirror wisdom. The first half of the second verse treats equality wisdom, while the second half discusses discernment wisdom. The first half of the third verse explains duty-fulfillment wisdom, while the second half is directed to the accompanying merits supported on these four wisdoms. The first half of the fourth verse explains the differences among the three bodies, which are the completion of these five factors.

A second opinion holds that these verses demonstrate that the Pure Dharma Realm has six descriptive marks which together support all the merits of the Buddha realm. They are 1) essence, 2) cause, 3) result, which are considered as 4) action, 5) associated qualities, and 6) differentiation. The first verse treats the first mark and then each half-verse treats one of the subsequent five marks.

The First Half of the First Verse

The Scripture says: "Suchness in all things is characterized by purification from the two obstacles."

The Commentary explains: According to the first opinion above, this treats the Pure Dharma Realm and means that suchness, manifested through the emptinesses and no-self of all things, is original purity, which is free from the two obstacles [of passion and to knowledge]. Being free from all defilement, it is able to be the support for all good states. Therefore it is termed the Pure 323a Dharma Realm. The phrase "all things" here means all transcendent and worldly, all contaminated and uncontaminated aggregates, spheres, and elements. Suchness is the true nature of all things, the indefectible nature, which is neither identical to nor different from all those things.

Although its essence is of one taste only, yet it is many, in virtue of the image-aspect [of sentient beings], and thus one may say that there are two suchnesses, the no-self of the emptiness of personhood and the no-self of the emptiness of things. However, suchness is not actually emptiness or no-self, for it is free from discrimination and severed from fabrication. It is called emptiness and no-self because in meditating on the insights of emptiness and no-self one destroys the clinging to "I" and "mine" that obstructs suchness.

One may say there are three suchnesses, good, bad, and morally neutral, for suchness is the true nature of these three states.

One may say that there are four suchnesses, those associated with the three realms and that not so associated, for suchness is the true nature of these four things.

One may say that there are five suchnesses, mind, mental states, unassociated things, material form, and the unconditioned, because suchness is the true nature of these five things.

One may say that there are six suchnesses, the five aggregates of material form, sensation, conceptualization, karmic formations, and consciousness, together with the unconditioned states, [because suchness is the true nature of these six things].

One may say that there are seven suchnesses, [as is explained in the *Scripture on the Explication of Underlying Meaning,*] the suchness of the flow of transmigration which is the true nature of that flow from the beginningless beginning, the suchness of descriptive marks which is the true nature of all things manifested by emptiness and no-self, the suchness of conscious construction–only which is the true nature of all things as conscious construction–only, the suchness of steadfastness which is the true nature of the truth of contaminated suffering, the suchness of wrong conduct which is the true nature of the truth of the origin of karmic torment, the suchness of purification which is the true nature of the truth of the cessation [of that torment] and which is good and uncontaminated, and the suchness of right practice which [is the true nature of] all conditioned and unconditioned good states.

Or one may say that there are eight suchnesses, [as is explained in the Perfection of Wisdom (Prajñāpāramitā) scriptures,] the suchness of no arising, the suchness of no destruction, the suchness of no annihilation, the suchness of no eternalism, the suchness of no unity, the suchness of no multiplicity, the suchness of no coming, and the suchness of no going, for suchness has been manifested through these eight negations.

Or one may say that there are nine suchnesses, suchness as manifested in the ninefold path which removes the nine obstacles.

Or one may say that there are ten suchnesses, suchness as manifested in the severance of the ten ignorances in the course of the ten stages. These are the ten Dharma realms explained in the *Summary of the Great Vehicle.*[60]

In this manner we could multiply the number indefinitely, for all things are different marks of suchness, and yet that suchness is neither one nor many. Discriminative language is entirely unable to explain this. But inasmuch as it is free from illusion and mistake, it is conventionally termed suchness. Inasmuch as it is able to support all good qualities, it is conventionally termed the Pure Dharma Realm. Inasmuch as it has nothing that can be negated, it is conventionally termed ultimate existence. Inasmuch as it has

nothing that can be affirmed, it is conventionally termed emptiness and nonexistence. We can analyze and examine all the idle
words of all teachings and, when we have finished, we still cannot
fathom it. It is ultimate meaning only, but by convention we call
it the limit of reality. This is the content realized by the eminently
holy path of nondiscrimination. By convention we call it the truth
of ultimate meaning, for such is its explanation.

323b   The phrase "the two obstacles" refers to the obstacle of passion and the obstacle to knowledge. The obstacle of passion is so
called because it torments and disperses the body and mind and
renders them agitated. The obstacle to knowledge is so called
because it covers over the indefectible nature of knowables and
causes them not to appear in the mind. The obstacle of passion has
as its principal element the belief in self that clings to "I" and
"mine," as well as the one hundred and twenty-eight basic passions together with their secondary passions. Both the acts they
engender and the results they attain are included [in this obsta-
cle] because they are rooted in passion. The obstacle to knowledge
has as its principal element the belief in self that clings to all imagined things, as well as to the mind and all the mental states of
ignorance, the love of things, together with affection for malicious
thoughts, and so forth. Both the acts they engender and the results
they attain are included [in this obstacle], for they are rooted in
clinging to things and in ignorance.

[There are however two opinions on the question of which consciousnesses have such clinging to things and ignorance.] A first
opinion holds that in contaminated minds and mental states,
whether good, bad, or morally neutral, in the mind and mental
states of those in the lower vehicles, both clinging to things and
ignorance are present because in such minds the no-self of things
cannot be understood and an image-aspect and insight-aspect similar to [those things and ignorant in their regard] arises.

But a second opinion holds that clinging to things and ignorance are present only in those contaminated minds and mental
states that are either bad or neutral, for, as the *Treatise on the*

Stages of Yogic Meditation teaches, "Ignorance is only of two kinds: bad or neutral, that is, defiled or undefiled." It does not mention good [states of mind] because it is impossible for that which is not good to be associated with the good mind, since their natures are incompatible.[61]

Furthermore, good states of mind must of necessity be associated with the good roots of the absence of delusion. Delusion is ignorance, and it is impossible for both delusion and the absence of delusion to coexist in the same mind, since they are incompatible, just as covetousness and the absence of covetousness or anger and the absence of anger [are incompatible]. And it is impossible for clinging to things [to be present in the good mind] unaccompanied by delusion, for in the absence of ignorance there would be no erroneous clinging at all. It is just as the clinging to a real self must be accompanied by ignorance.

Moreover, all good mental states have no illusory clinging. The understanding of no-self which accompanies the good mental states of faith and so forth have insight into the two emptinesses [of self and things] as their principal way of functioning. But it is impossible for clinging to things to lead to the insight of the emptiness of things because self-clinging does not permit such an insight to arise. Therefore, the good mind, whether contaminated or uncontaminated, is definitely not associated with these two clingings to self and to things, with ignorance, or with desire, because this would contradict the principles of the Dharma.

In the maturing, neutral mind and all its mental states (i.e., the container consciousness and the five sense consciousnesses) there is no clinging to things and no ignorance because their power of discrimination is insignificant and they are unable to engender attachment. If they did have such clinging and engendered a belief in real things and a real self, then the container consciousness, having ignorance, could be associated only with the five [universal] mental states [of contact, attention, sensation, conception, and volition], because it would be comprised in both ignorance and wisdom.

Furthermore, if clinging to things were present in the container consciousness, it would from moment to moment be annihilated, because it would not be permeable. Then this obstacle to knowledge could not be disciplined [by good permeations]. This constitutes a grave error. There is no question that such is not true in regard to the obstacle of passion, [for it certainly can be disciplined by the permeations of good seeds and practices].

Moreover, [if clinging to things were present in the container consciousness,] then when insight into the emptiness of things first occurred, this consciousness would be severed, since clinging to things is incompatible with the disciplining of the obstacle [to knowledge] and cannot function together with it. And, if it were so [severed], then the other contaminated seeds would have no support and the good states of meditation could not permeate it, for it would not be permeable. One cannot say that [these good states] permeate the pure mind associated with mirror wisdom because that mind is not undefined. Indeed it may not yet have even been attained. Therefore clinging to things is not present in the container consciousness.

[It is objected that] if this be the case, then would not the results of maturations which are present in the other active consciousnesses also be of the same nature, that is, without clinging to things?

[We answer that] clinging to things is not present in the five sense consciousnesses because they have no significant role in discriminating or examining [things]. The *Summary of the Great Vehicle* teaches that "It is only the thinking consciousness that is able discriminately to imagine."[62] We should then admit that these five [sense consciousnesses] do not have such discrimination as their content. Since they do not discriminate or gain insight by examining, they cannot imagine a self and, consequently, they cannot imagine any things [in contrast to that self]. Yet it is true that desire, hatred, and so forth, which arise from the imagined self and imagined things of the thinking consciousness, do engender in these five sense consciousnesses movements of desire, anger, and so forth, for those [movements] do not consist in insight.

323c

Although these consciousnesses do not have the ability to gain insight, yet they are supported on those states of desire, hatred, and ignorance, that is, by the two obstacles.

Therefore the discriminating and examination of the two clingings are present only in the sixth perceiving and the seventh thinking consciousnesses. If desire, anger, and so forth were not supported by the [deluded] insights [of these two consciousnesses], then such examination would also be absent in the five sense consciousnesses. Therefore the obstacle of passion in all its states of self-clinging is present essentially only in these two consciousnesses when they are bad, defiled, and undefined.

If in the state of no training of the lower vehicles the obstacle to knowledge, which engenders clinging to things, is present in that undefiled and undefined mind, then in that state of no training there would be no mental states that were bad, defiled, or undefined. Thus those in the two vehicles consider this mind to be undefiled [although it has the obstacle to knowledge]. But from the viewpoint of a bodhisattva it is yet impure, and they consider such a mind to be defiled. Thus the obstacle to knowledge is considered as both undefiled and as defiled, for its one essence is seen differently in these two viewpoints.

The obstacle to knowledge is [always] present within the obstacle of passion because it is the support for that obstacle of passion inasmuch as one necessarily imagines a self in clinging to imagined things as real. But, although they are essentially not separate one from the other they do function separately, just as, although the essence of consciousness is one, the functions of that consciousness in apprehending objects is differentiated. From such permeations there arises the seed [of these obstacles], which, while being one in essence, yet has many functions. Although [these obstacles] arise simultaneously, yet they are severed progressively because the power of the holy path is realized step by step.

[It is asked that] if the obstacle to knowledge is considered by those of the two vehicles to be undefiled and undefined, to which of the undefined categories does it pertain?

[We answer that] it pertains to the category of undefined maturation because it arises from the maturing consciousness.

[It is objected that] if this be so, then what might the categories that are not undefined consist of?

[We answer that] these include all other [undefined] categories, such as the enabling cause [of such undefined states], because the mind of undefined deportment and the other two undefined categories [of consciousness] have no tenacious clinging, are not universal, and in essence do not have the two obstacles.

[It is further asked that] if there is no clinging to things in the good, undefiled, undefined mind [of those in the two vehicles], why are they unable to understand the emptiness of things? If they have no self-clinging, why are they unable to understand the emptiness of birth?

[We answer that] they are unable to understand the emptiness of birth because of the presence of innate self-clinging in their thinking consciousness. They are unable to understand the emptiness of things because of the presence of innate clinging to things in their thinking consciousness. These innate clingings arise as an image-aspect, [which is mistaken for real objective things,] and an insight-aspect, [which is mistaken for a real subjective self].

324a   [The objection continues by asking,] why then do we not simply say that these two aspects [of image and insight] constitute clinging to things?

We do not state this because the uncontaminated wisdom of all Buddhas and bodhisattvas also has these two aspects.

How then is it that they do not cling to things?

They do not cling because their dependently co-arisen image-aspect and insight-aspect are comprised in the pattern of full perfection. Only if, because of these two aspects, they were to falsely imagine that fixed natures existed external to conscious construction, would we say that they cling [to things]. Therefore the obstacle to knowledge, present in the thinking consciousness, always accompanies the other six consciousnesses in all the triple world.

We are aware that this lengthy argumentation is not directly related to the text [of the Scripture], and so we will end it and return to interpreting the basic text of that Scripture.

The phrase "characterized by purification" means that the basic nature of suchness is pure. It is covered over by those two obstacles, just as pure space seems to become impure because of the obstacles of mists and clouds. But, when one attains the transcendent path wherein suchness is realized and the seeds of these two obstacles are gradually eradicated then, when diamond-like concentration appears, one destroys all the seeds of all obstacles entirely, just as a strong wind blows away mists and clouds, and then one attains the ultimate conversion of support to the Pure Dharma Realm. This is termed "the characteristic of purification" and is the Pure Dharma Realm of the five factors explained above [in the Scripture].

According to the second opinion [on the interpretation of these verses], this verse treats one of the six descriptive marks of the Pure Dharma Realm, that is, the mark of its essence. But the Commentary is the same as that given above.

The Second Half of the First Verse

The Scripture says: "Its mastery of doctrinal wisdom and in its content are characterized by inexhaustibility."

The Commentary explains: According to the first opinion [on the interpretation of these verses], this passage treats the factor of mirror wisdom. The other-dependent, conditioned factor of mirror wisdom is here called doctrinal wisdom. That mirror wisdom has as its content the conditioned pattern of other-dependency because it does manifest images and is not confused about them. The phrase "its content" refers to suchness and is not to be taken as indicating that doctrinal wisdom. Although suchness is beyond words, yet, inasmuch as it is associated with the ability to engender meaning, it is [the content of doctrinal wisdom] without thereby implying any logical contradiction. Because that doctrinal wisdom has as its content [suchness], the text uses the term "its content." This does not mean that doctrinal wisdom is itself the content.

Mirror wisdom has as its content the pattern of full perfection that consists of the truth of ultimate meaning, for it exhausts the limits of transmigration and internally realizes that [full perfection]. This means that mirror wisdom has as its content all the common and individual marks of all things, because its content includes the patterns both of other-dependency (*paratantra*) and of full perfection (*parinispanna*). In contrast, the pattern of clinging to the imagined is the illusory thinking of fools and is not included as a wisdom content. Therefore it is not said to be the content [of this wisdom]. As a treatise explains, "The pattern of clinging to the imagined is the content only of common understanding. The pattern of full perfection is the content only of holy wisdom. The pattern of other-dependency is the content both of common understanding and of holy wisdom." The imagined pattern is not realized by the arhats because it has no reality.

[It is objected that] if this be so, then the wisdom of the arhats does not know everything, for there would be some objects not known to wisdom.

[We answer that] the supposition of imagined things as really existing is erroneous. But if one understand that this pattern is not existent, then that [understanding] is not itself merely imagined. The appearance in the mind of really existing essences is comprised in the essenceless pattern of other-dependency, and the truth of suchness is comprised in the essenceless pattern of full perfection. Therefore holy wisdom takes the pattern of the imagined as its content only in the sense that it knows it to be nonexistent.

324b   The term "mastery" means that mirror wisdom is endowed with the ten masteries; and its various wondrous functionings are unhindered because it is the completion of the practice of the six perfections.

The phrase "characterized by inexhaustibility" means that it exhausts the limits of transmigration because, without cessation or interruption, it constantly perdures. The word "characterized" means that which is characterized (i.e., mirror wisdom as described) and that which so characterizes, (i.e., the mind that functions with this mirror wisdom), for [such descriptive characteristics] show the essence [of a thing]. Therefore this passage treats the mirror wisdom of the five factors.

According to the second opinion, this passage explains one aspect of the essence [of the Pure Dharma Realm]. The four wisdoms, which are the result of awakening, in one aspect constitute the essence. The state of conditioned merit is precisely mirror wisdom which, due to its enabling power, converts the container consciousness away from supporting the heavy dross [of defilement] and converts it into the pattern of purified other-dependency (*paratantra*), far removed from all discriminative thinking. Both the content of its understanding and its ability to so understand that content are universally equal and ineffable, for the dependently co-arisen reality nature neither increases nor decreases. Its mode of functioning, which is realized internally, is able to manifest all objects without discrimination. This is what the verse intends when it uses the term doctrinal wisdom.

That state of conditioned merit is [also] equality wisdom which, due to its enabling power, converts the thinking consciousness away from clinging and to the pattern of purified other-dependency. It takes as its content mirror wisdom, the other wisdoms, and the Pure Dharma Realm in universal equality. Because such a mode of functioning is realized internally, it is called wisdom, [that is, the term doctrinal wisdom refers to mirror wisdom and equality wisdom].

The phrase "its content" then refers to the other two wisdoms which, due to their enabling power, convert the other six consciousnesses away from worldly discrimination into the pattern of purified other-dependency. Whether in transcendent [nondiscriminative wisdom] or in [the subsequently attained wisdom] which is both worldly and transcendent, the content subsequently attained is both suchness and doctrinal wisdom, for the pattern of other-dependency is taken as their content. In a nonclinging discrimination, this content appears [in wisdom consciousness] and, by an internal discrimination, [wisdom knows] what is realized and what realizes, [in recognizing its own image- and insight-aspects]. As stated above, because this content is suchness, the verse says "its content."

In this fashion the wondrous activity of the four wisdoms is unhindered and therefore the verse says that "it has mastery." It is "characterized by inexhaustibility" inasmuch as that constant activity, which exhausts the limits of transmigration, never ceases. [That activity] is called inexhaustible because mirror wisdom and equality wisdom are constant and uninterrupted. Although discernment wisdom and duty-fulfillment wisdom are at times interrupted, yet, because the occasions on which they temporarily come to awareness are limitless, they are also said to be inexhaustible. The term "characterized" here refers to all the descriptive characteristics of the essence [of the Pure Dharma Realm], which arises conditionally, for it is pure other-dependency (*paratantra*). It is said to be pure because it is indefectible. The term "wisdom" means that the manifestation of such content consists in the functioning whereby that content is illumined and realized internally in the pattern of full perfection (*parinispanna*). Because these knowables are able to manifest the essence [of the Pure Dharma Realm], they are said to be its characteristics.

The First Half of the Second Verse

The Scripture says: "Because of the cultivation of suchness in all respects, full perfection is realized."

The Commentary explains: According to the first opinion [on the interpretation of these verses], this part of the [second] verse refers to equality wisdom. This means that with the first insight at the stage of joy, one attains nondiscriminative equality wisdom and gains insight into the universal equality of suchness. In the subsequent stages, it is progressively cultivated and becomes ever more purified, until in the stage of awakening one realizes full perfection. This ultimate purity is the realization of the Pure Dharma Realm, the realization that truth and its embodiment are entirely equal.

324c

214

According to the second opinion, this verse refers to the cause [of the Pure Dharma Realm]. This means that in the first stage of joy nondiscriminative wisdom gains an initial insight into that Pure Dharma Realm, and then in the path of insight the three consciousnesses (container, thinking, and perceiving) sever the one hundred and twelve fundamental passions and their secondary passions which must be severed by insight, and destroy part of the undefiled ignorance and the heavy dross of discriminative clinging to things. The seeds of wisdom, which reveal this initial insight into the Pure Dharma Realm, increase from this point on through the stages. In the path of practice this nondiscriminative wisdom gains insight into the other suchnesses of the Dharma realm. In all the other practices of hearing, reflecting, and meditating upon the Dharma, in the wisdoms of intensified practice, in its skillful methods, it progressively cultivates [these seeds]. As appropriate at each stage, [this wisdom] gradually suppresses the sixteen passions and their secondary passions which must be severed through meditation and, again as appropriate at each stage, gradually destroys that undefiled ignorance and that innate clinging to things in all of their aspects. The seeds of this wisdom, which manifest the other [aspects of] the Dharma realm, increase because of this causal power until in the land of awakening one realizes the full perfection of the Dharma realm and the four wisdoms.

The Second Half of the Second Verse

The Scripture says: "It establishes the two for all sentient beings and brings about inexhaustible results in all respects."

The Commentary explains: [According to the first interpretation], this passage refers to discernment wisdom. This means that discernment wisdom is able to enunciate the wondrous Dharma for sentient beings. The phrase "the two" refers to the benefit and happiness it establishes for sentient beings. The phrase "in all respects" refers to all the aspects of the two. They are "inexhaustible" because these two permeate the limit of transmigration and are always active without ceasing. Such is their "result" because this is the result of wisdom. Therefore this passage treats the discernment wisdom of the five factors.

According to the second opinion, this verse refers to the result [of the Dharma realm]. This means that the Pure Dharma Realm and the four wisdoms are all able to establish benefit and happiness for sentient beings. They are said to bring about benefit because they cause sentient beings to cultivate the causes of goodness. They bring about happiness because they cause them to attain the result of happiness. They are said to bring about benefit because, in causing them to support goodness, they lead [sentient beings] to avoid evil and to bring about happiness. Again they bring about benefit because they cause them to eradicate their suffering, and they bring about happiness because they cause them to elicit joy. Understand that this is [the result of the Dharma realm] in this world or in any other world, in this world or transcendent to this world. The phrase "in all respects" means that these two have many aspects. They are "inexhaustible" because such results will never come to an end. Indeed all the aspects of these two are inexhaustible because they arise from the Pure Dharma Realm and the four wisdoms.

The First Half of the Third Verse

The Scripture says: "It has the activity of the very skillful methods of the transformations of body, speech, and thought."

325a   The Commentary explains: According to the first opinion, this verse treats duty-fulfillment wisdom. This means that this wisdom is able to engender the transformations of body, speech, and thought. It is "skillful" because it is harmonious and appropriate. It is a "method" because the applications of its means are ceaseless. This is then what is meant by its "activity." Alternately, "activity" refers to this wisdom's skillful method whereby it can engender the three transformations of body, speech, and thought.

According to the second opinion, this verse treats the action [of the Dharma realm]. This means that the Pure Dharma Realm and the four wondrous wisdoms can engender the three transformed actions of body, speech, and thought, as well as their accompanying skillful methods. Duty-fulfillment wisdom engenders the three actions of body, speech, and thought. Discernment wisdom engenders skillful activity, for it examines which methods would be most appropriate [in given circumstances]. The other two wisdoms and the Pure Dharma Realm engender the activity of skillful methods because they are spontaneously able to relate to all actions as skillful methods.

The transformations of the body are three. The first is the transformation of one's own body; for example, the changing of one's own body into that of a universal monarch or the creations of various material forms from former existences. The second is the transformation of the bodies of others; for example, the changing of King Māra into a Buddha body or the changing of Śāriputra into the daughter of a god, for in these bodies of others are manifested various kinds of transformed appearances.[63] The third is that not joined to any body, such as the manifestation of the great earth as the seven-jeweled [palace of the Pure Land], the manifestation of immeasurable Buddha bodies, or the emitting of a light to illumine limitless realms. These creations are not joined to any body at all. They manifest transforming action in acting upon the various kinds of sentient beings and nonsentient material forms; for example, a shaking of the earth, an emitting of light, a raising up of a fragrant wind, for such things are done in order to benefit sentient beings. All these are termed the actions of the Buddha in transforming bodies.

In a similar fashion the transformations of speech are three. The first is that of one's own body, for the Buddha, by transforming his own body, does manifest a Brahmā voice and universally addresses himself to unlimited world-realms in various kinds of speaking. The second is that of the bodies of others, for he causes word-hearers and his great sons to proclaim the deep Dharma of the Great Vehicle through the Brahmā voice of the Buddha. It is thus that word-hearers and all bodhisattvas speak, for previously they were incapable of [enunciating] such a deeply wondrous

Dharma. Their ability is created by the Tathāgata's transforming activity and not through their own power. The third is that not joined to any body, such as the creations of various mountains, seas, grasses, trees, and so forth, even of empty space, which emit voices and enunciate the great Dharma. All these are termed the action of the Buddha's transformation of speech.[64]

The transformation of thought is of only two kinds. The first is that of one's own body, which consists in the transformation of various images in the mind and mental states of one's own mind. The second is that of the bodies of others, which means that one causes various images to appear in the mind and mental states of others. These are only images, but they do appear as if they have been elicited from the insight-aspect of the minds of those beings.

According to one opinion, that which is called the transformation of one's own thought is that which in virtue of meditation leads to the understanding in one's own mind of Dharma beyond one's own ability [to understand]. That which is termed the transformation of the thought of others consists in the exercise of an assisting activity upon sentient beings so that the dull-witted may understand the deep, subtle Dharma and so that the forgetful may attain correct recollection.

325b   [It is objected that] thought cannot be so transformed because it has no material form. A treatise explains, "Because thought has no material form, it cannot be transformed." Again it is taught, "The transformation body is without mind and mental states."

[We answer that] these texts refer to the concentration powers of those in the lower vehicles and common worldlings, which is slight and incapable of manifesting things without an [already given] material form. The inconceivable concentration of all Buddhas and bodhisattvas is entirely capable of creating and manifesting [such things without any preexisting material form]. Otherwise, how could the Tathāgata manifest desire, hatred, and so forth? How could word-hearers and animals know the thought of the Tathāgata? How could this Scripture teach that he creates immeasurable kinds [of transformation bodies] and causes them to be conscious?

218

How could it teach that he creates the activity of thinking? How could it teach that he has other-dependent mind? All these created material forms have the same effect [on the senses of beings] as do real material forms, but inasmuch as these images appear in the mind through the modification of the senses, they do not actually operate in the same way as real material forms. Furthermore, it was for the sake of lower kinds [of beings] that the [Buddha] made those statements [in the texts cited above in the objection].

[The objection continues by stating that] if this be so, then why does he not transform the unconscious gods and cause images to appear in their minds?

[We answer that] these unconscious beings already have the image-aspect in their minds and mental states, [although it is dormant]. Why would he again cause such images to arise in their minds and make them conscious? When images appear, they do become sentient and are no longer reckoned among the unconscious. Therefore the transformations of thought are of only the two kinds explained above.

Discernment wisdom is able to examine and understand the lands of recollective formulae and concentrations. It is able to diagnose the basic lineages and desires of sentient beings and enunciate the medicine of the wondrous Dharma. Thus it is said to be "skillful." The other three wisdoms (duty-fulfillment, equality, and mirror wisdoms) and the Pure Dharma Realm, as well as all their qualities, are the basic support for the engendering of these benefits for sentient beings. Therefore this verse speaks of an "activity of methods."

The Second Half of the Third Verse

The Scripture says: "It is fully endowed with the two limitless doors of concentration and recollective formulae."

The Commentary explains: According to the first interpretation, this verse treats the accompanying merits supported by the four wisdoms.

According to the second interpretation, it refers to the associated qualities [of the Dharma realm].

"Concentration" refers to the eighty-four thousand concentrations, while "recollective formulae" refer to the eighty-four thousand recollective formulae. They are called "doors" because they engender all conditioned merits and all uncontaminated states, and bring about benefit for sentient beings through the supernatural powers they call forth. These "two are limitless" because of their two adornments of merit and wisdom. They are "limitless" because their varieties consist of the eighty-four thousand merits and wisdoms, or because they are perfected through the practice of meditation for immeasurable eons. The first five [of the ten] perfections are termed merit, while the last five are termed wisdom. Or, as appropriate to the nature of each, they are all accompanied and endowed with these two [aspects of merit and wisdom]. Each of the four wisdoms is endowed and always associated with these two adorned doors [of concentration and recollective formulae].

The verse says that "it is fully endowed" because they also have the Pure Dharma Realm as their support, since [concentrations and recollective formulae] are not apart from the Pure Dharma Realm.

The First Half of the Fourth Verse

325c

The Scripture says: "It displays the differentiations of essence, enjoyment of Dharma, and transformation."

The Commentary explains: According to the first interpretation, this verse refers to the differentiation of the three bodies, which is the perfection of the five factors.

According to the second interpretation, it refers to the differentiation [of the Dharma realm]. Although the Pure Dharma Realm, which is the basic support for all Tathāgatas, is undifferentiated, yet, because of the evolutions of the various marks of the three bodies, the verse uses the term "differentiations" [in its regard].

The term "essence" means that the essence of the Tathāgata's first body of his own essence is eternal and unchanging, and thus is called the essence. It is also called the Dharma body because it is the support for all the [Buddha] qualities, such as the fearlessnesses, the powers, and so forth. The "enjoyment of Dharma" means that the next enjoyment body is able to enjoy various kinds of great doctrines both for itself and for others. The term "transformation" means that the transformation body is able to manifest various kinds of creations because he desires to benefit and gladden sentient beings. The term "body" here means essence, basis, an accumulation of various qualities. This is the general interpretation of the meaning of the three bodies.

Moreover, the Dharma body is characterized by suchness as the ultimate conversion. It is the support for the equality of all Buddha qualities, and it is able to engender all masterful activity which becomes revealed in the increase of stainless doctrines. It is the essence of the equality of all Tathāgatas. It is subtle, wondrous, and difficult to fathom. It destroys all discrimination and abolishes all fabrication. Thus a scripture teaches, "The Dharma body of all Buddhas is not associated with reflective thinking and is not an object for reflection. It surpasses all reflective thinking and fabrication."

The enjoyment body is characterized by the fullness of all merit. It is the accumulated completion of all Buddha qualities. It is thus able to engender all masterful activity, which is elicited from the increase of all stainless doctrines. The essence of each Tathāgata is subtle, wondrous, and difficult to fathom. These [enjoyment bodies] dwell in Pure Lands, and their spontaneity is profound. They never come to an end, and each experiences the joy of the Dharma. They manifest various forms and enunciate various doctrines in order to cause the great bodhisattvas also to experience such joy in the Dharma.

The transformation body is characterized by the fullness of all supernatural creations. It is the accumulated completion of all transforming activity. It manifests all masterful activity, which is elicited from the increase of all stainless doctrines. Such transforming activity of each Tathāgata is subtle, wondrous, and difficult to fathom. These [transformation bodies] dwell in this world, manifest various forms, and enunciate various doctrines. They mature the multitude of lower bodhisattvas, those in the two vehicles, and common worldlings, and cause them respectively to enter that great land, to transcend the triple world, and to be delivered from evil destinies.

This is the general interpretation of the activity that characterizes the three bodies.

Chapter XV

A Discussion on the Three Bodies of the Buddha

First Theme: The Five Factors and the Three Bodies

As stated above, the five factors support the three bodies. According to one opinion, the first two [factors of the Pure Dharma Realm and mirror wisdom] support the essence body. The next two [factors of equality wisdom and discernment wisdom] support the enjoyment body. Finally, duty-fulfillment wisdom supports the transformation body.

This is so because a scripture teaches that suchness is the Dharma body [and thus the Pure Dharma Realm supports that Dharma-essence body]. And a treatise explains that one attains the essence body through the conversion of the container consciousness in the attainment of mirror wisdom that issues from that conversion of the container consciousness.[65] Therefore we know that these two support the essence body.

This Scripture teaches that duty-fulfillment wisdom engenders all the creative activities. The *Ornament of the Scriptures of the Great Vehicle* teaches that in all realms duty-fulfillment wisdom engenders all the various kinds of immeasurable, inconceivable creations.[66] Therefore we know that this last of the four wisdoms supports the transformation body.

Another treatise explains that equality wisdom is able to manifest various Buddha bodies in accord with the predilections of the bodhisattvas in the Pure Lands. It also states that discernment wisdom is able to manifest all masterful activity in the great assemblies and to enunciate the Dharma without doubt. Furthermore it is said that one attains the enjoyment body because of the con-

326a

version of the active consciousnesses. Therefore we know that these middle two [of the four] wisdoms support the enjoyment body.[67]

Furthermore, of all the ten meanings of the three bodies of Buddha, wisdom is the preeminent support. Therefore we know that all of the three bodies attain wisdom.

According to a second opinion, it is only the first of the five factors, the Pure Dharma Realm, which supports the essence body. The four wisdoms are all associated with that essence and are manifested to bodhisattvas in the stages. In one aspect their subtle marks support the enjoyment body, while, inasmuch as they are manifested to bodhisattvas not yet in those stages, in another aspect the functioning of their crude marks manifests the transformation body.

All the scriptures teach that pure suchness is the Dharma body. The *Treatise in Praise of Buddha* (*Buddhastotra-śāstra*) expounds that the Tathāgata's Dharma body has no arising and no passing away. The *Ornament of the Scriptures of the Great Vehicle* teaches that the basic nature of the Buddha's essence body is eternal.[68] The *Treatise on the Diamond Scripture* (*Vajracchedikā-prajñāpāramitā-śāstra*) teaches that the good qualities propounded and discussed in the scriptures mean that the Dharma body does have a cause whereby one is enabled to realize it, while the other two bodies have a cause whereby one is enabled to produce them.[69] All the scriptures and treatises state that the ultimate conversion of support is the Dharma body. This conversion of support is precisely purified suchness. Since this is not the path of word-hearers, we know that the Dharma body has as its nature only the suchness of the Pure Dharma Realm.

Also the *Ornament of the Scriptures of the Great Vehicle* teaches that mirror wisdom is the enjoyment body.[70] The *Treatise on the Summary of the Great Vehicle* says that the conversion of the active consciousnesses attains the enjoyment body, but that the conversion of the container consciousness attains the Dharma body.[71] This means that one manifests and attains the Dharma body through the conversion away from the seeds of the two obstacles in that container consciousness. This passage does not mention mirror wisdom because it teaches that mirror wisdom is an enjoyment, [and thus that mirror wisdom supports the enjoyment body, not the Dharma body].

Furthermore, there are two kinds of enjoyment body. The first is one's own enjoyment body, which is the completion of practices for three innumerable eons. The second is the enjoyment body for others whereby all the bodhisattvas [are enabled to] enjoy Dharma. Therefore the enjoyment body includes all the characteristics commonly associated with the four wisdoms [inasmuch as it is one's own enjoyment body], and one aspect of creative transformation [of duty-fulfillment wisdom, inasmuch as it is the enjoyment body for others].

All the scriptures and treatises teach that the transformation body is the manifestation of various images for sentient beings who have not yet entered the stages leading to conversion, for its images constitute knowable objects for those sentient beings. Therefore we know that these images are not the qualities of ultimate meaning, but only its creative functioning. The scriptures and treatises state only that duty-fulfillment wisdom is able to engender this creative functioning and not that that [wisdom itself] is the transformation body.

Although the three bodies are comprised in the preeminence of wisdom, yet the Dharma body is said to be wisdom only by convention because it is a realization supported by wisdom, while the transformation body is said to be wisdom only by convention because it is the functioning of wisdom and because in its mani-   326b
festation it appears like wisdom. For these reasons there is no logical error in calling these bodies wisdom.

[The enjoyment body, being the experience of joy in the Dharma, is wisdom,] but both the enjoyment body and the transformation body are involved in arising and passing away, for they are involved in the realm of transmigration.

225

The Second Theme:
The Three Bodies as Eternal

[It is objected that] if this is so, then how can the scriptures teach that all the Buddha bodies are eternal?

[We answer that] they are eternal because of the Dharma body which is the support for the other two. Although the enjoyment body and the transformation body are characterized by arising and passing away, yet they are also said to be eternal because [the enjoyment body] always experiences joy in various doctrines without ceasing, and [the transformation body] manifests numerous creations in the ten realms without interruption. Therefore they always experience joy and always take on human form.

The *Ornament of the Scriptures of the Great Vehicle* teaches that the three bodies are eternal in basic nature, in the state of not resting, and in continuity.[72] The term "basic nature" refers to the essence body because the basic nature of this body is eternal. The phrase "state of not resting" refers to the enjoyment body because it always experiences joy in the Dharma without interruption. The term "continuity" refers to the transformation body because it manifests an inexhaustibility of creative transformations. Therefore, the Dharma body is eternal because it is free from all discrimination and fabrication and has no arising nor passing away. Although the other two bodies from moment to moment do arise and pass away, yet they are also said to be eternal because they rely on that eternal body without interruption and continue without ceasing. As a scripture teaches, "The aggregates of material form, sensation, and so forth, as they pertain to the Tathā-gata, are all eternally abiding." From this doctrinal principle, [the Tathāgata's transformation bodies] do not arise and do not pass away because they arise from the cultivation of uncontaminated seeds. Still, we have the absolute declaration that that which arises is destined to pass away because all material form and mind are seen to be impermanent, and an eternally abiding material form or mind has never yet been seen.

The Third Theme:
The Dimensions of the Three Bodies

What are the dimensions [of these bodies]?

The Dharma realm has suchness as its essence, and suchness is the real nature of all things. Since things have no limit, the Dharma body has no limit. It pervades all things, and there is no place wherein it is not present. It is like empty space, and one cannot say that its dimensions are either large or small. However, from its perceptible marks we say that it pervades all places.

The enjoyment body both has material form and does not have material form. All things that have no material form have no dimensions and cannot be said to be either large or small. Just like the [Dharma] body on which it is supported and which is its content, so [this enjoyment body] may be said to pervade everywhere.

Now there are two kinds of material form: concrete form and magically created form. Concrete form indicates those actions of the major and minor marks of the form body produced by practice for three incalculable eons (i.e., the historical form of an historical Buddha, such as Śākyamuni). Through the conversion of the five sense organs, a contaminated form body attains the form of the Buddha's uncontaminated five sense organs, adorned with its immeasurable major and minor marks. Such a body encompasses the Dharma realm and is called the true Pure Land. But in transmigration its actions do have limitations. The dimensions of this body, which is a creative transformation of the container consciousness, are not determined as to size. Rather they are similar to that of the realm [in which they appear]. Because the good actions of humans in Jambudvīpa are minimal, a form body attained therein would be at most six feet and four inches. Good actions in Pūrvavideha are more eminent, and a body there would be twelve feet and eight inches. In such a fashion, as the good actions progressively increase, the dimensions of the body thereby realized will become progressively larger until a body in the final heaven of the world of form attains a dimension of sixteen thousand leagues 326c because the actions that produce forms therein are preeminent. The dimensions of such bodies become so large because of the accumulated permeations of good and pure roots [cultivated] during the bodhisattva practices in the ten stages. As a scripture explains, "At the realization of diamond-like concentration, the body attained fills the entire Dharma realm and pervades the true Pure Land because all obstacles are destroyed and the measure of the power of such good roots is infinite." This is because the transformed body and land of the pure consciousness associated with mirror wisdom are unlimited. The consciousnesses of all Buddhas create [these bodies and lands] at the same place and the same time so that the similarity of their characteristics is not mutually incompatible. They will never come to an end, be interrupted, or cease. Thus they are able to cause all Buddhas to experience broad delight and are thus called enjoyment bodies and enjoyment lands. Such bodies and lands are known only by Buddhas and are not realized through the five senses of any bodhisattva. But the material organs of [Buddhas] are able to perceive all sense objects because they are without obstacle. These excellent marks of all Buddhas, which are beyond the sight [of all sentient beings], the limitless proclamation of Dharma, and the functioning of all their sense organs are so unlimited because they are universally perfected.

Magically created material form is the manifestation of various kinds of bodies and various kinds of major and minor marks through the power of the compassionate vow [of Buddhas] for the sake of leading the multitudes of bodhisattvas to enter that great land. "Various kinds" here means that their voice depends upon the kind of land and their dimensions are not determined.

Transformation bodies are the manifestation of magically created bodies through that same power of the compassionate vow for the sake of converting all sentient beings who have not yet entered the stages. [Such a transformation body] both has a material form and does not have a material form. It does not have form because it is the action of the transformation of thought [and thought has no material form], and because the marks of all such qualities, such as the supernatural powers, the fearlessnesses, and so forth, have no material form; thus [those bodies] have no material form and no dimensions. But it does have material form because it is the action of the transformation of body and speech, brought about in accord with the occasion, place, and multitude [of sentient beings to be converted, for speech has material form]. As the Scripture explains, such a manifested body is not determined as to its size.

The Fourth Theme:
Differentiation and the Three Bodies

Are all the Tathāgatas differentiated from one another or not?

They are undifferentiated because the true nature of the Dharma body is common to all Tathāgatas. But we conventionally say that they are differentiated because the causes that render them experientially present are differentiated.

The other two bodies are each influenced by different causes, and their different compositions are distinct from one another. But they do not cling to these differentiations, and we say that they are undifferentiated because, being [all] similar in the same place, their actions of benefiting and gladdening are equal one to the other. Therefore we say that all Tathāgatas in the three bodies are undifferentiated because the Dharma realm, which supports them in the action of their basic aspiration, is undifferentiated, because their intention of benefiting and gladdening is undifferentiated, and because all the phenomenal activity they perform in unison is undifferentiated.

The Fifth Theme:
Individual Qualities and the Three Bodies

But do [Tathāgatas] have conditioned and individual qualities or not?

The Tathāgata's Pure Dharma Realm is characterized by the conversion of support to suchness. It is ultimately true, good, and original purity because it is far removed from all defiled states,

327a because it is the basic support for all good qualities, and because
it is the true nature of all good qualities. Therefore it is said to be
endowed with all those good qualities, but it does not have any of
the qualities whereby one differentiates material form from mind.
The Buddha's enjoyment body is endowed with all its true material and mental qualities and manifests these transformed qualities for the sake of others. The Buddha's transformation body is
endowed only with those qualities associated with the magical creations of its manifested material and mental [attributes]. Therefore each of the three bodies is said to have qualities surpassing
in number the sands of the Ganges River.

The Sixth Theme:
The Relationship of Beings with Tathāgatas

Are all the beings to be converted common to all Tathāgatas
or not?

According to one opinion, they are common [to all Tathāgatas]
because each and every Tathāgata is able to convert and save each
and every sentient being. They are all equal in merit and wisdom.
For three incalculable eons they have all cultivated the course of
their vows. They have all in the same identical manner sought
wisdom in order to save all beings. Therefore it is said that the
beings converted by one Buddha are converted by all Buddhas.

But according to another opinion they are not common [to all
Tathāgatas] because there is a basic relationship between a particular Buddha and all those beings he is to convert. Thus at the
time of the Buddha Tiṣya, the Tathāgata [Śākyamuni] and
Maitreya were both his disciples. That Buddha [Tiṣya] saw that
the good roots of the sentient beings to be converted by Śākyamuni would come to maturation before the good roots of those sentient beings to be converted by Maitreya. He also saw that the
preparatory course of Maitreya would be completed before that of
Śākyamuni. Thus he entered into the concentration of fire and
caused Śākyamuni to witness it. For seven days and seven nights
Śākyamuni, while standing on one foot, praised that Buddha in a

single verse and was thus led to surpass Maitreya and become a Buddha before him.[73]

Furthermore, when the Buddha was about to enter cessation, he said, "All those who were to be saved by me have already been saved." Also another scripture teaches, "At the time of his cessation, the Buddha saw that one who was to have been converted by him was actually found to be in the realm of no conceptualization and no nonconceptualization, and that therefore he had [first] to be reborn into this [conscious] world in order to be converted by him. He then created a transformation body which in a concealed fashion continued to dwell in this world, and then in the [birth] body he had first received [from his mother], the Buddha appeared to enter into cessation. That being in the realm of no conceptualization and no nonconceptualization died and did come to be reborn into this world. That transformation body created by the Buddha taught him the wondrous Dharma and he became an arhat, whereupon that transformation body disappeared and was not seen again.

Moreover, all the scriptures in many passages teach that there is a determined relationship between the one who converts and those whom he converts. Therefore those to be converted are not common to all Buddhas.

The third and correct opinion is that they are both common to all Buddhas and are not common to all Buddhas. In the basic natures of the lineages [of sentient beings] there is a relationship whereby either many [sentient beings] are related to one [Buddha] or one [sentient being] is related to many [Buddhas]. During their preparatory course bodhisattvas, whether in common or not, have not matured sentient beings in the identically same manner; thus, on becoming Buddhas, they either convert in common or they convert singly. If all the beings to be converted were common to all Buddhas, then why would there be many Buddhas? One Buddha alone would be adequate to convert all beings. Since then there would be but a single Buddha dwelling always in the world and through his teaching converting sentient beings, then any other Buddha would have entered quiescence. Then even that single

Buddha would not convert all beings by leading them to enter the Great Vehicle, for that would be rendered useless [since there would be no need for anyone to realize Buddhahood because no further Buddhas would be necessary to convert anyone]. Rather that single Buddha would convert beings by leading them to enter the other vehicles and attain quiescence, for that would be the easiest course of action. What sensible person would reject what was easy and hold onto what was difficult? Who would light a lamp to assist the sun? Therefore the beings to be converted are not common [to all Tathāgatas].

327b

On the other hand, if the beings to be converted were never common [to many Tathāgatas], then bodhisattvas would not elicit their broad vows nor successively attend upon all the Buddhas. They would not cultivate the Great Vehicle, persons like Sudhana would encounter no spiritual friends, and Buddhas would not entrust those they have converted to later Buddhas.[74] This refutes the opinion that those to be converted are never common to all Buddhas. Therefore it is not true that those beings are never common [to all Tathāgatas].

Therefore, although each and every Buddha has the ability to convert all sentient beings, nevertheless, sentient beings are not disposed to being converted by all those Buddhas with whom they have no relationship, for they have never seen or heard [those Buddhas]. But though each and every Buddha never comes to an end and always abides in the world, teaching and converting innumerable kinds of sentient beings, yet they manifest particular transformation [bodies] as appropriate, whether they manifest wisdom or cessation, whether they are called Śākyamuni or Maitreya, or anything else. The sentient beings to be saved through these transformations say that all [Buddhas] save them.

The abiding of the transformation left behind in the case of the being who was reborn into the realm of no conceptualization [and no nonconceptualization,] and who finally attained salvation by seeing the appropriate transformation of Śākyamuni, is not incompatible [with this principle that transformations are shared by all Buddhas].

How is this so? [it is asked.] If that particular being was converted by all Tathāgatas [who created that transformation body for his sake], then what Buddha was it who came before him to convert him?

[We answer that] all Buddhas have the power of their compassionate vows, and it is impossible that just a single Buddha would convert him while all the others remained inactive. Each Buddha with which he has a relationship manifests a transformation body at the same place and at the same time through his subsequently attained wisdom. Since the visible qualities [of those transformation bodies] are all similar one to the other, they are not mutually opposed. Therefore [these Buddhas] in unison were the enabling cause that led the consciousness of that being to be converted and changed so that he might witness one Buddha manifesting his supernatural powers and teaching the Dharma. These things are inconceivable and cannot be understood by those who deny the principle of conscious construction–only.

The Seventh Theme:
Differences between the Three Bodies

Moreover, the essence body is quiescent and peaceful, for it is the support for merits that directly relate to self-benefit. But inasmuch as it is the enabling cause of benefit to the multitudes it is also related to benefit for others. Therefore it is included in the benefit of the other two bodies inasmuch as it is the support for the benefit and merit of those two bodies.

The enjoyment body has two aspects. The first is the aspect of one's own enjoyment of the Dharma and is the actual form body, which is realized in the completion of self-benefiting practices and which leads to one's own experience of wondrous joy. The second is the aspect of the enjoyment of the Dharma for others, which consists in the form bodies that are magically created so that the great multitude of bodhisattvas might enter that great land and which are realized by the full perfection of the practices of benefiting others cultivated for three incalculable eons. It manifests various forms and teaches various doctrines to lead all bodhisattvas to experience joy in the great Dharma. Because of these two aspects, there is no contradiction in saying that this enjoyment body consists only in self-benefit, or in saying that it consists only of benefit for others, or in saying that it consists of both.

The transformation body consists of benefiting others because it manifests all the descriptive marks of transformation in order to benefit others.

327c Thus the three bodies have four aspects which can be expressed in four phrases. The first is enjoyment without transformation, for that is the true enjoyment body of self-benefit. The second is transformation without enjoyment, for that is the transformation body for the sake of those not yet in the stages. Whether gross or subtle, whether productive of joy or alarm, its variations are undetermined. It is said to be transformation and not enjoyment because such a body does not necessarily lead to the enjoyment of joy in the Dharma. The third is both transformation and enjoyment, for that is the varied transformation body manifested to bodhisattvas in the stages. [It is said to be] experience because such a body does cause all those bodhisattvas to enjoy the Dharma. It is changed according to circumstances and is undetermined. The fourth is neither experience nor enjoyment, for it is the essence body.

Other texts say that the Buddha has two kinds of bodies: his birth body and his Dharma body. Here the Dharma body includes both the essence body and the true enjoyment body, for the first is the support for all meritorious doctrines and the second is the accumulated perfection of all those meritorious doctrines. The birth body here includes both the transformation body and the enjoyment body for others because they both manifest birth, for sentient beings and for bodhisattvas respectively, as appropriate.

Furthermore, another scripture says that there are ten kinds of Buddhas: Buddhas of full wisdom, Buddhas of earnest vow, Buddhas whose actions have matured, Buddhas of masterful power, Buddhas of transformation, Buddhas of the Dharma realm, Buddhas of mind, Buddhas of concentration, Buddhas of essence, and Buddhas of masterful activity. The first five of these are conventional, while the last five are ultimate meaning. They are included, as appropriate, in the three bodies, and in this manner one should understand their varieties and their descriptions.

The Second Half of the Fourth Verse

The Scripture says: "This Pure Dharma Realm is enunciated by all Buddhas."

The Commentary explains: This Pure Dharma Realm of all Tathāgatas is enunciated in the same fashion by all Buddhas. That fully perfected Buddha land is differentiated in the five kinds of factors and in the three bodies.

Alternately, [according to the second interpretation of these verses,] it is differentiated into the six characteristics of essence, cause, result, action, associated qualities, and functioning. Therefore these four verses summarize all the marks of the Buddha land. As explained above, this is the overall theme enunciated in this sacred teaching.

The Concluding Passage

The Scripture says: "At that time the Bhagavat finished teaching this Scripture and the entire assembly of the wondrously born bodhisattvas, great beings, all the great word-hearers, gods, humans, and *devas* in this world all heard this doctrine of the Buddha and all of them elicited great joy, received it in faith, and upheld it in practice."

The Commentary explains: This passage explains that, upon hearing this teaching, that multitudinous assembly relied upon its doctrine and received it in faith. Drawn on by the compassionate vow of the Buddha's pure consciousness and changed by the enabling power of this Scripture, the good roots in their minds matured and became manifest, as described above in the text. This means that upon hearing this Buddha teaching, they all "elicited joy, received it in faith, and upheld it in practice." All those word-hearers and so forth, whether they were creations [of the Buddha or of bodhisattvas] or were actually word-hearers, heard this doctrine while each remained in his own place either in the land of enjoyment or in the land of transformation. Although what that assembly of word-hearers heard was the same, what they saw was different. There is no incompatibility in this. Those above did see those below, but those below did not see those above. [In this manner] each one realized benefit and happiness.

328a

The Concluding Verses of the Commentary

I have now expounded all the deep words and meanings of this *Scripture on the Buddha Land* according to my ability.

May the merits [thus attained] spread among all kinds of beings, and may they all quickly realize the unexcelled result.

May all the merits that arise from the writing of this Commentary afterward issue in excellent results.

And may they continue without end to benefit and glad den all sentient beings.

Notes

1   See Hakamaya Noriaki, "Asvabhāva's Commentary on the *Mahāyāna-sūtrālaṃkāra* IX. 56–76," JIBS XX (Dec. 1971: 1): 471–2, for a parallel presentation of these commentaries.

2   The priority of the *Buddhabhūmi-sūtra* is assumed, on the basis of the passages from Asvabhāva and Sthiramati, throughout Nishio Kyōo's *Butsujikyōron no kenkyū* (Tokyo 1939; reprinted 1982): 1–32. Hakamaya also follows this judgment in his "Shōjō hokkai kō," *Nanto Bukkyō* XXXVII (Nov. 1976): 1, n. 3.

3   Takasaki Jikidō in his "Hōshin no ichigenron Nyoraizō shisō no hō kannen," *Bukkyō ni okeru hō no kenkyū*, Shunjūsha: Tokyo, p. 239, n. 38 and in his *Nyoraizō shisō no keisei*, Shunjūsha: Tokyo, pp. 346–7.

4   I have attempted to indicate the additional material in my dissertation, "A Study of the *Buddhabhūmyupadeśa:* The Doctrinal Development of the Notion of Wisdom in Yogācāra Thought." For the most part this was not a difficult task, as the additional sections have been inserted rather mechanically, but on occasion the text has been reworked to such an extent in the Bandhuprabha version that precise identification of new material becomes problematic.

5   These descriptions of wisdom stress that the universal Buddha wisdom entails both full understanding and full engagement. It is not merely transcendent, but also involved in all aspects of phenomenal living.

6   Such an analysis of the literary forms of Buddha discourse show not only an awareness of hermeneutical method but also of the underlying issue of just how the content of awakening relates to its verbal expression. Note that here none of these four "discourses" is described as literal.

7   That is, the passions that lead to attachment, the impermanence of the aggregates that constitute a human person, fear of death, and the demon or devil who dwells within the cycle of transmigration, ensconced in the highest heaven of pleasure.

8   This passage is also found in other Yogācāra texts, such as *The Scripture on the Explication of Underlying Meaning (Saṃdhinirmocana-sūtra)* (translated by John P. Keenan, Numata Center, 2000) and *The Summary of the Great Vehicle (Mahāyānasaṃgraha)* (translated by John P. Keenan, Numata Center, 1992).

9   The issue under discussion here is the authority of the text. If the transformation body of Buddha preached it in a transformed land, then it is

empirical speech, but if an enjoyment body of Buddha preached it in an enjoyment land, then its teaching is deemed much deeper and more profound, for that body—newly developed in Yogācāra three-body (*trikāya*) teaching—is the experienced presence of the Buddha to bodhisattvas in deep practice of meditation.

[10] That is, no fabrication of ideas or images mistakenly clung to as imagined. Yet, dependent on the pure mind of wisdom, they do embody Buddha wisdom in images and ideas, in order to carry out the tasks of compassion. The issue is basic to the text.

[11] Abhidharma thinkers taught that fifteen of the eighteen realms (the six sense organs, their six objects, and the six resultant consciousnesses) are defiled, and also that eight (the five sense organs of eyes, ears, nose, tongue, and body, plus smell, taste, and touch) can be morally neutral. This Abhidharma argumentation relates to the basic issue of the present text: how can pure Buddha consciousness be involved in an obviously defiled world? Yet, if not so involved, what relevance does it have to the world? If involved, how then can it be completely pure?

[12] This objection and its answer, as many others, are almost unintelligible without consulting Dharmapāla's *Ch'eng wei-shih lun*. See the discussion on Dharma Body in Louis de la Vallée Poussin, *Vijñaptimātratāsiddhi,* pp. 693–716. Also consult the English translation by Francis H. Cook, "Demonstration of Consciousness Only," in *Three Texts on Consciousness Only* (Numata Center, 1999), pp. 355–67. Since this is a more recent English translation, readers will find it more accessible than de la Vallée Poussin's French translation. This *Ch'eng wei-shih lun* figures more than any other text in the large portion of the *Interpretation of the Buddha Land* extant only in Chinese, and apparently added either by Bandhuprabha or by Hsüan-tsang. Parallels will be indicated.

[13] That is, the Western Paradise of Amitābha Buddha.

[14] The four causes are: 1) the direct cause, the cause for the production of a result, 2) the antecedent cause, the immediately preceding linkage in an ongoing continuity, 3) the object cause, the object of consciousness which, being understood, brings to mind to be what it is, and 4) the dominant, enabling cause, which, although it cannot produce the result, yet enables the direct cause to issue in the result. The issue here is whether nondiscriminative and subsequently attained wisdoms are the direct cause or the dominant cause of the Pure Land.

[15] This objection appears to be that of the Sarvāstivādins, as reported in the *Ch'eng wei-shih lun*. See de la Vallée Poussin, *Vijñaptimātratāsiddhi,* pp. 44–5; Cook, "Demonstration of Consciousness Only," p. 25.

[16] Kapphina is accounted to have been a king in the frontier city of Kukkuṭavati. In his search for wisdom, he heard of the Buddha. Upon

listening to and pondering the Buddha's teaching, he was converted and became an eminent disciple. The *Discipline of the Original Sarvāstivādins (Mūlasarvāstivāda-vinaya)* (Taishō Vol. 23, No. 1442, p. 670a) reports that at the moment of Kapphina's conversion the Buddha was surrounded by all sorts of marvelous beings, among which were many universal monarchs (*cakravartins*).

17 This listing of the Buddha's merits is the subject of many commentaries, two of which are contained in this commentary. It is also found in commentaries on *The Scripture on the Explication of Underlying Meaning* and on *The Summary of the Great Vehicle*.

18 The six times are divisions of the times of day into early morning, midday, sunset, evening, night, and late night—that is, all day long.

19 This is the first appearance of this argument in Mahayana thinking.

20 The "six branches" are perhaps the six kinds of moral discipline treated in the the *Treatise on the Stages of Yogic Meditation (Yogācārabhūmi)* (Taishō Vol. 30, No. 1579, p. 522): discipline that orients one toward awakening; discipline that extensively covers all that is to be learned; discipline that abides in stainless joy; discipline that perseveres until death; discipline that fortifies against covetousness; and discipline fully adorned with perfected moral observances.

21 This passage is one of the many Bandhuprabha has apparently added to the earlier text translated into Tibetan by Śīlabhadra. It emphasizes that all previous teachings on wisdom are summarized and subsumed in this teaching of the five factors of wisdom.

22 This commentary agrees almost word for word with the *Ch'eng wei-shih lun*. See de la Vallée Poussin, *Vijñaptimātratāsiddhi*, pp. 130–5 and Cook, "Demonstration of Consciousness Only," pp. 62–5.

23 One of the earliest explicit discussions of the debate about whether awakened wisdom has images or not, i.e., *sākārajñānavāda* or *nirākāra-jñānavāda*. All Yogācāra thinkers agreed that defiled, samsaric consciousness functioned in images, but, as above, did not agree on whether the mind of wisdom needed an image to function.

24 In the *Ocean Wisdom Scripture (Sāgaramati-sūtra)* contained in the *Mahāsaṃnipāta-sūtra* (Taishō Vol. 13, No. 397, p. 58a–b), the Buddha discusses the teaching of wisdom and draws the following simile: "Were a person to paint images in the empty sky—a man, a woman, an elephant, a horse—would such a person be conceivable or not?" [Sāgaramati answered,] "He would not be conceivable, Bhagavat. Just so, you can believe that the Tathāgata Bhagavat knows [the reality of awakening] is ineffable, and yet is able to explain it in detail."

25 The original purity of mind will shortly be expressed in terms of the *tathāgatagarbha,* the inner seed or embryo which constitutes the pure mind of all beings.

26 The notion that discrimination is adventitious (*āgantuka*) follows from the assertion of original purity. Such a notion is not in harmony with the classic Yogācāra texts of Asaṅga and Vasubandhu, for whom discrimination is indeed the very other-dependent nature (*paratantra*) or consciousness.

27 The *Ornament of the Scriptures of the Great Vehicle* (*Mahāyānasūtrālaṃkara,* Taishō Vol. 31, No. 1604), 9:37 has: "Not being discriminated in any regard, suchness has reached purity, the state of all-Tathāgata. Therefore all embodied beings are the embryo (*garbha*) of that [*tathāgata*]."

28 The preceding paragraph, present only in Bandhuprabha's Chinese version and not in Śīlabhadra's Tibetan, harmonizes this discussion about original purity with the former treatment of the five lineages (*gotra*). It does seem to weaken the impact of original purity by restricting its compass.

29 The *Summary of the Great Vehicle,* 10:28 has: "The Bhagavat is not seen because of the faults of sentient beings, just as the moon [is not reflected] in a broken basin, [but] like the sun he fills all worlds with the light of Dharma."

30 The *Ornament of the Scriptures of the Great Vehicle,* 9:29 and 19 has: "Just as the rays [of light] are all blended into the disk of the sun, and with one action, make the world visible...." And "Just as a gem shows forth its brightness without purposeful activity, so the Buddha's effortless activity is manifested."

31 The Sāgaramati chapter of the *Mahāsaṃnipāta-sūtra* (Taishō Vol. 13, No. 397, p. 67c) has: "Good sons, just as if before a monk were to enter the concentration of destruction he were to vow: 'I will enter concentration but when the bell sounds I will awaken.' Although there is no bell sound in concentration, yet because of the force of that vow, when the bell sounds, he does awaken from concentration."

32 The *Great Vehicle Scripture of the Luminescent Adornment of the Wisdom of Entering All Buddha Realms* (*Sarvabuddhaviṣayāvatārajñānālokālaṃkāra-sūtra*) (Taishō Vol. 12, No. 359, p. 255a) has: "The Tathāgata then said, 'According to this teaching on birth and nonbirth, Mañjuśrī is he who is not born and does not perish; this description is the appellation of a Tathāgata.'"

33 A frequent Mahayana claim to priority not only in importance, but also in time.

34 The *Diamond Scripture* (*Vajracchedikā-prajñāpāramitā-sūtra*) has: "Because the Tathāgata has no place to come from nor any place to go to, he is called the Tathāgata."

35 Scriptures were often presented to kings and rulers; here an unidentified text, and thus unknown king.

36 The term "excellent women," literally, "jewels of women," is here meant to include the entire list of seven jewels of a universal monarch: golden wheels, elephants, swift horses, a queen, good ministers, excellent women, and fine generals.

37 The *Great Vehicle Scripture on the Inconceivable Mystery of the Tathā-gata (Tathāgataguhya-sūtra)* (Taishō Vol. 11, No. 312, p. 718a) has: "Good sons, conventional usage exhausts all metaphors without being able analogically to express the various merits of the discipline, concentration, wisdom, liberation, and liberation-wisdom of all Buddhas and Tathāgatas. All these metaphors, whether of body, speech, or thought, are unable analogically to express them, because those Tathā-gatas transcend them. The sole exception is [the metaphor] of empty space, which is able to express them analogically, because the Tathā-gatas' discipline, concentration, wisdom, liberation, and liberation-wisdom are all just like empty space."

38 The thesis that all wisdom states are characterized by an inner image—*sākāra*, for images of all knowable things are present to mirror wisdom.

39 Perhaps the reference is to the *Ch'eng wei-shih lun:* "Thinking consciousness ceases to exist at the stage of arhatship, in the concentration of destruction, and on the transcendent path" (de la Vallée Poussin, *Vijñaptimātratāsiddhi*, p. 267; Cook, "Demonstration of Consciousness Only," p. 139). Frequently the *Interpretation of the Buddha Land* is difficult to understand apart from the *Ch'eng wei-shih lun.*

40 This section is quoted almost verbatim from the *Ch'eng wei-shih lun,* the third argument for the nondefiled thinking consciousness. See de la Vallée Poussin, *Vijñaptimātratāsiddhi,* p. 269; Cook, "Demonstration of Consciousness Only," p. 141.

41 A citation from a Pure Land text, perhaps included to incorporate Pure Land thinking within a Yogācāra perspective.

42 The *Ornament of the Scriptures of the Great Vehicle,* 9:16 has: "Just as the image of the moon is not seen in a broken pot, so the image of Buddha is not seen in sinful beings." Vasubandhu's prose *Commentary* contained in that text explains: "It is shown by simile...that the Buddha image is not seen in those beings who are unfit vessels."

43 The *Diamond Scripture* has: "The Tathāgata's possession of thirty-three marks is a no possession of thirty-three marks, and this is called his possession of thirty-three marks." (Taishō Vol. 8, No. 235, p. 750a)

44 The *Perfection of Wisdom Scripture (Prajñapāramitā-sūtra)* (Taishō Vol. 8, No. 227, p. 579a) has: "If bodhisattvas do not revert, they will attain the power of skillful means, which is called the bodhisattva practice of the perfection of wisdom whereby they see that the twelve dependent co-arisings include all things. When bodhisattvas gain this insight, they do not see anything that does not co-arise dependently."

⁴⁵ The *Great Vehicle Scripture of the Luminescent Adornment of the Wisdom of Entering All Buddha Realms* (Taishō Vol. 12, No. 359, p. 261c) has: "If one sees into dependent co-arising, then one sees reality, and if one sees reality, then one sees Tathāgata."

⁴⁶ The *Treatise on the Stages of Yogic Meditation* (Taishō Vol. 30, No. 1579, p. 499b) has: "Thus the Tathāgata at the six times, the three [divisions] of day and the three [divisions] of night, constantly by means of his Buddha-eye, perceives the world."

⁴⁷ The *Great Vehicle Scripture on the Inconceivable Mystery of the Tathāgata* (Taishō Vol. 11, No. 312, p. 716c) has: "Both gods and humans delight in seeing the golden colors of the Buddha. This is because he causes them to see his golden-colored body."

⁴⁸ Discussed in the *Treatise on the Stages of Yogic Meditation* (Taishō Vol. 30, No. 1579, pp. 542c–543a).

⁴⁹ In defiled consciousness insight is gained into sensed image, and thus the trigger is the image. In Buddha consciousness, wisdom insight employs images and thus reverses the process.

⁵⁰ The *Ornament of the Scriptures of the Great Vehicle,* 9:58 has: "Its action is the skillful means that employ the transformations of body, speech, and thought."

⁵¹ The *Ornament of the Scriptures of the Great Vehicle,* 12:9 has a detailed description of these sixty qualities of the Buddha's speech.

⁵² The *Ornament of the Scriptures of the Great Vehicle,* 12:4 has: "The teaching of superior beings comes from scripture, understanding, and mastery. It issues forth from the mouth, from all things, and from space."

⁵³ The *Scripture Elucidated by Vimalakīrti (Vimalakīrtinirdeśa-sūtra)* (Taishō Vol. 14, No. 475, p. 538a) has: "Buddha by means of one sound explains the teaching, and sentient beings, according to their level of understanding, all receive that action and obtain benefit."

⁵⁴ See *Hsien-chüeh-ching,* Taishō Vol. 14, No. 425, which thematizes states of meditation and concentration.

⁵⁵ Similar passages occur in the *Flower Ornament Scripture (Avataṃsaka-sūtra),* Taishō Vol. 9, No. 278, p. 623a and Taishō Vol. 10, No. 279, p. 272a, as well as in the *Scripture on the Tathāgata's Appearance (Tathā-gatotpattisambhavanirdeśa-sūtra),* Taishō Vol. 10, No. 291, p. 600a.

⁵⁶ A parallel passage is found in the *Mahāratnakūṭa* (Taishō Vol. 11, No. 310, p. 633b), Samantaprabhāsa Bodhisattva Assembly, Kāśyapa Paripṛcchā: "Kāśyapa, just as the thirty-threefold gods, when they enter that garden of equality, are all equal in the things they employ, just so bodhisattvas, because of the purity of their minds, teach and transform with equality among sentient beings."

57 The *Ornament of the Scriptures of the Great Vehicle,* 9:82–5 appears to be the source for this simile.

58 The *Ornament of the Scriptures of the Great Vehicle,* 9:77 has: "Because of the divisions of the lineage [of Buddhas], because they are not without use, because they are beginningless, because they have no divisions, in the uncontaminated ground there is neither one Buddha nor many Buddhas."

59 These four verses are identical with verses 56–9 from the *Ornament of the Scriptures of the Great Vehicle,* chapter 9, and thus have been commented upon by Sthiramati and by Asvabhāsa in their commentaries to that text.

60 The theme of chapter 5 of the *Summary of the Great Vehicle.*

61 The *Ch'eng wei-shih lun* has: "The obstacle to knowledge is associated only with bad or neutral thoughts. The *Treatise [on the Stages of Yogic Meditation]* says: "Ignorance includes only bad and neutral states; delusion and non-delusion are incompatible." See de la Vallée Poussin, *Vijñaptimātratāsiddhi,* pp. 570–1; Cook, "Demonstration of Consciousness Only," p. 300.

62 The *Summary of the Great Vehicle* (Taishō Vol. 31, No. 1594, p. 139a) has: "Understand that thinking consciousness is able to imagine, because it has discrimination."

63 See the Devadatta chapter of the *Scripture of the Lotus Blossom of the Wonderful Dharma (Saddharmapuṇḍarīka-sūtra) (The Lotus Sutra,* translated by Tsugunari Kubo and Akira Yuyama, Numata Center, 1993) for the story of Śāriputra and the dragon girl.

64 The *Treatise on the Perfection of Wisdom (Ta chih-tu lun)* has: "Many people do not believe when they listen to a teaching taught by a human. But they would believe a teaching taught by an animal. This is why bodhisattvas teach in the form of animals, as seen in the *Accounts of Previous Births (Jātakas),* for the hearers believe because it is extraordinary and because in their judgment animals are of a true mind without craftiness. Others perhaps do think that animals are liars and crafty, and this is why Buddha makes trees to speak. Everybody will believe the trees, which are devoid of thought [and cannot deceive anyone]." See de la Vallée Poussin, *Vijñaptimātratāsiddhi,* p. 797.

65 The *Summary of the Great Vehicle,* 10:7 has: "By the conversion of the storehouse consciousness one attains the Dharma body."

66 The *Ornament of the Scriptures of the Great Vehicle,* 9:74 has: "duty-fulfillment wisdom in all realms, by means of all kinds of immeasurable, inconceivable transformations, brings benefit to all sentient beings."

67 The *Summary of the Great Vehicle,* 10:35 explains that the essence body and the enjoyment body differ "because the conversions of the

active consciousnesses and of the storehouse (i.e., container) consciousness [differ]."

[68] The *Ornament of the Scriptures of the Great Vehicle,* 9:66 has: "[The three bodies] are equal in their basic nature, disposition, and actions. In their basic nature, state of resting, and continuity, they are eternal."

[69] Vasubandhu's *Treatise on the Diamond Scripture* (*Vajracchedikā-prajñāpāramitā-śāstra*) 1:14 says that "although there is no cause for the production of the Dharma body, there is a cause for its realization."

[70] The *Ornament of the Scriptures of the Great Vehicle,* 9:69 has: "[mirror wisdom] is the image of the wisdom of an enjoyment Buddha, from which it arises."

[71] See note 67, above.

[72] See note 68, above.

[73] The *Vibhāṣāśāstra* (Taishō Vol. 27, No. 1545, p. 890b–c) reports: "There once was a Buddha named Tiṣya or Puṣya. That Buddha had as his disciples two bodhisattvas, Śākyamuni and Maitreya. When asked which would mature first, that Buddha saw that it would be Maitreya. But asked when the beings to be converted by these two would mature, he saw that Śākyamuni's would be first. So he thought, How can I arrange it that those to be converted will actually meet their converters? Indeed, it is easier to mature one person than many. So he took up his mat and walked the road to the top of a mountain, where he entered a cave, spread his mat, sat with his legs crossed, and entered the concentration of fire, wherein for seven days and nights he experienced the most sublime joy. Śākyamuni took himself immediately to that mountain and sought that Buddha from place to place, just as a calf would seek its mother. Finally he arrived at the cave and, [stopping in mid-step, remained standing on one foot for seven days and praised the Buddha with one verse, at the end of which he had matured to full awakening before Maitreya]."

[74] Sudhana is the youth of the *Gaṇḍavyūha-sūtra* who, on Mañjuśrī's instructions, seeks wisdom through encounters with diverse spiritual friends.

Glossary

Abhidharma: A collection of treatises explaining some of the contents of the Buddha's teachings. One of the three divisions (Tripiṭaka) of Buddhist scriptures, along with the Sutras (the teachings of the Buddha) and the Vinaya (rules of monastic discipline).

arhat: One who has freed himself from the bonds of birth and death by eliminating all passions. The highest spiritual ideal of the Hinayana. *See also* Hinayana.

asura: A class of superhuman beings that are in constant conflict with the gods.

bīja. See container consciousness.

bodhisattva: In the Mahayana, a selfless being with universal compassion who sees the universal emptiness of phenomena and has generated the profound aspiration to achieve enlightenment (*bodhicitta*) on behalf of all sentient beings. *See also* emptiness; Mahayana.

Buddha-nature: The basic enlightened nature of sentient beings, which is chronically obscured by their ignorance. The complete unfolding of the Buddha-nature is enlightenment itself.

chiliocosm: A system of thousands of world-realms.

concentration: A mental state of concentration involving focusing on one object.

conscious construction–only (*vijñapti-mātra*): The central teaching of the Yogācāra school of Buddhism, which indicates that we mistakenly take mental constructions (*vijñapti*) as presenting realities external to the consciousness (*vijñāna*) in which they appear, yet they are only mental constructs and not ultimate truth. *See also* two truths; Yogācāra.

container consciousness (*ālayavijñāna*): The latent, seminal consciousness that supports karmically defiled awareness; the storehouse of all the seeds (*bījas*), imprints of mental defilements, that generate delusion.

conventional truth. *See* two truths.

dependent co-arising (*pratītyasamutpāda*): The doctrine that all things come into being only in dependence upon other things.

deva: A god; a divine being.

dhāraṇī. *See* prayer formulae.

emptiness (*śūnyatā*): The quality that all things have of being devoid of independent, real existence. All phenomena are devoid of independent, permanent existence, self-nature (*svabhāva*), and instead exist only in dependence on a complex web of causes and conditions and go on existing only as long as those causes and conditions prevail. The doctrine of emptiness is the central teaching of Mahayana Buddhism. *See also* dependent co-arising; Mahayana.

four kinds of birth: According to Buddhism, the four possible ways that a being may be born, i.e., 1) from a womb, 2) from an egg, 3) from moisture, or 4) through metamorphosis or spontaneous generation.

Four Noble Truths: The basic teaching of the Buddha. They are: 1) Existence is characterized by suffering; 2) craving and attachment are the cause of suffering; 3) all suffering can be ended; 4) the way to end suffering is by following the Buddha's eightfold path (right view, right thought, right speech, right action, right livelihood, right effort, right mindfulness, and right concentration).

four wisdoms: The four types of transformed consciousness discussed in Yogācāra philosophy. They are: 1) mirror wisdom (*ādarśa-jñāna*), 2) equality wisdom (*samatā-jñāna*), 3) discernment wisdom (*pratyavekṣanā-jñāna*), and 4) duty-fulfillment wisdom (*kṛtyānuṣṭhāna-jñāna*). These wisdoms emerge from the eight forms of consciousness when illusion is destroyed and enlightenment is realized.

gandharva: A class of mythical beings, celestial musicians.

garuḍa: A mythological being in the form of a giant bird.

Hinayana ("Lesser Vehicle"): The name given by Mahayanists to early Buddhist teachings that had as their ideal the arhat; the two kinds of Hinayana practice, that of the word-hearers (*śrāvakas*) and of the individually enlightened ones (*pratyekabuddhas*), are known as the two vehicles. *See also* arhat; Mahayana; individually enlightened one; lower vehicles; word-hearer.

individually enlightened one (*pratyekabuddha*): A sage who attains enlightenment by directly observing the dependent co-arising of phenomena, without the guidance of a teacher. An individually enlightened one intends neither to guide others nor to expound the teaching to others. One of the two kinds of Hinayana sages. *See also* Hinayana; word-hearer.

kalpa: An immense period of time, an eon.

kiṃnara: A class of mythical beings, either half human and half bird or half human and half horse, that make celestial music.

lower vehicles: The two Hinayana soteriological paths of the word-hearers and the individually enlightened ones, said to be "lower" by adherents of the Mahayana, which upholds the ideal of the bodhisattva. *See also* bodhisattva; Hinayana; Mahayana; individually enlightened one; word-hearer.

Mahayana ("Great Vehicle"): A form of Buddhism that developed in India around 100 B.C.E. and which exalts as its religious ideal the bodhisattva, great beings who are willing to delay their own enlightenment until they can save all sentient beings. Such selfless compassion becomes possible only when the practitioner grasps the central Mahayana doctrine of emptiness and so realizes that "self" and "others" are not separate. *See also* bodhisattva; emptiness.

mahoraga: A class of snake-like mythical beings.

One Vehicle: The single teaching, given in the *Lotus Sutra,* by which all sentient beings can attain Buddhahood. It is contrasted with the three-vehicles teaching, which addresses the bodhisattva vehicle, the individually enlightened ones' vehicle, and the word-hearers' vehicle separately as skillful means to guide all sentient beings to the One Vehicle.

perceiving consciousness (*manovijñāna*): The mind that perceives that which has been contacted through a sense organ and its corresponding sense consciousness. *See also* sense consciousnesses.

Prajñāpāramitā ("perfection of wisdom"): The name of a body of Mahayana scriptures that emphasize the doctrine of emptiness, and which served as the fundamental texts for a number of important Buddhist schools, including Yogācāra. *See also* emptiness; Mahayana; Yogācāra.

prayer formulae (*dhāraṇī*). A special verbal formula that contains the essence of a teaching in short phrases and that is believed to hold great power. In this text the terms mystic formulae, prayer formulae, and recollective formulae are used interchangeably to refer to *dhāraṇī*s.

primal vow: The vows made by bodhisattvas at the outset of their religious careers; especially, a vow made to save all sentient beings and establish a Pure Land for them. *See also* Pure Land.

Pure Dharma Realm (*dharmadhātu*): The sphere of ultimate truth or ultimate reality. *See also* two truths.

Pure Land: A Buddha land, a world or realm in which a particular Buddha dwells. In the teachings of the Pure Land school, a major East Asian Mahayana Buddhist tradition, the term refers to Sukhāvatī ("Land of Bliss") in the western quarter, which was produced by the bodhisattva Dharmākara who became Amitābha Buddha upon fulfillment of his vows. In the context of this text, the term Pure Land refers to Buddhahood comprised of the Pure Dharma Realm and the four wisdoms. *See also* four wisdoms; Pure Dharma Realm.

sense consciousnesses: The consciousnesses, i.e., visual consciousness, aural consciousness, olfactory consciousness, gustatory consciousness, and tactile consciousness, that arise from contact between the five sense organs of the eyes, ears, nose, tongue, and body with their respective objects.

suchness: The state of things as they really are; the truth of ultimate meaning; ultimate reality. The content of the perfect wisdom (*prajñā-pāramitā*) insight into the nature of reality just as it is, i.e., empty of self-nature and dependently arisen. Apprehension of this state is enlightenment. *See also* dependent co-arising; emptiness; two truths.

Tathāgata: An epithet for the Buddha. It means "one who has gone to (*gata*) and come from (*āgata*) the truth of suchness (*tathā*)," i.e., "one who embodies the truth of suchness (*tathā*)." *See also* suchness.

tathāgatagarbha: Another name for the Buddha-nature that is within all beings, conceived of as a kind of storeroom or receptacle where the embryo of the Tathāgata is retained and matured. *See also* Buddha-nature; Tathāgata.

thinking consciousness (*manas*): Each of the sense organs, including the perceiving mind, has a corresponding consciousness by which its objects are known. The thinking function of the mind arises from and leads to defilement by giving rise to discriminative thoughts and false ideas. *See also* container consciousness; perceiving consciousness; sense consciousnesses.

three bodies (*trikāya*): The three bodies of the Buddha, 1) the Dharma body (*dharmakāya*), which is the Buddha as suchness or the truth of ultimate meaning, 2) the enjoyment body (*saṃbhogakāya*), acquired by Buddhas through absolute perfection of their practice; this body can go everywhere, is omniscient, etc., and 3) the transformation body (*nirmāṇakāya*), whereby, out of infinite compassion, the Buddha reveals himself in an infinite number of forms in order to assist sentient beings. *See also* suchness; two truths.

Three Jewels: The Buddha, the Dharma (teachings), and the Sangha (followers).

three realms: 1) The realm of desire (*kāmadhātu*), this world of desires, 2) the realm of form (*rūpadhātu*), the realm experienced by one in this world who has severed all desires but still experiences the world as form, and 3) the formless realm (*arūpadhātu*), the realm that has no form but consists of only the other four of the five aggregates; the realm of experience of one who has severed all desires and attachment to form but has still not experienced enlightenment.

three vehicles. As opposed to the doctrine of the One Vehicle, advocates of the three vehicles doctrine hold that each of the soteriological paths—the bodhisattva vehicle (i.e., the Mahayana), the individually enlightened ones' vehicle, and the word-hearers' vehicle—are all skillful means to guide sentient beings to liberation according to their capacities. *See also* bodhisattva; individually enlightened one; lower vehicles; Mahayana; One Vehicle; word-hearer.

triple world: *See* three realms.

two truths: 1) Ultimate truth, or the truth of ultimate meaning, the transcendent truth that is beyond conceptualization, and 2) conventional truth, the truth that can be put into words. Ultimate truth or ultimate reality is the apprehension of things as they really are (suchness), the state of enlightenment; conventional truth or conventional reality represents a limited understanding of things based in mental constructs. *See also* suchness.

ultimate truth. *See* two truths.

word-hearer (*śrāvaka*): Originally, a disciple of the Buddha, one who directly heard his teachings; later generally used to mean so-called Hinayana Buddhists, as opposed to Mahayana Buddhists who follow the bodhisattva path. *See also* Hinayana; Mahayana.

yakṣa: A class of demonic beings.

Yogācāra: A major Mahayana Buddhist philosophical school, founded by the Indian masters Asaṅga and Vasubandhu in the fourth century C.E., which advocates the doctrine of conscious construction–only. *See also* conscious construction–only; Mahayana.

Bibliography

Cook, Francis H. *Three Texts on Consciousness Only* ("Demonstration of Consciousness Only" by Hsüan-tsang; "The Thirty Verses on Consciousness Only" by Vasubandhu; and "The Treatise in Twenty Verses on Consciousness Only" by Vasubandhu). Berkeley, CA: Numata Center for Buddhist Translation and Research, 1999.

de la Vallée Poussin, Louis. *Vijñaptimātratāsiddhi: La Siddhi de Hiuan-Tsang*. Paris: Librairie Orientaliste Paul Geuthner, 1928.

Hakamaya, Noriaki. "Asvabhāva's and Sthiramati's Commentary on the *Mahāyānasūtralaṃkāra* IX 56–76." *Indogaku Bukkyōgaku Kenkyū* XXVII (1978): 12–16.

—. "Shōjō hokkai kō." *Nanto Bukkyō* XXXVII (1976): 1–28.

Katsumata, Shunkyo. *Bukkyō ni okeru shinishikisetsu no kenkyū*. Tokyo: Sankido Busshorin, 1978.

Keenan, John P. "A Study of the *Buddhabhūmyupadeśa*: The Doctrinal Development of the Notion of Wisdom in Yogācāra Thought." Doctoral dissertation, University of Wisconsin, 1980.

Nishio, Kyōo. *Butsujikyōron no kenkyū*. 1940. Tokyo: Kokusho Kankokai, 1982. Reprint.

Takasaki, Jikidō. "Hōshin no ichigenron nyoraizō shisō no hō kannen." In Hirakawa Akira hakase kanreki kinen ronshu: *Bukkyō ni okeru hō no kenkyū*. Tokyo: Shunjyūsha, 1975.

—. *Noraizō shisō no keisei*. Tokyo: Shunjūsha, 1974.

Index

A

Abhidharma 127, 238
abode(s) 2, 11, 13, 29–30, 35, 36, 40, 42, 53, 57
  of the Buddha 35, 40, 42, 46
  of the Tathāgata 2, 11, 29
Accounts of Previous Births (*see also Jātakas*) 243
aggregates 6, 8, 19, 29, 37, 82, 90, 95, 113, 117–9, 120, 121, 147, 150, 156, 204, 226, 237
  five 29, 94, 118–9, 156, 204
ālayavijñāna. See consciousness, container
Amitābha 238
Aparagodānīya 163
arhat(s), arhatship 56, 61, 71, 79, 129, 157, 212, 231, 241
arupadhātu. See three realms; triple world
Asaṅga xiv, 240
aspiration 13, 85, 91, 92, 229
  for awakening, wisdom 61, 62, 67, 76, 92, 94, 150, 194
"A Study of the *Buddhabhūmyupa-deśa:* The Doctrinal Development of the Notion of Wisdom in Yogācāra Thought" 237
asura(s) 26
Asvabhāva xiii, 237, 243
Avataṃsaka-sūtra. See Flower Ornament Scripture

B

Bandhuprabha xiv, 237, 238, 239, 240
Bhadrakalpika-sūtra. See Scripture of the Fortunate Eon
Bhagavat (*see* also Buddha; Tathā-gata) 2, 5, 8–9, 11, 14, 15, 23, 32, 35–47, 49, 51, 54, 62, 75, 100, 126–7, 142, 148, 153, 171, 189, 191, 203, 235, 239, 240
bhikṣu(s) (*see also* monk) 149, 180
bīja. See seed
birth(s) (*see* also destinies; rebirth; transmigration) 12, 30, 31, 39, 48, 57, 61, 108, 115, 151, 166, 167, 179, 180, 181, 210, 234, 240
bodhi 65
bodhicitta. See aspiration, for awakening
bodhisattva(s) xv, 5, 11, 13, 15, 16, 18, 19, 20, 23, 26, 27, 29, 30, 32, 33, 35, 39, 40, 45, 51, 52, 53, 54, 55, 62, 65–73, 75, 76, 93, 109, 118, 119, 131, 138, 140, 148, 150, 157, 158, 160, 162, 163, 164, 170, 177, 188, 191–201, 209, 210, 217, 218, 222, 223, 224, 225, 228, 231, 232, 233, 234, 236, 238, 241, 242, 243, 244
  great 11, 19, 23–4, 51, 177, 221

N

A List of the Volumes of
the BDK English Tripiṭaka
(First Series)

Abbreviations

Ch.:	Chinese
Skt.:	Sanskrit
Jp.:	Japanese
Eng.:	Published title
T.:	Taishō Tripiṭaka

Vol. No.	Title	T. No.
1, 2	*Ch.* Ch'ang-a-han-ching （長阿含經） *Skt.* Dīrghāgama	1
3–8	*Ch.* Chung-a-han-ching （中阿含經） *Skt.* Madhyamāgama	26
9-I	*Ch.* Ta-ch'eng-pên-shêng-hsin-ti-kuan-ching （大乘本生心地觀經）	159
9-II	*Ch.* Fo-so-hsing-tsan （佛所行讚） *Skt.* Buddhacarita	192
10-I	*Ch.* Tsa-pao-ts'ang-ching （雜寶藏經） *Eng.* The Storehouse of Sundry Valuables	203
10-II	*Ch.* Fa-chü-p'i-yü-ching （法句譬喻經） *Eng.* The Scriptural Text: Verses of the Doctrine, with Parables	211
11-I	*Ch.* Hsiao-p'in-pan-jo-po-lo-mi-ching （小品般若波羅蜜經） *Skt.* Aṣṭasāhasrikā-prajñāpāramitā-sūtra	227
11-II	*Ch.* Chin-kang-pan-jo-po-lo-mi-ching （金剛般若波羅蜜經） *Skt.* Vajracchedikā-prajñāpāramitā-sūtra	235

Vol. No.		Title	T. No.
45-II	*Ch.*	Yu-p'o-sai-chieh-ching （優婆塞戒經）	1488
	Skt.	Upāsakaśīla-sūtra (?)	
	Eng.	The Sutra on Upāsaka Precepts	
46-I	*Ch.*	Miao-fa-lien-hua-ching-yu-po-t'i-shê （妙法蓮華經憂波提舍）	1519
	Skt.	Saddharmapuṇḍarīka-upadeśa	
46-II	*Ch.*	Fo-ti-ching-lun （佛地經論）	1530
	Skt.	Buddhabhūmisūtra-śāstra (?)	
	Eng.	The Interpretation of the Buddha Land	
46-III	*Ch.*	Shê-ta-ch'eng-lun （攝大乘論）	1593
	Skt.	Mahāyānasaṃgraha	
	Eng.	The Summary of the Great Vehicle	
47	*Ch.*	Shih-chu-p'i-p'o-sha-lun （十住毘婆沙論）	1521
	Skt.	Daśabhūmika-vibhāṣā (?)	
48, 49	*Ch.*	A-p'i-ta-mo-chü-shê-lun （阿毘達磨俱舍論）	1558
	Skt.	Abhidharmakośa-bhāṣya	
50–59	*Ch.*	Yü-ch'ieh-shih-ti-lun （瑜伽師地論）	1579
	Skt.	Yogācārabhūmi	
60-I	*Ch.*	Ch'êng-wei-shih-lun （成唯識論）	1585
	Eng.	Demonstration of Consciousness Only (In Three Texts on Consciousness Only)	
60-II	*Ch.*	Wei-shih-san-shih-lun-sung （唯識三十論頌）	1586
	Skt.	Triṃśikā	
	Eng.	The Thirty Verses on Consciousness Only (In Three Texts on Consciousness Only)	
60-III	*Ch.*	Wei-shih-êrh-shih-lun （唯識二十論）	1590
	Skt.	Viṃśatikā	
	Eng.	The Treatise in Twenty Verses on Consciousness Only (In Three Texts on Consciousness Only)	
61-I	*Ch.*	Chung-lun （中論）	1564
	Skt.	Madhyamaka-śāstra	
61-II	*Ch.*	Pien-chung-pien-lun （辯中邊論）	1600
	Skt.	Madhyāntavibhāga	

Vol. No.		Title	T. No.
61-III	*Ch.*	Ta-ch'eng-ch'êng-yeh-lun （大乘成業論）	1609
	Skt.	Karmasiddhiprakaraṇa	
61-IV	*Ch.*	Yin-ming-ju-chêng-li-lun （因明入正理論）	1630
	Skt.	Nyāyapraveśa	
61-V	*Ch.*	Chin-kang-chên-lun （金剛針論）	1642
	Skt.	Vajrasūcī	
61-VI	*Ch.*	Chang-so-chih-lun （彰所知論）	1645
62	*Ch.*	Ta-ch'eng-chuang-yen-ching-lun （大乘莊嚴經論）	1604
	Skt.	Mahāyānasūtrālaṃkāra	
63-I	*Ch.*	Chiu-ching-i-ch'eng-pao-hsing-lun （究竟一乘寶性論）	1611
	Skt.	Ratnagotravibhāgamahāyānottaratantra-śāstra	
63-II	*Ch.*	P'u-t'i-hsing-ching （菩提行經）	1662
	Skt.	Bodhicaryāvatāra	
63-III	*Ch.*	Chin-kang-ting-yü-ch'ieh-chung-fa-a-nou-to-lo-san-miao-san-p'u-t'i-hsin-lun （金剛頂瑜伽中發阿耨多羅三藐三菩提心論）	1665
63-IV	*Ch.*	Ta-ch'eng-ch'i-hsin-lun （大乘起信論）	1666
	Skt.	Mahāyānaśraddhotpāda-śāstra (?)	
63-V	*Ch.*	Na-hsien-pi-ch'iu-ching （那先比丘經）	1670
	Pāli	Milindapañhā	
64	*Ch.*	Ta-ch'eng-chi-p'u-sa-hsüeh-lun （大乘集菩薩學論）	1636
	Skt.	Śikṣāsamuccaya	
65	*Ch.*	Shih-mo-ho-yen-lun （釋摩訶衍論）	1688
66-I	*Ch.*	Pan-jo-po-lo-mi-to-hsin-ching-yu-tsan （般若波羅蜜多心經幽贊）	1710
	Eng.	A Comprehensive Commentary on the Heart Sutra (Prajñāpāramitā-hṛdaya-sūtra)	
66-II	*Ch.*	Kuan-wu-liang-shou-fo-ching-shu （觀無量壽佛經疏）	1753
66-III	*Ch.*	San-lun-hsüan-i （三論玄義）	1852

Vol. No.		Title	T. No.
66-IV	*Ch.*	Chao-lun （肇論）	1858
67, 68	*Ch.*	Miao-fa-lien-hua-ching-hsüan-i （妙法蓮華經玄義）	1716
69	*Ch.*	Ta-ch'eng-hsüan-lun （大乘玄論）	1853
70-I	*Ch.*	Hua-yen-i-ch'eng-chiao-i-fên-ch'i-chang （華嚴一乘教義分齊章）	1866
70-II	*Ch.*	Yüan-jên-lun （原人論）	1886
70-III	*Ch.*	Hsiu-hsi-chih-kuan-tso-ch'an-fa-yao （修習止觀坐禪法要）	1915
70-IV	*Ch.*	T'ien-t'ai-ssŭ-chiao-i （天台四教儀）	1931
71, 72	*Ch.*	Mo-ho-chih-kuan （摩訶止觀）	1911
73-I	*Ch.*	Kuo-ch'ing-pai-lu （國清百録）	1934
73-II	*Ch.* *Eng.*	Liu-tsu-ta-shih-fa-pao-t'an-ching （六祖大師法寶壇經） The Platform Sutra of the Sixth Patriarch	2008
73-III	*Ch.*	Huang-po-shan-tuan-chi-ch'an-shih-ch'uan- hsin-fa-yao （黃檗山斷際禪師傳心法要）	2012A
73-IV	*Ch.*	Yung-chia-chêng-tao-ko （永嘉證道歌）	2014
74-I	*Ch.* *Eng.*	Chên-chou-lin-chi-hui-chao-ch'an-shih-wu-lu （鎮州臨濟慧照禪師語録） The Recorded Sayings of Linji (In Three Chan Classics)	1985
74-II	*Ch.* *Eng.*	Wu-mên-kuan （無門關） Wumen's Gate (In Three Chan Classics)	2005
74-III	*Ch.* *Eng.*	Hsin-hsin-ming （信心銘） The Faith-Mind Maxim (In Three Chan Classics)	2010
74-IV	*Ch.*	Ch'ih-hsiu-pai-chang-ch'ing-kuei （勑修百丈清規）	2025

Vol. No.		Title	T. No.
75	*Ch.*	Fo-kuo-yüan-wu-ch'an-shih-pi-yen-lu （佛果圜悟禪師碧巖録）	2003
	Eng.	The Blue Cliff Record	
76-I	*Ch.*	I-pu-tsung-lun-lun （異部宗輪論）	2031
	Skt.	Samayabhedoparacanacakra	
76-II	*Ch.*	A-yü-wang-ching （阿育王經）	2043
	Skt.	Aśokarāja-sūtra (?)	
	Eng.	The Biographical Scripture of King Aśoka	
76-III	*Ch.*	Ma-ming-p'u-sa-ch'uan （馬鳴菩薩傳）	2046
	Eng.	The Life of Aśvaghoṣa Bodhisattva (In Lives of Great Monks and Nuns)	
76-IV	*Ch.*	Lung-shu-p'u-sa-ch'uan （龍樹菩薩傳）	2047
	Eng.	The Life of Nāgārjuna Bodhisattva (In Lives of Great Monks and Nuns)	
76-V	*Ch.*	P'o-sou-p'an-tou-fa-shih-ch'uan （婆藪槃豆法師傳）	2049
	Eng.	Biography of Dharma Master Vasubandhu (In Lives of Great Monks and Nuns)	
76-VI	*Ch.*	Pi-ch'iu-ni-ch'uan （比丘尼傳）	2063
	Eng.	Biographies of Buddhist Nuns (In Lives of Great Monks and Nuns)	
76-VII	*Ch.*	Kao-sêng-fa-hsien-ch'uan （高僧法顯傳）	2085
	Eng.	The Journey of the Eminent Monk Faxian (In Lives of Great Monks and Nuns)	
76-VIII	*Ch.*	Yu-fang-chi-ch'ao: T'ang-ta-ho-shang-tung- chêng-ch'uan（遊方記抄: 唐大和上東征傳）	2089-(7)
77	*Ch.*	Ta-t'ang-ta-tz'ŭ-ên-ssŭ-san-ts'ang-fa-shih- ch'uan （大唐大慈恩寺三藏法師傳）	2053
	Eng.	A Biography of the Tripiṭaka Master of the Great Ci'en Monastery of the Great Tang Dynasty	
78	*Ch.*	Kao-sêng-ch'uan （高僧傳）	2059
79	*Ch.*	Ta-t'ang-hsi-yü-chi （大唐西域記）	2087
	Eng.	The Great Tang Dynasty Record of the Western Regions	
80	*Ch.*	Hung-ming-chi （弘明集）	2102

Vol. No.		Title	T. No.
81–92	*Ch.*	Fa-yüan-chu-lin （法苑珠林）	2122
93-I	*Ch.*	Nan-hai-chi-kuei-nei-fa-chʻuan （南海寄歸內法傳）	2125
	Eng.	Buddhist Monastic Traditions of Southern Asia	
93-II	*Ch.*	Fan-yü-tsa-ming （梵語雜名）	2135
94-I	*Jp.*	Shō-man-gyō-gi-sho （勝鬘經義疏）	2185
94-II	*Jp.*	Yui-ma-kyō-gi-sho （維摩經義疏）	2186
95	*Jp.*	Hok-ke-gi-sho （法華義疏）	2187
96-I	*Jp.*	Han-nya-shin-gyō-hi-ken （般若心經秘鍵）	2203
96-II	*Jp.*	Dai-jō-hos-sō-ken-jin-shō （大乘法相研神章）	2309
96-III	*Jp.*	Kan-jin-kaku-mu-shō （觀心覺夢鈔）	2312
97-I	*Jp.*	Ris-shū-kō-yō （律宗綱要）	2348
	Eng.	The Essentials of the Vinaya Tradition	
97-II	*Jp.*	Ten-dai-hok-ke-shū-gi-shū （天台法華宗義集）	2366
	Eng.	The Collected Teachings of the Tendai Lotus School	
97-III	*Jp.*	Ken-kai-ron （顯戒論）	2376
97-IV	*Jp.*	San-ge-gaku-shō-shiki （山家學生式）	2377
98-I	*Jp.*	Hi-zō-hō-yaku （秘藏寶鑰）	2426
98-II	*Jp.*	Ben-ken-mitsu-ni-kyō-ron （辨顯密二教論）	2427
98-III	*Jp.*	Soku-shin-jō-butsu-gi （即身成佛義）	2428
98-IV	*Jp.*	Shō-ji-jis-sō-gi （聲字實相義）	2429
98-V	*Jp.*	Un-ji-gi （吽字義）	2430
98-VI	*Jp.*	Go-rin-ku-ji-myō-hi-mitsu-shaku （五輪九字明秘密釋）	2514
98-VII	*Jp.*	Mitsu-gon-in-hotsu-ro-san-ge-mon （密嚴院發露懺悔文）	2527